UR

'OF THE CHALDEES'

UR
'OF THE CHALDEES'

A Revised and
Updated Edition of
Sir Leonard Woolley's
Excavations at Ur
by P. R. S. Moorey

Cornell University Press
Ithaca, New York

Originally published as *Ur of the Chaldees* 1929
Second edition 1950
Expanded edition published as *Excavations at Ur* 1954
Second edition 1964
This revised, updated edition first published 1982 by
Cornell University Press

International Standard Book Number 0-8014-1518-7
Library of Congress Catalog Card Number 81-86557

Designed by Pauline Harrison
Set, printed, and bound in Great Britain
by Jolly and Barber Limited,
Rugby, Warwickshire

Contents

Colour Plates

Editor's Note for the Reader

The editors of the posthumously published final reports of the Ur excavations, cited in the bibliographies here, have generally not revised the spellings of ancient names to bring them into line with current usage. I believe such a step is unavoidable here and I have used the forms of names, usually royal ones, now more usual. Even then there is not a universally accepted spelling, even in the English-speaking world. The revised building names will be found in the concise topographical glossary on pp. 267–8.

The crucial personal names likely to confuse the reader passing from this book to Woolley's own reports are given here with the older form used by Woolley in brackets:

Amar-Sin (Bur-Sin)
Ennigaldi-Nanna (Bel-Shalti-Nannar)
Ḥendursag (Pa-sag)
Kudur-Mabuk (Kudur-Mabug)

Puabi (Shubad)
Shulgi (Dungi)
Shu-Ilishu (Gimil-Ilishu)
Shu-Sin (Gimil-Sin)

The following abbreviations have been used:

PG Private Grave   RT Royal Tomb

Acknowledgements

The plates on pages 70, 72, 74, 90, 103, 121, 127, 175 are reproduced by permission of the University Museum, University of Pennsylvania, Philadelphia

The drawing on page 71 is reproduced by permission of the *Illustrated London News*

The drawing on page 37 and the plan on page 107 are from the Editor's own collection

All other black and white plates, drawings, and plans are taken from the Ur Excavation Reports and are reproduced by permission of the Trustees of the British Museum

The maps were drawn by Kenneth Clarke

Editor's Preface

There are few archaeological excavations which have had such an abiding interest for the general public as those at Ur in modern Iraq directed by Sir Leonard Woolley between 1922 and 1934. His unusual skill as a writer for the non-specialist and the fascination of his discoveries have continued to sustain the demand for copies of *Excavations at Ur: A record of twelve years' work* (1954), written twenty years after the close of work at Ur when Woolley was already well over seventy years old. Even then he was largely rewriting a book which was first published in 1929 as *Ur of the Chaldees: A record of seven years of excavation*. 'The facts', he wrote in 1954, 'of course, remain [i.e., as in the earlier book], and the description of them cannot be radically altered, but the conclusions which were formed about them may have been modified by later discoveries so that there must always be a certain amount of re-writing'. In accepting the publishers' invitation to produce a revised edition of this book, under its original main title, I have followed the lines indicated here by Woolley for his own account in 1954. I have striven to retain the immediacy and vivid quality of his original text, in which nothing was made too difficult for the general reader, whilst presenting the record of a fifty-year-old excavation in the context of modern study. This has inevitably involved changes, some of them sub-stantial. In fairness both to Woolley and to the reader my treatment of three primary aspects of Woolley's approach to his work requires some explana-tion here. These are his strong Biblical bias in general interpretation, his vivid historical imagination, and his lifelong independence of thought on controversial matters. I will consider them in turn.

Woolley was the son of a clergyman and when young considered going into the church himself. For analogies and comparisons he turned instinc-tively to the Bible, as did many of the generation of readers for whom he was writing. His popular books were full of Biblical allusions and he was ever ready to bring the Old Testament to bear on his archaeological discoveries. In 1954, a number of reviewers commented unfavourably on the Biblical references, many of which seemed to them inappropriate. Here they have largely been edited out. But there is one Biblical connection which still requires special attention, not least because in 1936 Woolley devoted a whole book, entitled *Abraham*, to Ur and the patriarchal narratives.

Ur's fame as the birthplace of Abraham has given it a special position in the literary legacy of Judaism and Islam. Contrary to the view consistently argued by Woolley, there is no actual proof that Tell el-Mukayyar, the Ur of this book, was identical with 'Ur of the Chaldees' in *Genesis* 11:29–32. Nor is there any agreed opinion on the existence of Abraham himself, on his social and ethnic origins, on his history and chronology, above all on his relationship to the enigmatic chapter 14 of *Genesis*. The specialist literature debating all these questions has recently grown considerably. In view of the impossibility of providing the reader with any consensus it seemed best to write of the excavations at Ur at this time without mention of Abraham. Even if Tell el-Mukayyar should eventually be shown to have been the Biblical 'Ur of the Chaldees', we still have no firm evidence from this site for the period in which Abraham might have lived. He and his people were unknown to the scribes of Ur whose tablets have so far been recovered from the site.

Another aspect of my editing and revising is less precisely justified, and far less easy to apply, since it goes to the very heart of Woolley's distinctive style and personality. The most difficult single problem facing any editor of Woolley's popular books is his vivid historical imagination which, though it may not stray too far from probability, sometimes stretches the available archaeological information to its limits in complete reconstructions of individual buildings, known only from excavated foundations, and in memorable evocations of daily life in them. There is so much that we do not know about the ancient world that controlled writing of this kind is unavoidable in general surveys. My limits of inference, it will be clear, are less flexible on occasion than were Woolley's, but wherever possible I have given him the benefit of our common ignorance. Sir Max Mallowan, who was in a much better position than anyone else to comment on this side of Woolley's character, has provided, in *Mallowan's Memoirs* (London, 1977), a particularly intimate glimpse of Woolley in the role of guide. This was a task he relished, both on the site at Ur, when taking visitors round his excavations, and on the printed page when he imagined a similar audience.

'There is the Headmaster's house', wrote Mallowan, recalling his master's voice,

> take care of the bottom step, it is much too high to be practicable. There was once a wooden step in front of it, but this has long ago perished. You see, the owner had to have the maximum possible rise before the turn of the stairs which ran over the lavatory behind you; in that way he was able to avoid bumping his head'. 'Now take a look at the roof', he would say, as we stared up at the empty sky. 'I know you cannot see it, but we know everything

about it that matters. The evidence is mostly on the floor in front of you'. He would point to the brick base of a vanished column, one of four, which could only have been used to support a balcony three feet wide which allowed the rain to drip into an impluvium in the middle of the court; he would then point to the only possible place for the gutters and explain how a raised coping must have run along the gentle slopes between them. So it went on as we passed through the bazaar ...

This passage admirably evokes Woolley's skill as a raconteur and his ability, all too rare among archaeologists addressing a wide public, to write a lively, clear account of his discoveries constantly illuminated by intimate flashes of memory, rich in significant detail, which leaves an enduring impression on the reader's mind. All this I have striven to retain, whilst seeking to set Woolley's remarkable finds within a general framework acceptable to a new generation of students and general readers.

Then, finally, there is the matter of Woolley's lifelong independence of academic involvement, which brought a welcome freshness of approach, but at times left him out of step with the current consensus based on a wider range of evidence than he had at his disposal. Reviewers in 1954 were struck by how few changes there had been in Woolley's basic opinions since 1929. Although very ready to write 'I was wrong' or 'my colleagues have called me seriously to account' in questions of detail, Woolley had strong ideas on some crucial general questions of interpretation. These were little modified by fresh evidence and changing perspectives over the quarter of a century up to 1954 during which much happened in Meso-potamian archaeology. Even more has happened in the next twenty-five years. Woolley was inclined, as Mallowan tells us, 'to play a lone hand and was reluctant to consult authority, particularly when he had built up a chronological framework which he considered to be satisfactory'. He was, understandably, keen to establish the high antiquity of his finds and sometimes pressed his case overhard to that end, particularly if in doing so he was able to give Mesopotamia precedence over Egypt in cultural developments. Time has inevitably modified even his less controversial positions, and his chronology, and had indeed already done so by the early 1950s, though it is not apparent in the pages of the original edition of this book. Thus my revisions in the early chapters will seem more radical than those in the later ones, where Woolley's historical framework conformed more closely to current understanding.

The criticisms implied by this necessary explanation of my procedures must not for a moment be allowed to overshadow my profound respect for Woolley's achievements at Ur. He excavated the site with remarkable skill in the face of intimidating problems and he had his whole excavation report ready for publication within five years of completion, although by then he was already engaged on new excavations in Syria. For reasons entirely beyond Woolley's control this monumental publication of his work was not completed until sixteen years after his death. It made Ur one of the very few satisfactorily published Near Eastern excavations. It is to these volumes that any reader must go who wishes to pursue further his interest in the work surveyed in the following pages. His effort will be richly rewarded, since they are unique in being both readable and fully comprehensible to any reader with a basic knowledge of Mesopotamian archaeology. To aid such a reader I have added brief bibliographical notes to each chapter. Detailed footnotes would, I felt, have defeated Woolley's purpose and run counter to the spirit of the book. It is to be hoped they will be found one day in the comprehensive survey of both the archaeological and the textual evidence from Ur that remains to be written. I have dropped the original appendix in which the Sumerian King-List was summarized. This seemed inappropriate for the lay reader, adding nothing to his appreciation of the book and being too concise for a true understanding of this difficult, but vital document. I have put in its place a quick topographical guide to ancient Ur.

Woolley died in 1960, within weeks of his eightieth birthday, and the last word in this preface may most appropriately be left to Sir Max Mallowan, whose help at Ur Woolley acknowledged in his own preface.

> For his work at Ur alone our debt to Woolley is immeasurable. In three things he excelled. First, his recognition of how much a knowledge of architectural development can contribute to our understanding of ancient society. Next I think comes his incomparable sense of craftsmanship, for which he had a genuine love. I remember standing alone with him one day and seeing the sudden collapse of a Kassite wall which had stood its ground for thirty-three centuries: 'It grieves me', he said, 'to watch the end of any good work to which men have given much thought and skill'. Whenever he found something produced by human hands he tried to visualise the process of creating it, and to share the aspirations of its maker. Lastly, he was a most gifted writer with a fluency of style which has entranced a multitude of readers the world over. His books may well serve as a model to all archaeologists, an immortal reminder that good writing, which can only be achieved through good reading and clear thinking, should be the crown for our endeavours.
>
> (*Iraq* 12 (1960), p.16)

Ashmolean Museum, Oxford, 1981   P.R.S.M.

Introduction

Ur lies about half-way between Baghdad and the head of the Gulf, some 10 miles west of the present course of the Euphrates. A mile and a half to the east of the ruins runs the single line of railway which joins Basra to the capital of Iraq, and between the rail and the river there is sparse cultivation and little villages of mud huts or reed-mat shelters are dotted here and there; but westwards of the line is desert blank and unredeemed. Out of this waste rise the mounds which were Ur, called by the Arabs after the highest of them all, the Ziggurat hill, 'Tell el-Mukayyar', the 'Mound of Pitch'.

Standing on the summit of this mound one can distinguish along the eastern skyline the dark tasselled fringe of the palm-gardens on the river's bank, but to north and west and south as far as the eye can see stretches a waste of unprofitable sand. To the south-west the flat line of the horizon is broken by a grey upstanding pinnacle, the ruins of the staged tower of the sacred city of Eridu which the Sumerians believed to be the oldest city upon earth, and to the north-west a shadow thrown by the low sun may tell the whereabouts of the low mound of al-'Ubaid; but otherwise nothing relieves the monotony of the vast plain over which the shimmering heat-waves dance and the mirage spreads its mockery of placid waters. It seems incredible that such a wilderness should ever have been habitable for man, and yet the weathered hillocks at one's feet cover the temples and houses of a very great city.

As long ago as 1854 Mr J.E. Taylor, British Consul at Basra, was employed by the British Museum to investigate some of the southern sites of Mesopotamia, and chose for his chief work the 'Mound of Pitch'. Here he unearthed inscriptions which for the first time revealed that the name-less ruin was the site of ancient Ur. Taylor's discoveries were not at the time appraised at their true worth and his excavations closed down after two seasons; but more and more the importance of the site came to be recognized, and though, partly through lack of funds and partly because of the lawless character of the district into which foreigners could penetrate only at their own risk, no further excavations were undertaken, yet the British Museum never gave up hope of carrying on the work which Taylor had begun.

Towards the end of the nineteenth century an expedition sent out by the University of Pennsylvania visited Ur and contrived to do a little excavation of which the results have never been published, and then again the site lay fallow until the Great War brought British troops into Mesopotamia and gave an opportunity for long-cherished hopes to be realized. In 1918 Mr R. Campbell Thompson, formerly assistant in the British Museum and then on the Intelligence Staff of the Army in Mesopotamia, excavated at Eridu and made soundings at Ur. The British Museum was encouraged to put a regular expedition into the field, and when Dr Leonard King, who was to have led it, fell ill, Dr H.R. Hall took his place and during the winter of 1918–19 dug at Ur, Eridu, and al-'Ubaid. Dr Hall's work at Ur was of an experimental nature, richer in promise than fulfilment, but his expedition was of prime importance in that he discovered and partly excavated the mound of al-'Ubaid with its fine remains of early architectural decoration.

Again the want of pence which vexes public institutions brought matters to a standstill. Then, in 1922, Dr G.B. Gordon, Director of the University Museum of Pennsylvania, approached the British Museum with the proposal of a joint expedition to Mesopotamia; the offer was accepted, and Ur was chosen as the scene of operations. The directorship of the Joint Expedition was entrusted to me and I carried on the field-work without interruption for the next twelve winters. We could not in that time excavate the whole of Ur, for the site is immense and to reach the earlier levels we often had to dig very deeply so that, although work was always done at high pressure and the number of men employed was the maximum consistent with proper supervision—at one moment it topped the four hundred—only a minute fraction of the city's area was thoroughly explored. None the less, we did secure a reasonably detailed picture of Ur throughout its five thousand years of existence and by 1934 had made discoveries far surpassing anything we had dared to expect; now there was the danger that more digging would yield results more or less repetitive, and the preparing of our material for publication, an imperative duty, could not be undertaken while field-work was still in progress; it was therefore decided to close down the Expedition.

This is a book about excavation, about the buildings and the objects that we unearthed, and the wealth of our archaeological material is so great that I do not propose to deal with anything outside it. So far as is possible I shall treat of things in historical order, but I am not writing a history of Ur. In 1929 Mr C.J. Gadd published a pioneering attempt at this, entitled *The History and Monuments of Ur*, during the course of our work. This is now completely outdated and no attempt has yet been made to produce a

13

synthesis of the information so far gleaned from the many thousands of tablets and other inscriptions which the excavations recovered. I am not qualified to draw upon the literary sources and I shall do no more than try to show how our finds illustrate or supplement the historical framework established for Ur by Gadd and other scholars working on the documentary evidence. But the introduction to my book does seem to be the appropriate place in which to describe the positive additions to history afforded by our work in the field.

When the Expedition was being planned, I was told that we might expect to recover monuments taking us back so far in time as the reign of King Ur-Nammu, founder of the Third Dynasty of Ur c. 2112 B.C., but should probably find nothing earlier. King Ur-Nammu was indeed almost

Map of the Near and Middle East

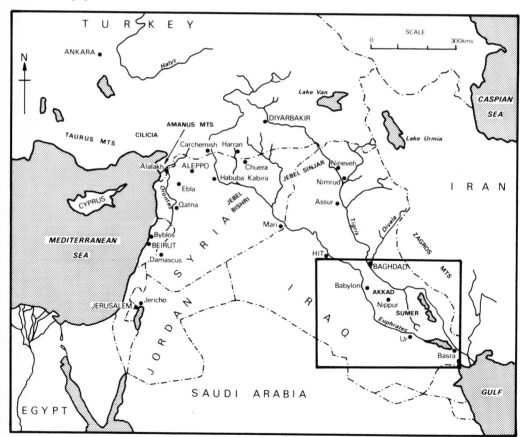

the first character in the history of Mesopotamia acknowledged by scholars to be historically authentic. It was known that cities went back far beyond Ur-Nammu; there were in museums actual monuments of earlier kings with their names written against them—but there was no means of saying when they reigned; about one great figure, Sargon of Akkad, there were poems and legends—but as late as 1916 Dr Leonard King found it necessary to argue at length the real identity of one who had been discounted as a mere hero of romance. There was even a list of kings which had been drawn up by Sumerian scribes about 1800 B.C., a sort of skeleton of history not unlike the King-list 'William I, 21 years, William II, 13 years....' of our English school-books, whose value depended on more archaeological research. While its arrangement, the succession of various families (or dynasties), can be considered a later construction of uncertain significance, it includes material of high historical value from which only exaggerated reigns for some of the earliest rulers have to be excluded.

The recovery from Ur of contemporary inscriptions of kings of the dynasty of Akkad (c. 2334–2154 B.C.), including a relief and an inscription of Sargon's daughter, who was High-Priestess of the Moon-god, and personal seals of some of her officials, opened a new era in understanding early Mesopotamian history. Even more significant was the discovery at al-'Ubaid of a stone foundation-tablet of the small temple there which stated that it had been built by Aanepada, king of Ur, son of Mesanepada, king of Ur; the latter appears in the Sumerian King-List as the founder of the First Dynasty of Ur, and with the discovery that First Dynasty, which had until then been regarded as mythical, emerged into history. The find also cleared up a minor difficulty. Owing to the similarity of the two names that of Aanepada had dropped out of the Sumerian King-List and Mesanepada was credited with the unlikely reign of eighty years; as soon as it became evident that the figure had to be divided between father and son, the improbability vanished and the record could be accepted as authentic. The written history of Sumer had been carried back for something like five hundred years; although nothing could justify the swollen chronology of the earlier kings named in the List, one could suspect that behind it all there lurks an element of historical reality. At an archaeological congress of excavators held at Baghdad in 1929 it was agreed that the early stages of human settlement in south Mesopotamia could be classified in successive phases which should be called, after the places where the evidence for each was first discovered, the al-'Ubaid period, the Uruk period, the Jamdat Nasr period, and then the Early Dynastic period, towards the end of which (in IIIb) comes the First Dynasty of Ur.

Archaeological excavation provides us with a relative sequence for these phases, but it does not of itself offer an absolute chronology in years B.C./A.D. Even when written records provide information upon which such an absolute chronology can be constructed, the further this goes back in time the greater grows the possible margin of error. Any system we adopt still has to be regarded as tentative and liable to revision, possibly major ones before the middle of the second millennium B.C., relatively minor ones thereafter. The absolute dates given here for the rulers of Mesopotamia from Sargon of Akkad onwards are those of Professor J.A. Brinkman in his 'Mesopotamian Chronology of the Historical Period' in A.L. Oppenheim, *Ancient Mesopotamia: Portrait of a Dead Civilization* (revised edition, Chicago, 1977). Measurements of residual radioactivity in carbon specimens (Carbon-14) have added a source of absolute chronology for periods before Sargon of Akkad. Unfortunately this technique has not been so widely applied to samples from Mesopotamia as we might wish, but sufficient determinations are available to allow us to date the early historic and prehistoric periods within broad limits. The Early Dynastic period, conventionally divided into three (I,II,III), extends from about 3000 B.C. ($\pm$ 150 years) to about 2330 B.C., with the royal tombs at Ur, usually attributed to Early Dynastic IIIa, falling about 2650–2550 B.C. The Uruk and Jamdat Nasr periods between them cover the fourth millennium B.C., with the earlier Uruk period, in which writing was invented in Mesopotamia, being much the longer of the two. The various phases of the 'Ubaid period embrace the fifth millennium B.C., with the earliest recognized settlements in southern Mesopotamia, the Eridu or 'Ubaid I phase, going back to about the middle of the sixth millennium B.C.

Now no single dig, however successful, can give a complete picture of the history even of its own site, much less of the whole country. Sites may be very large, so that the excavations cannot cover their entire area, or may be very complicated so that digging has to be done down to great depths in order to reach the earlier levels, and the expense of such work may be prohibitive. Part of a site may at one time have been deserted, with the result that excavation in that part will fail to produce any evidence of a cultural phase which elsewhere on the site may be well represented; in preparing the foundation of an important building the old builders may have swept away a whole series of earlier strata and so have made a gap in our archaeological series which we have no reason to suspect; or that building may have stood unaltered throughout a period of time that saw many vicissitudes in the town's history—but if our excavation is limited to the building, it will tell us nothing of those vicissitudes. These excava-

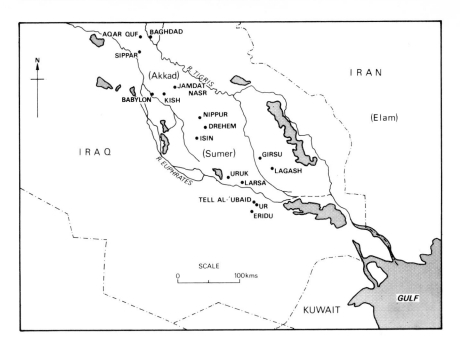

Map of lower Mesopotamia

tions therefore do not give us the full story of Ur; what they do give has to be amplified and sometimes modified by the results of the many other digs on other sites; but since the subject of this book is the Ur excavation and not a complete history, I shall refer to the other digs only when such reference is necessary for the proper understanding of what we found. If then I say little or nothing about the discoveries made by fellow archaeologists working in Iraq, it is not because I underrate their importance but because they do not fall within my province. But I should indeed be doing injustice if I failed to acknowledge the debt that I owe my own staff. In the course of twelve years I had the help of a large number of assistants; my wife was with me for ten seasons, Professor Mallowan for six, others for four or less; if they are not mentioned individually in the course of this book, it is because the work was team-work throughout and each was prone to sink his personality in the common task; looking back now, I am surprised to find how seldom I can say of a particular job 'So-and-so did that'; nearly always it was a joint affair. And perhaps that is the highest praise I can give to a staff which deserves all my praise and gratitude; they did not do this job or that—they were the Expedition, and its success was the measure of their devotion.

The Beginnings of Ur

Lower Mesopotamia, the Sumer of the ancient world, is no more or less than the river-valley of the Tigris and the Euphrates; it does not include the high Syrian desert to the west, because that is desert—a waterless expanse of gravel barren for most of the year at least—where the wandering Bedouin may pitch their tents for a brief space, but no man claiming to be civilized could make his home; and it does not include the Persian mountains that fringe it on the east because always those mountains were held by warlike tribes more ready to raid the cultivated fields of the valley people than to submit to their sway. The people of Sumer themselves believed that the oldest of their cities was Eridu, which lies about 12 miles south of Ur, and excavation there by an Iraqi government expedition between 1947 and 1949 went far towards confirming this belief; nowhere in lower Mesopotamia proper have there yet been found traces of a settlement so ancient as that at Eridu. Clearly this requires explanation, and we must look carefully at the physical geography of our area.

Geologists long thought it to be a land of recent origin. The arm of the sea now called the Gulf was believed to have extended far inland, to the north of modern Baghdad, and it was only at a relatively late date, since about 4000 B.C., that salt water gave place to dry land, a change due not to any sudden cataclysm, but to the gradual deposit of river silt filling the great rift between mountain and desert. When the vast quantities of alluvium removed annually by the Tigris and the Euphrates were taken into account, the hypothesis of a coastline moving steadily in a southerly direction seemed not improbable. It was, however, radically modified by

LEFT *View of pit 'X', one of a number of deep pits through which Woolley investigated the prehistory of Ur; he is to be seen among his Arab workmen, distinguishable by hat and jacket* the researches of two oil company geologists, Lees and Falcon, published 1952. In their view continuous sedimentation by rivers feeding the lower Mesopotamian plain has been finely balanced by intermittent subsidence in the floor of the river basin producing a virtual equilibrium between land and sea levels. In the last six thousand years at least, they argued, there has been no substantial movement in the shoreline at the head of the Gulf, though there has been a complex pattern of advance and retreat along this line. More recent evidence would go further. Borings in the region of modern Basra have revealed sediments and fauna partly marine in origin and of recent geological age. This suggests that even into historic times the shoreline may have run, in part at least, anything from 80 to 175 miles north-west of its present line. When ancient texts speak of Ur and Eridu 'on the sea', they may well have meant just that rather than an extended lake tortuously linked with the sea by channels through marshy swamps, as some scholars have argued. Only further analysis of steadily accumulating geological data will bring greater precision to answering this question.

In 1919 Dr H.R. Hall, who was carrying out an experimental dig at Ur on behalf of the British Museum, discovered and partly excavated a little mound called by the Arabs Tell al-'Ubaid, which lay some 4 miles to the north of Ur; the results were so important that the complete excavation of the site was one of the first items in the programme of the Joint Expedition when it took the field three years later. The most sensational discovery was that of the First Dynasty temple which will be described hereafter (p. 104); what interests us now was something entirely different and very much older. About 60 yards from the temple ruins there was a low mound—it rose no more than 6 feet above the plain—the surface of which was strewn with flint implements and fragments of hand-made painted pottery, of a sort which had already been found at Eridu, south of Ur, and had been recognized as 'prehistoric', though little more than that was known about it. We excavated the mound and were somewhat taken aback to find how little work it required—everything lay quite close to the surface. Under a few inches of light dust mixed with potsherds there came a stratum not more than 3 feet thick composed of hard mud in which were quantities of sherds of painted ware, flint and obsidian tools, and bits of reed matting plastered with clay mixed with dung or, less often, with a mixture of earth and bitumen; below this was clean water-laid soil. This was, in fact, an island of river silt which originally rose above the marshy plain and had been seized upon by immigrants who had erected on it their primitive hut dwellings of reeds plastered with clay. The village had later been deserted and the dust and potsherds of the top-most layer represented its ruins; at one point we found in this layer the foundations of a mud-brick wall contemporary with the First Dynasty temple close by, and since this lay immediately in and over the older remains from which it was separated by an unknown length of time, we could conclude that our village had been definitely abandoned and that its site remained for long uninhabited. The 3 feet of hard mud and household rubbish had accumulated during the village's lifetime, as the flimsy huts fell down and others were erected over them; the lighter soil above represented the last buildings, but much of it had been eroded by the desert winds (which accounts for the mass of potsherds exposed on the surface) and this must have happened during the time when the site lay desolate. But, scanty as the remains were, they were enough to tell us a great deal about the people who lived there.

At al-'Ubaid not a trace of metal was found, though it is known elsewhere at this time. The larger tools, such as hoes, were chipped from the flint or chert that can be got from the upper desert; knives and awls might be of rock crystal or obsidian—volcanic glass—both of which had to be imported from abroad; beads were made from rock crystal, carnelian, pink pebble, and shell, and these were all chipped into shape and not polished; but one or two ear- or nose-studs of polished obsidian found on the surface may date from this period and, if so, show that a finer working of stone was not beyond the powers of the al-'Ubaid craftsman. But that in which they excelled was their pottery. The vessels were hand-made without the use of the wheel, but were thinly walled and finely shaped, and the characteristic ware was decorated with designs in black or brown paint on a ground which was intended to be white but often, through over-firing, assumed a curious and rather effective greenish tint. The patterns were all geometrical, built up from the simple elements of triangles, squares, wavy or vandyke lines, and chevrons which might be filled in solidly or with hatching, but these were most skilfully combined and in all cases the design was admirably adapted to the shape of the vessel. At al-'Ubaid the pottery seems to be from the outset fully developed; it is not of local growth. In more recent times excavations at Eridu have brought to light an earlier phase of the same ware, but the difference is one of degree only, not of kind, and the essential characteristics of the al-'Ubaid pottery are already there.

If we accept, as most scholars now do, that the overall character of southern Iraq was established much as it is today by soon after 6000 B.C., then relatively settled communities with a hunting and fishing economy, and a way of life much like that of the modern Marsh Arabs of the region, could have been established in the lagoons and marshes long before the

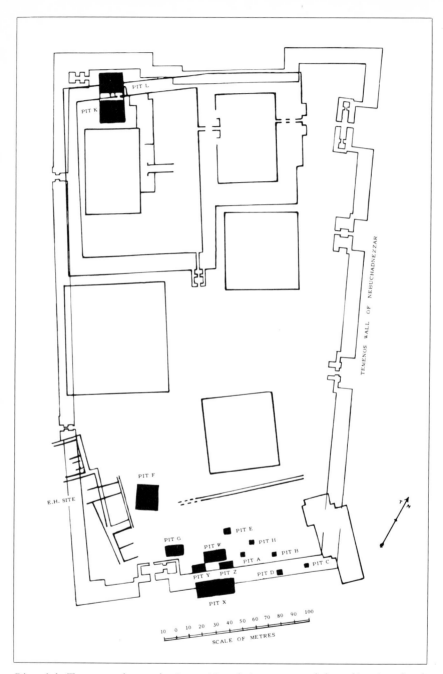

PIT L

PIT K

TEMENOS WALL OF NEBUCHADNEZZAR

PIT F

E.H. SITE

PIT G   PIT E

PIT W   PIT H

PIT A   PIT B

PIT Y   PIT Z   PIT D   PIT C

PIT X

10 0 10 20 30 40 50 60 70 80 90 100
SCALE OF METRES

Plan of the Temenos enclosure, showing position of pits cut to reveal the prehistoric and early historic settlements

earliest traces now evident to archaeologists. Heavy silting, and the shifting pattern of rivers and marshes, greatly hamper archaeological research. Remains of very early settlements may lie far below the modern surface, even where that is above water, leaving no indication of their presence. The novelty in the way of life of the people of 'Ubaid times, their cultivation of cereals like wheat and barley with the aid of simple irrigation techniques, could well have been derived from external contacts, like the pigments with which they painted their pottery. This seems more probable than the alternative view that the appearance of 'Ubaid painted pottery necessarily involves the arrival of large groups of intruders from outside the area.

Quite definitely the 'Ubaid period people were agriculturalists; the commonest stone implement is the hoe; many of the small flints seem to come from the sledges used for threshing grain; stone querns and pounders show that this was used for bread. But the most curious evidence is that given by the sickles, which, or rather the fragments of which, litter the site of the village. These sickles were made of baked clay. Clay would seem to be the very last material that one would use for a cutting instrument, but the shape is indisputable, and the clay is so hard-baked and the jagged edge of the blade so keen that they would cut more or less; and if it be argued that they would certainly break, the answer is that they did, only too easily, and that is why we find them in such numbers, and hardly ever one of them intact. The people then tilled the ground, and they kept domestic animals—the cow-dung in the mud plaster of their huts is evidence for that, and we found a clay figurine of a pig; spindle-whorls of baked clay or of bitumen prove that thread was spun, woollen thread presumably, and heavy clay discs pierced with two holes are almost certainly loom-weights. Fishbones found in the hut ruins show that fish were eaten, as one would expect in a village close to river and marsh; some were so small that the fish must have been taken in nets, and a number of grooved pebbles that we found may have been net-sinkers; we found also a clay model of an open boat with canoe-like body and curled prow. We have seen that nose- or ear-studs were worn, and beads; part of a painted clay figurine shows a woman wearing a very wide necklace and on the shoulders there are painted lines which may represent drapery; another figurine fragment, the lower part of the body, shows either tight-fitting breeches laced down the front or else tattoo marks on the flesh.

One day two Arabs came to the expedition house at Ur and from a folded handkerchief produced four or five big flint hoes which they had picked up, they said vaguely, 'in the desert'. They received a good *baksheesh* and, as I had hoped, returned a day or two later with more hoes, but again would not specify where they were found. When they came for the fourth time, I refused any reward, protesting that I had hoes enough, but told them that they would be well paid if they would guide us to the find-spot; which, seeing that that was the only chance of making any more money, they agreed to do. The site, called by the Arabs Rajeibeh, lay some 6 miles to the north-east of Ur; it was so low a mound as to be hardly noticeable, but as soon as we came to it, the mystery of our visitors' hoe-harvest was explained; one could not walk a step without setting one's foot on worked flints and painted potsherds lying so thick as to hide the desert surface. It was a site exactly like al-'Ubaid but much larger. No excavation would have availed here, for directly below the stone and pottery refuse was the clean silt of the island on which the settlers had made their homes; nobody in later times had ever built upon the site so that there were no upper strata to protect it, and the wind had carried away everything that wind could carry. Probably there had been here successive building levels representing a fairly long period, and the flints, etc. (too numerous to be all of one date) must have been distributed throughout a deposit of consider-able depth; but as the process of wind erosion went on, the heavier debris of the upper levels had settled down until all the dust of the decomposed dwellings had been blown away and the flints and potsherds of many generations had sunk to one common level which was virtually flush with the surrounding desert and so offered no challenge to the winds. Rajeibeh did not give us any information beyond what al-'Ubaid had given, but its importance lay in the fact that it repeated exactly the al-'Ubaid story; in both cases we have a natural island in the marshland inhabited by immigrants of the same stock and culture and in both, after a period of continuous occupation, the site is completely and finally deserted. Why this was, we were to learn from the excavations at Ur itself. And another point on which we needed evidence was the relative date of these village settlements.

In the year 1929 the work of excavating the Royal Cemetery at Ur was drawing towards its end. On the evidence then to hand I was convinced that the cemetery came before, but only just before, the First Dynasty of Ur; the treasures recovered from its graves illustrated a civilization of an astonishingly high order and it was therefore all the more important to trace the steps by which man had reached that level of art and culture. That meant, presumably, that we had to dig deeper; but it was just as well to begin by a small-scale test of the lower levels which could be carried out with a minimum of time and cost. Starting then below the level at which the graves had been found we sank a little shaft, not more than 5 feet square at the outset, into the underlying soil and went down through the mixed rubbish that is characteristic of old inhabited sites—a mixture of decomposed mud-bricks, ashes, and broken pottery, very much like that in which the graves had been dug. This went on for about 3 feet and then suddenly, it all stopped; there were no more potsherds, no ashes, only clean water-laid mud, and the Arab workman at the bottom of the shaft told me that he had reached virgin soil; there was nothing more to be found, and he had better go elsewhere.

I got down and looked at the evidence and agreed with him; but then I took my levels and discovered that 'virgin soil' was not nearly so deep down as I had expected, for I had assumed that the original Ur was built not on a hill but on a low mound rising only just above the surrounding swampy land; and because I do not like having my theories upset by anything less than proof, I told the man to get back and go on digging. Most unwillingly he did so, again turning up nothing but clean soil that yielded no sign of human activity; he dug through 8 feet of it in all and then, suddenly, there appeared flint implements and fragments of painted al-'Ubaid pottery vessels. I got into the pit once more, examined the sides, and by the time I had written up my notes was quite convinced of what it all meant; but I wanted to see whether others would come to the same conclusion. So I brought up two of my staff and, after pointing out the facts, asked for their explanation. They did not know what to say. My wife came along and looked and was asked the same question, and she turned away remarking casually, 'Well, of course, it's the Flood'. That was the right answer. But one could scarcely argue for the Deluge on the strength of a pit a yard square; so in the next season I marked out, on the low ground where the graves of the Royal Cemetery had been, a rectangle some 75 feet by 60 and there dug a huge pit which went down, in the end, for 64 feet. Now the graves, which had been pretty deep-lying, had been dug down, from a ground-surface much higher than the level at which our pit started, into rubbish-mounds heaped against the flank of the old town; we had cleared away the graves and the rubbish and the level of the pit's mouth therefore was necessarily older than the graves by the (unknown) length of time required for so much rubbish to accumulate; it was probably quite a long time.

Almost as soon as the new dig started we came upon the ruins of houses. The walls were built of mud-bricks of the 'plano-convex' type—rectangular but rounded on the top instead of flat—which we had found alike in the First Dynasty temple at al-'Ubaid and in the Royal Cemetery, and such pottery as lay in the rooms was of the sort common in the graves higher up.

Below these ruins came a second building stratum, and then a third; in the first 20 feet we dug through no fewer than eight levels of houses, each built above the ruins of the previous age; but in the lowest three the wall-bricks were not plano-convex but flat-topped, and there were types of pottery different from any that the Royal Cemetery had produced. Then, abruptly, the house-ruins stopped and we were digging down through a solid mass of broken pottery which continued for about 18 feet and in it, at different levels, were the kilns in which the pots had been fired. It was the site of a vase-factory; the sherds represented the pots which went wrong in the firing—were cracked or distorted—and having no commercial value were smashed by the potter and the bits left lying there until they were heaped so high that the kiln was buried and a new kiln had to be built on top of them; an accumulation of 18 feet of wasters meant that the factory was in production for a long time, and the changes of fashion during that time could be traced from its discards. The sherds in upper debris were for the most part similar to the few found in the lower house levels, but amongst them were fragments painted in red and black on a buff ground identical with a ware which on a site called Jamdat Nasr, 150 miles to the north of Ur, had shortly before been found associated with written clay tablets of a most primitive sort; but Jamdat Nasr, like al-'Ubaid, was as yet an isolated discovery whose relation to Sumerian history was a matter of guesswork only. Lower down in our kiln stratum the character of the potsherds changed, the polychrome wares disappeared and in their place all the distinctive fragments showed a monochrome decoration, plain red produced by a wash of haematite or grey or black resulting from the use of the

Two spouted pottery jars of the 'Ubaid period

'smother-kiln' in which the smoke is retained to carbonize the clay; this was a ware which the German excavators at Uruk (the ancient Erech) had been finding in the lowest levels they had yet reached. Low down in this 'Uruk' stratum we found a remarkable object, a heavy disc of baked clay about 3 feet in diameter with a central pivot-hole and a small hole near the rim to take a handle; it was a potter's wheel as used by the makers of the Uruk vases, the earliest known example of that invention whereby man passed from the age of pure handicraft into the age of machinery. And only a foot or so below the point at which the wheel was found the character of the pottery changed again and we were digging through sherds of the hand-turned painted ware of al-'Ubaid. But this was al-'Ubaid with a difference. The hand-made pots were of the same clay and had the same whitish or greenish surface, but in most the decoration in black paint was reduced to a minimum—plain horizontal lines or the simplest patterns perfunctorily and carelessly drawn; clearly they belonged to the last stages of decadence. Then—it was only a thin stratum—all the pottery came to an end and we had, as we expected, the clean silt piled up by the Flood. A few graves had been dug down in the silt, and in them was al-'Ubaid pottery of a richer sort than that in the kiln rubbish above; in one of them there was a copper spear-blade, the earliest example we have found of metal being used for weapons or tools; the bodies all lay on their backs, rigidly extended, with the hands crossed below the stomach, a position not found in Mesopotamian graves of any later date until the Greek period; such a difference in the ritual of burial is most important in that it implies a difference in the basic religious beliefs of the people. In some of the graves

Painted pottery of the 'Ubaid period

*Clay figurine of a woman
suckling a baby: 'Ubaid period*

LEFT *Baked clay female
figurines of the 'Ubaid period*

there were terracotta figurines of the type also found in the al-'Ubaid house ruins; they were always female and nude, sometimes showing a woman suckling a child but more often a single figure with the hands brought in front of the body very much in the attitude of the dead beside whom they lay. These graves, dug into the silt deposit, were of course later than the Flood, but they had been made before the vase-factory occupied the area in the last phase of the al-'Ubaid period.

At this point the clean silt measured about 11 feet in thickness and except for one scarcely noticeable stratum of darker mud was absolutely uniform throughout; microscopic analysis proved that it was water-laid, subject to the action of gentle currents, and it was composed of material brought down from the middle reaches of the Euphrates. Below it came the level of human occupation—decayed mud-brick, ashes, and potsherds, in which we could distinguish three successive floor-levels; here was the richly decorated al-'Ubaid pottery in abundance, flints, clay figurines, and flat rectangular bricks (preserved because they had been accidentally burnt) and fragments of clay plaster, also hardened by fire, which on one side were smooth, flat or convex, and on the other side bore the imprint of reed stems, the daub from the walls of the reed huts which, as we saw at al-'Ubaid, were the normal houses of the pre-Flood people, as they are of the Marsh Arab today.

The first huts had been set up on the surface of a belt of mud which was clearly formed, for the most part, of decayed vegetable matter, in it were the potsherds (thicker at the bottom of the belt) all lying horizontally as if they had been thrown there and had sunk of their own weight through water into soft mud; below this again, 3 feet below modern sea-level, there was stiff green clay pierced by sinuous brown stains which had been the roots of reeds; here all traces of human activity ceased and we were at the bottom of Mesopotamia.

The digging of so great a pit was a long and expensive matter, but it amply repaid us in historical results; it confirmed the sequence which had been tentatively drawn upon the strength of our own and other excavations—particularly those of Uruk—and it added a lot of valuable detail.

The green clay at the bottom was the floor of the original marsh bordering the island which was occupied by the first settlers in this part of the valley; it was dense with reeds, and with the decay of their stems and leaves and with the rubbish thrown into the water from the island the bottom rose and gradually dry land was formed; when it was dry enough people set up their huts on it at the foot of what was by now the city mound. All this low-lying quarter was overwhelmed by a great flood and buried beneath its silt.

The appearance in the kiln stratum of the red, black to grey 'Uruk' pottery marks a new chapter in the history of lower Mesopotamia. Its origins are still obscure. At the site of Uruk itself German archaeologists have sunk a number of pits deep into the soil, as at Ur, revealing a sequence of levels in which a gradual change may be observed from the last type of painted 'Ubaid pottery to the mass-produced, often wheel-made, plain pottery taken to be characteristic of the Uruk period. Attractive red and grey burnished pottery is less common than the plain wares. Here also a monumental building of the later 'Ubaid period is ancestral to the complex series of shrines, ceremonial and administrative buildings of the culminating level of the Uruk period (level IV). In this phase (IVa) appeared the oldest written records yet found anywhere in the world. They decisively mark the emergence of complex urban communities in southern Iraq. Their pictographic script gradually evolved into the cuneiform (wedge-shaped) script used by later Sumerian scribes. Above the Uruk potsherds at Ur come the levels containing painted Jamdat Nasr pottery. Then, high up in our pit, with the fourth stratum of house ruins, Jamdat Nasr ware disappears, round-topped bricks (the so-called plano-convex bricks) replace the old flat type, and the pottery is that ancestral to what we find in the Royal Cemetery—it is the beginning of the Early Dynastic period, divided by archaeologists into three phases. But the houses were to decay and be rebuilt three times, and thereafter the site of them was abandoned and turned into a rubbish-heap before the first grave of the Royal Cemetery was dug; that cemetery therefore, and the First Dynasty of Ur which immediately succeeded it, do not introduce the first historic period at Ur but come relatively late in it, in what is currently known as Early Dynastic III.

Such is the outline of prehistory given by the stratification of our great pit. It shows, beyond all question, the order of the ceramic phases, and until we know that order there is no possibility of explaining the sequence of events; but it does not necessarily tell us much about any one phase; the picture has to be completed from the results not of one dig but of many. Thus from the three superimposed floor-levels found below the Flood silt it might be argued that the Flood happened when the settlement was still young; but that is far from being the case to judge by the depth of deposits revealed by excavations at Eridu. There the lowest level of human occupation recognized by the excavators was numbered XIX down from the surface; the highest level attributed to the 'Ubaid period was number VI.

Within this range various subdivisions were made on the basis of the pottery. Levels XIX–XVI produced pottery, painted in what has become known as the 'Eridu' style. The geographical distribution of related archaeological material is wide, extending north and east to the frontiers of modern Iran. The succeeding levels XV–XIII at Eridu, represent a phase distinguished by a painted pottery style named after the site of Hajji Muhammad (near Uruk). From Ur came many sherds both of 'Eridu' and of 'Hajji Muhammad' pottery, indicating that there was indeed a village there at this time (equivalent to Eridu: levels XIX–XIII) missed by our deep excavation shafts. These sherds came from the area near the Ziggurat, where they had arrived with earth brought from elsewhere to level up the great temple platform in the second millennium B.C. The pits we dug had been sunk down into the edge of the mound formed by successive prehistoric villages, inevitably missing the earliest one, as that would have lain at the centre of the mound, at a point not yet reached by any deep excavation at Ur.

The evidence from Eridu involves a reappraisal of the three subdivisions of the 'Ubaid period defined at Ur and numbered I to III, from early to late. 'Ubaid I in our Ur terminology, the archaeological material from below the 'Flood-level', is possibly as late as level IX in the sequence at Eridu and certainly no earlier than level XII there, whilst 'Ubaid II at Ur is equivalent to the latest phase of the 'Ubaid period at Eridu. In the confused sequence of graves attributed to 'Ubaid III at Ur, high up in, or above, the top of the 'Flood-deposit', painted pottery was reduced to a minimum. More significantly there had been a change in burial position. The bodies were now fully extended rather than slightly flexed as they had been earlier. Information from other sites indicates that these graves belong not to the 'Ubaid but to the following Uruk period.

The range of distribution of the decorated pottery of Ur–'Ubaid II (levels XII–VIII at Eridu), the final phase of the 'Ubaid period proper, when pottery was more simply decorated than before, is enormous. It stretches throughout modern Iraq, into Syria in the west, Iran in the east, and down the western shores of the Gulf into Saudi Arabia. How are we to explain this apparent diffusion of so distinctive a ware from a nuclear region in lower Mesopotamia around Ur in the second half of the fifth millennium B.C.? If it were merely a matter of pottery, as it primarily is outside Mesopotamia, this might well be explained by the diffusion of potting fashions through trade, as the inhabitants of lower Mesopotamia sought the raw materials, metals, stones, and timber, unavailable to them at home. But within Mesopotamia by this time there are close parallels between religious buildings in north and south. This could well mean that the peoples of the south were exercising some kind of military or political authority over the north in order to ensure a regular flow of vital and desirable raw materials, perhaps even some manufactured goods, from the already well-developed farming communities of the region. In the south along the western shores of the Gulf, including the island of Bahrein, the 'Ubaid peoples of Ur were making contact with less fully developed communities to secure perishable commodities like dried fish. Among offerings found in the contemporary shrines at Eridu were the bones of salt-water sea-perch. Whether or not the inhabitants of Ur in the 'Ubaid period should properly be called Sumerian is still a matter of debate; but this much at least may be safely said, the culture which they evolved was not a sterile growth. It contributed not a little to the Sumerian civilization which in later times was to flower so richly.

The 'Flood-deposit' in the deep sounding at Ur also has to be seen in a much wider context of geographical conditions, of myth and of history. Mesopotamia is remarkably flat. In the distance of over 300 miles which separates Baghdad from the head of the Gulf it drops only about 35 metres. This has two important consequences. First, natural drainage is rarely very effective and large areas of lake and marsh have always been part of the landscape. Second, throughout their course below Baghdad the rivers Tigris and Euphrates meander through the alluvial plain, gradually raising their own beds, as do all sediment-bearing rivers moving at such a low gradient. Thus, flowing at a higher level than the surrounding plain, their flood potential, even without the impact of any tectonic movement, is greatly increased. In an exceptionally rainy season they would rise and burst their banks. Were this to occur in the spring, when the rivers were already swollen by melting snows and rain in their upper reaches among the mountains of eastern Turkey, the effect in the plain would be devastating, with the countryside submerged under hundreds of miles of standing water. It is, then, not surprising that archaeologists have found flood deposits of various dates on ancient sites in Iraq from Kish, near Babylon, southwards through Fara to Ur.

Among the many things which the Sumerians handed down to their successors was the story of a devastating flood. This was incorporated in the *Epic of Gilgamesh*, reconstructed by modern scholars from texts, some written as early as the early second millennium B.C. Previous to that it was known only through related Hebrew traditions, the familiar Biblical story of Noah's Ark, in the Book of *Genesis*, and through scattered fragments preserved by quotations in Greek and Latin writers. The Sumer-

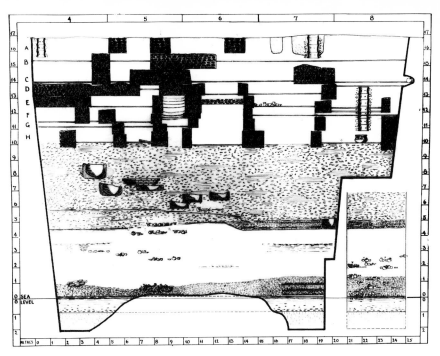

*Section of Pit 'F' (*The Flood-pit*), extending from the third millennium* B.C. *at the top (with later vertical drains) to the 'Ubaid period at the bottom*

ian legend, not yet known in its original third-millennium version, is in the form of a religious poem reflecting the beliefs of a pagan people, and if that were all that we were told about the Flood, we might dismiss it out-of-hand as a piece of fantastic mythology. But it does not stand alone. In some of the ancient copies of a document now known as the *Sumerian King-List*, giving the rulers of Mesopotamia from earliest times to about 1800 B.C., there is an antediluvian section listing rulers with reigns of fabulous length. 'The Flood came. After the Flood came, kingship again was sent down from on high'. The list gives a dynasty of kings immediately after this statement whose capital was at Kish. This is followed by a dynasty whose capital was at Uruk, and then by the First Dynasty of Ur, the historical reality of which has been proved by our excavations at Ur (see p. 15). As textual research has proceeded, it has become evident that the antediluvian kings were at first an independent tradition only later prefixed to the official Sumerian King-List, though the balance of evidence still indicates that the original King-List began with the mention of a flood.

33

View of part of the 'Flood-deposit' with two of Woolley's Arab workmen

Does this very ancient memory recall a single, overwhelming flood in a certain year in still remoter antiquity or has the Sumerian literary tradition telescoped the memories of a number of natural disasters, to which the region was clearly prone, into one major event? It is clear that the idea of a universal flood engulfing all humanity, as portrayed both in the Old Testament and the *Epic of Gilgamesh*, is an unreal extension of a very real natural hazard in Sumer. But what of more specific references? Late Assyro-Babylonian literary sources speak of the 'Flood which was in Shuruppak' and the hero of the Flood in the *Epic of Gilgamesh* is Ziusudra, king of Shuruppak, which is now identified with the site of Fara. This reference is of great interest to the archaeologist, since excavators at Fara found evidence of a flood-deposit towards the end of Early Dynastic I, which may be dated about 2750 B.C. This corresponds well with the fact that the name of the penultimate ruler of the First Dynasty of Kish after the Flood in the Sumerian King-List, Enmebaragisi, has been found in an archaeological context dated to Early Dynastic II (*c.* 2750–2650 B.C.). It is still the oldest inscription of an historically attested ruler found in Mesopotamia. Whether or not the Fara Flood-deposit is indeed surviving witness to the actual flood which found its way into Sumerian history and tradition, it is now generally agreed that the 'Flood-deposit' at Ur in the 'Ubaid period is too remote in time to be the one enshrined in local memory.

Further Reading

The basic description of the 'Ubaid period occupation at Ur is in C.L. Woolley, *Ur Excavations* IV (London, 1955), pp.7–22. The broader implications of these discoveries were considered in two papers in the special volume of the journal *Iraq* entitled *Ur in Retrospect* (*Iraq* 22, 1960): S. Lloyd, 'Ur-Al'Ubaid, Uquair and Eridu', pp.23ff.; J. Oates, 'Ur and Eridu, The Prehistory', pp.32ff.

The range and nature of commercial contacts in the 'Ubaid period have been investigated through the scientific examination of pottery sherds from southern Mesopotamia and Arabia: J. Oates and others, 'Seafaring Merchants of Ur?', *Antiquity* LI (1977), pp.221ff.

The continuing debate about the formation of Lower Mesopotamia was reviewed by C.E. Larsen and G. Evans, 'The Holocene Geological History of the Tigris–Euphrates–Karun Delta' in *The Environmental History of the Near and Middle East since the Last Ice Age* (ed. W. Brice, Academic Press, 1978), pp.227ff. A challenging interpretation of Mesopotamian and Gulf land formation, before 5500 B.C., has been presented by W. Nützel, 'On the Geographical Position of as yet Unexplored Early Mesopotamian Cultures: Contribution to the Theoretical Archaeology', *Journal of the American Oriental Society* 99 (1979), pp.288ff.

The significance of the 'Flood' in Sumerian archaeology was examined in detail by M.E.L. Mallowan, 'Noah's Flood Reconsidered', *Iraq* 26 (1964), pp.62ff. and in literature by W.G. Lambert and A.R. Millard, *Atrahasis: The Babylonian Story of the Flood* (Oxford, 1969).

From the Uruk to the
Early Dynastic III Period
c. 4000–2600 B.C.

Apart from the levels in the Flood-pit distinguished by pottery in the Uruk style (pp. 26–7), we found very little at Ur from this important period. Had our digging been inside the walls of the ancient town we should presumably have found plenty of remains, for in digging far below the Ziggurat of later times we found vestiges of an Uruk period temple-platform. Between 1930 and 1933 we were working in the Ziggurat area, trying to trace its history previous to the time when Ur-Nammu, of the Third Dynasty of Ur (*c.* 2112–2004 B.C.), built the great structure whose ruins, now much restored, are today the outstanding feature of the site. Since we were obliged to respect the monument and its dependent buildings, the investigation of the underlying levels was none too easy. Though we were in the end able to work out a good deal of the plans of two successive buildings, both belonging to the Early Dynastic period, that will be described later (pp. 113ff), it was seldom that we could, in the confined space, dig down to an earlier stratum. But a cutting made in the west corner of the Ziggurat terrace gave us just the evidence we wanted. Underneath, and partly cut away by the foundations of the earlier walling of the Dynastic period, there was a length of wall whose sharply sloped face proved it to be the retaining wall of a terrace.

This terrace was built of a peculiar small-sized type of mud-brick which at Uruk is characteristic of the Uruk period construction, but it had been covered by the addition of a new facing with bricks of a different type resembling those of the Jamdat Nasr period house-walls in our 'Flood-pit'. Behind the walls stretched a mud-brick floor which was littered with thousands of small cones of baked clay, pointed at one end and blunt at the other, rather like crayons, most of them about $3\frac{1}{2}$ inches long and half an inch in diameter, they were of light whitish-yellow clay and while some were plain, others had the blunt ends covered with red or black paint.

Now in the 1850s the English traveller and archaeologist Loftus discovered at Uruk a mosaic-covered wall, part of a building which has since
been unearthed by the German excavators there. This was part of a temple
complex with huge mud-brick columns and recessed or niched walls, but
that rather prosaic material was entirely disguised by the surface decoration. The walls and columns were thickly plastered with mud and into the
mud were pressed little baked clay pegs such as we found at Ur; they were
deeply driven in, so that only the flat ends showed, touching each other,
and the pegs of different colours were so arranged as to produce elaborate
patterns, vandykes, lozenges, triangles, etc., in unending variety over the
whole building. In the light of this we can safely say that at Ur in the Uruk
period, and probably also in the following Jamdat Nasr period, there was a
temple set on an artificial platform, of which we found the terrace wall, and
richly decorated with a mosaic of coloured cones. Its position, in the area of
the later Ziggurat, illustrates the continuity of religious building on the
same site so evident in many Sumerian cities.

But while we have to look to Uruk for examples of the architectural
grandeurs of this early time, Ur has given us a cemetery which illustrates
very well the domestic crafts of the late prehistoric period. Our deepest

Cone mosaic columns, restored
from evidence at Uruk (cf. p.38)

Scattered baked clay cones from a wall mosaic; see figure p.37 for reconstruction

digging in the Royal Cemetery area had already brought to light a few graves which seemed to belong to the Jamdat Nasr period and had also produced quantities of inscribed tablets and seal-impressions of a very early type scattered in rubbish tips just above these graves, but below the debris into which the graves of the Royal Cemetery had been cut.

In the season of 1932–33 in order to obtain more of these important tablets and seal-impressions, we resumed work in pit 'W' and at once found fresh examples; but the stratum was relatively thin and below it came the ordinary mixed soil of the old rubbish mounds. In this nothing of great interest could be expected, but there was a possibility of graves lower down, and in any case to carry on the work down to virgin soil would give us a useful check on former results and theories; so we went down. At 4 feet below the seal-impression stratum we came upon numbers of large clay bowls—the rough hand-made bowls characteristic of the Jamdat Nasr period—set upside down in the ground, and two feet below those the graves of the Jamdat Nasr period with which the bowls were associated by some ritual of burial. The graves, most of which were poor, lay thickly together and one above another, and the lowest of them contained pottery vases decorated with red and black paint on a buff ground of the sort found at Jamdat Nasr itself. The discovery was so important that excavation on a larger scale was called for, and therefore in the following season I marked out over what I hoped would be the centre of the graveyard an area of some 1200 square yards and started to dig a pit which, since our graves lay 56 feet below the modern surface, was almost a rival to the Flood-pit. Close to the surface was the Temenos wall built by Nebuchadnezzar and part of a contemporary building lying inside it; lower down there were the ruins of Kassite period houses, two layers of them (see p.214). Dug down into their ruins were burials in clay coffins of the Persian period and a few Neo-Babylonian burials with the bodies doubled up inside two large clay jars set mouth to mouth; below the Kassite floors were burials in brick vaults or under inverted clay coffins which had belonged to the dwellers in the houses. Thus far then we had a very satisfactory historic sequence, but below that there were no buildings; the site had been used for dumping builders' rubbish and had lain derelict throughout all the days of Ur's greatness.[1] At about 18 feet down, on a line following the slope of the rubbish-mound, were hundreds of graves of the time of Sargon of Akkad and his dynasty, an extension of the great cemetery wherein we had dug in former seasons; below these were the outlying graves of the Royal Cemetery, also on the slope, and then, under the tailend of our 'seal-impression stratum', the 'Jamdat Nasr cemetery', grave above grave so that sometimes they lay eight deep, the lowest dug down to and into the silt of the Flood.

Because the cemetery was in use for a long time and the graves super-imposed, more than half, perhaps two-thirds, of them had been destroyed; the diggers of a late grave, happening on an old burial, made off with any objects of value that it contained and smashed the rest without the least compunction; but even so we recorded three hundred and fifty graves in all.

In most cases the body to be buried was wrapped in matting—this may indeed have been general, for where we recorded a 'simple burial' because we could see no trace of matting, this may have been due simply to the decay of the fragile material; one only was in a rectangular wickerwork coffin. Most of the graves lay roughly N.N.E. by S.S.W., but the uniformity was probably due only to the need of economizing space in an over-crowded graveyard; inside the grave it was a matter of indifference at which end the dead man's head was placed. What was interesting was the attitude of the body. Whereas in the al-'Ubaid graves the dead lay extended on their backs, and in the Royal Cemetery lay on one side with the legs slightly bent in the position of sleep, here the body, lying on its side, was tightly flexed, the head bent forward over the breast, the legs brought up so that the knees were at right-angles to the body or might even almost touch the chin, while the heels came against the buttocks; the hands were held in front of the face and a little way from it, usually holding a cup or small vessel; apart from the complication of the cup it was the embryonic attitude—'as a man came out of his mother's womb so shall he return whence he came'.

Since the graves were often superimposed, they could not all be of precisely the same date—the lower were necessarily the older— and it was possible to draw up something like a sequence within the general period represented by the cemetery. The difference in the contents of graves at the successive levels showed a cultural development which required a considerable length of time; a whole range of vase types common in the lowest graves disappears altogether in the higher; there is an intermediate phase in which many of the old types vanish and no new ones are introduced but stone vessels preponderate instead of clay, and a third phase marks the appearance of numerous pottery types not found before. At the beginning we constantly get large clay pots over whose mouths are inverted plain lead tumblers; there are examples of black or smoky grey pottery produced in a 'smother-kiln', and others with a plain red wash highly burnished; with them come simple bowls or cups of white limestone. In the next stage the stone vessels were more numerous and more varied and amongst the pottery vases a good many were of 'reserved slip ware', that is, vessels which after making had been dipped in a bath of watery clay of a different colour from the body-clay of which the pot was made, and then this 'slip' had been wiped off in stripes so as to expose the body-clay. The slip, standing out in slight relief and contrasting with the body-clay in colour and texture, produces an unambitious but rather pleasing decorative effect. In the topmost graves pottery was almost entirely lacking and its place was taken by an astonishing wealth of cups, bowls, and vases in limestone, steatite, diorite or basic diorite, gypsum, and alabaster. It will be noticed that all this material had to be imported, much of it from far away—Mosul in the north, the Gulf and the Persian mountains to the east; but the vases were made at Ur. In the rubbish-mounds over the graves we found examples of the stone drill-heads used in vase manufacture; for the hollowing-out of a steatite bowl a start might be made with a narrow-edged metal chisel, steatite being a soft stone, but even in that case the finishing, or in the case of a harder stone the whole of the work would be done with a bow-drill whose head was of diorite. The vase-makers were certainly masters of their craft; many of the shapes are really beautiful, and constantly the shape is modified to suit the character of the material; thus, with a semi-transparent stone like alabaster the wide flat rim may be cut to almost paper-like thinness, while the solidity of the big black diorite vases with the severe strength of their outlines, would have done credit to an Athenian artist of the early fifth century B.C. Certainly the vase-maker of Ur could produce a beautiful thing without having recourse to surface decoration, and the great majority of the vessels are plain or at most bear a band of rope moulding in relief; but a few are more elaborately carved, and these show the Sumerian predilection for animal motifs. A curious example of this is an alabaster lamp in the form of a large shell (we found in the graves several real shells of the sort cut open to make lamps), the five projecting horns

Pottery of the Jamdat Nasr to Early Dynastic I period

Stone vessels of the Jamdat Nasr to Early Dynastic I period

serving as troughs to take the wicks; but moved by some whim of fancy the maker has added underneath a bat's head carved in the round, and seen from below the lamp has all the appearance of a flying bat, the horned 'shell' becoming its ribbed extended wings. One alabaster toilet-box is supported by the figure of a ram; two limestone cups have the outside decorated with a procession of oxen carved in low relief; but none of them are very well worked. It has to be remembered that the objects placed in graves would be of the kind normally used by the man in his lifetime, and our graves do not seem to have been those of people of the wealthier class (our pit did *not* hit the centre of the cemetery as I had hoped it would; the better graves lay at the south-west limits of the pit, and presumably the best lay beyond) so that we could not expect to find in them masterpieces of contemporary art such as adorned the temples and palaces of Uruk and were found there by the German expedition. Actually the finest example of Jamdat Nasr sculpture that we got came not from the cemetery but from one of the houses in the Flood-pit; this is a steatite figure of a wild boar made as a support for some object and originally set into a stand—the deep grooves on the sides suggest that the animal was crouched between flat-leafed reeds perhaps of bronze or gold—and as such is truly statuesque; there is a touch of realism in the wrinkling of the upper lip over the tusks, but otherwise all accidentals have been deliberately eliminated in favour of an abstract balance of mass; it is indeed a most successful composition. The bull bowls were crude, as I have already said, but that is because they were

42

cheap 'bazaar' goods not claiming to be works of art and reproducing only the general idea of the real masterpieces; the magnificent steatite bowl shown on p.48 may rank as one of the latter. It is not dated by any external evidence, for it was found in the ruins of a Persian period house and certainly does not belong to that period, nor can one guess how it got into such surroundings; it was probably made in the Jamdat Nasr period.

The decorated stone vases, indeed the vast bulk of the stone vases in general, came from the later graves in the upper levels of the cemetery (one of these contained no less than thirty-two stone vessels), but since the three-coloured clay vases which are the hall-mark of Jamdat Nasr occurred throughout the whole series, the differences between the early and the late graves denote no more than stages of progress in a single period. One peculiarity they had in common. Whereas most of the graves produced beads, of carnelian, shell, lapis lazuli, haematite, glazed frit, and gold, which were worn generally as necklaces, sometimes as bracelets or bangles, and fairly often as belts round the waist, and beads are, of course, strictly personal belongings, there were no tools or weapons such as are normally found in the graves of other periods. Metal was freely used—we found plenty of copper pots, especially in the lower levels—and therefore metal weapons must have been common enough; our excavations at Ur certainly produced much more material of the Jamdat Nasr period than of the previous Uruk period, but admittedly it did not amount to a great deal—in the Flood-pit the piled sherds of the kiln stratum and the ruins of houses which replaced them, in the Ziggurat area a mere scrap of religious architecture, and finally the cemetery. Does this contribute anything to history?

Clearly it only does so, if the information from Ur is assimilated with the results of excavations at other sites in the region. In attempting to understand the course of events in south Mesopotamia in the fourth millennium B.C. it is easiest to take the Uruk and Jamdat Nasr periods together, as was done by Henri Frankfort, who called them the 'Protoliterate period'. This was the time when urban societies may first be recognized. Marked concentrations of population in certain places now have monumental mud-brick architecture, stone sculpture, luxury goods in a growing range of imported raw materials, and above all a writing system steadily developed from a pictographic means of accounting to a flexible instrument of record for the business of daily life and for literature. The specialization and centralization inherent in such developments were stimulated by the high agricultural potential of southern Mesopotamia and an almost total lack of other material resources. This encouraged ever more distant trading enterprises and possibly also the establishment of colonies at sites in Syria like Habuba Kabira on the Euphrates, controlling the access routes to vital raw materials. In this walled settlement the pottery was virtually indistinguishable from that at Uruk itself in levels V–IV; the same form and size of building brick were used; tablets, seals, and seal-impressions were identical to those found in southern Mesopotamia. Away to the east, deep into Iran, Jamdat Nasr type pottery jars have been found as they have also along the Gulf as far south as Oman. From these regions came the metals, stones, and timber, required by growing towns like Ur.

The cemeteries of this period so far excavated, as at Ur, do not reveal any substantial social differentiation by marked variations of value in grave gifts. Nor are there individual items which might be taken to denote that the recipient had had outstanding status in contemporary society. We are little better informed about the precise nature of government and authority at this time. It is generally argued that religious institutions were paramount, with little scope for the political supremacy of individuals outside them, or for the manipulation of economic forces by private persons rather than by corporations controlled through the temple hierarchies. Every major settlement had at its architectural heart a substantial group of religious buildings; but to what extent their personnel controlled the daily life of the town is not yet properly understood.

By the end of the fourth millennium B.C. Sumerian civilization was fully developed. This statement involves a question which has often been discussed, 'Who were the Sumerians?'. The adjective 'Sumerian' has been formed by modern scholars from the place-name 'Sumer' which from the latter part of the third millennium B.C. was the name regularly used for southern Mesopotamia as opposed to 'Akkad', the northern part of the river valley; but the inhabitants did not call themselves 'Sumerians', they were simply 'The people of Sumer'. For the modern historian the invention of the adjective 'Sumerian' was convenient for distinguishing a particular language, a particular people, and a particular civilization. This language, that of the earliest tablets we can read from Sumer, is different from that used later in Mesopotamia (but to what family of languages it belongs has not been determined) and thanks to the rich harvest of excavation we know exactly what we mean by 'Sumerian civilization'. But the problem 'Who were the Sumerians' remains. Ought we to apply the term to the inhabitants of the 'Ubaid period settlement at Ur? Undoubtedly they contributed much to the civilization which we know as Sumerian, but they were submerged before it had developed far. To the people of the Uruk period? They introduced mass-production, wheel-made pottery and writing; but we know little more about them. To the people who produced the 'Jamdat

Nasr' painted pottery? Were they all of the same stock or had there been infiltration of fresh peoples, perhaps from south-west Iran, marked by changes in the material culture? There was a Sumerian legend that a race of monsters, half human and half fish, had come from the Gulf, led by one Oannes, and settled in the cities of Sumer, to which they introduced the arts of writing, of agriculture, and of working metal 'and since that time no further inventions have been made'. Sumerian civilization was composed of elements derived from diverse sources, reflected in their language, where some philologists have detected words from an earlier tongue, and their varied material culture. But the strong continuity of religious institutions, as in the sequence of prehistoric temples at Uruk and Eridu, suggests that at the core was a single strand so ancient that archaeology has not yet been able to trace its complex roots. We should, I think, reserve the name 'Sumerians' for the hybrid stock whose disparate forebears had made Sumer but who, by the Early Dynastic period, had merged their individuality in a civilization common to all.

Steatite statuette of a wild boar; Jamdat Nasr period (see p.42)

The beginning of the Early Dynastic period, at Ur as elsewhere in Sumer, is conventionally signalized by the general and virtually exclusive adoption of a brick rounded on the top like a loaf of bread, the 'plano-convex' brick of our archaeological jargon. Constructionally speaking this is a thoroughly bad brick. Various suggestions have been put forward to account for its adoption by people who had plenty of experience of the better type, e.g., that it is an imitation of building in stone brought in by people accustomed to using mud and pebbles or rounded boulders; but there is no evidence that the Early Dynastic occupants of Sumer were other than the age-old inhabitants of lower Mesopotamia who had no such traditions of stone building and no knowledge of it. Moreover, the builder in stone has a natural preference for flat stones and would never have been at pains to mould his mud substitutes into so uncongenial a form, nor could so absurd an imitation, if that was all it was, have been imposed uniformly upon every builder in the land and have been employed exclusively, as the plano-convex brick was, for centuries. There must have been a much more compelling reason that still escapes us.

The earlier part of the Early Dynastic period (*c.* 3000–2650 B.C.) was not well represented in the excavations at Ur. On the temple-platform new buildings were erected on a quite different plan to their predecessors and with a different orientation. The underground foundations of the new walls contained a mixture of flat Jamdat Nasr period bricks and the plano-convex bricks characteristic of the new period; but the proportion of the former quickly diminished and by the time the walls rose above ground-level, they consisted almost entirely, if not entirely, of plano-convex bricks. And the other outstanding feature was the mud mortar used by bricklayers. Mortar should be, and in every other building at Ur was, reasonably clean and smooth; but in this case it was mixed with a mass of small sherds of 'Ubaid pottery. Later building made it impossible to trace any coherent plan.

Below the Ziggurat, above the ruins of the cone-decorated late prehistoric temple, we were able to trace religious buildings of the Early Dynastic period but only in a few fragments left untouched by the later structures. The more recent and best preserved of the two main phases we detected ('Archaic I') belonged to the time of the First Dynasty of Ur (about 2550–2450 B.C., see pp.104ff). Below it lay an earlier structure ('Archaic II') to very much the same ground plan. There was a massive retaining-wall for the terrace with a range of chambers along its north-east side and small buildings in the north and east corners. The interior buildings had been ruined down below their floor-levels and only their foundations remained; such features therefore as doors had always disappeared, the rooms could contain nothing, and complete excavation was scarcely worthwhile. Since no objects were found in the building, and no inscriptions, its date can only be approximately fixed by the character of its brickwork, which is curious and illuminating, for it includes a variety of brick types such as is very rarely found.

The flat sorts of brick, used in the later prehistoric period, were employed only in the lower parts of the foundations, the superstructure having been built consistently with bricks of a strongly plano-convex shape. There is no possibility of explaining this as due to successive reconstructions, because courses of the different types alternate. Nor can it be due to reuse of old material, as is often true where burnt bricks are concerned, because it is extremely difficult to extract a single mud-brick intact from its place in a wall and to extract them in any number would be out of the question. It follows that our 'Archaic II' temple terrace was constructed when plano-convex bricks were first coming into use, but the builders had still by them stocks of the old-fashioned bricks which they did not want to waste. Most of the wall-bricks were of fairly clean material, but those of the floor packing contained many sherds of painted 'Ubaid period pottery, as did the mud mortar. As it is unlikely the brick-makers dug very deep for their raw material, 'Ubaid period remains must have been relatively close to the surface at this time, somewhere in the vicinity of the temple terrace.

In excavating below the graves of the Royal Cemetery (pp.51ff) we found layers of debris from burnt buildings, coloured from red to sooty black. In them were quantities of clay tablets, inscribed in a script earlier in character than that associated with the royal graves, and clay jar-stoppers and other clay fittings bearing seal-impressions. The buildings whence this debris had come lay further to the north, closer to the temple-platform, in a part of the site which we did not excavate. We numbered all these rubbish strata from 1 at the top to 8 at the bottom. Strata 1–3 overlay the royal graves (pp.6off); 4–8 underlay them, extending back to the very end of the prehistoric period. Thus they spanned the first part of the Early Dynastic period, contemporary with 'Archaic II' on the temple terrace, and provide the best evidence we have at present for the material culture of Ur at this time, meagre as it is.

There were two main groups among the more than 350 tablets which we catalogued, many of them small fragments. By far the greater number are administrative records. The rest are 'school texts' indicating that the scribes were being trained in the same complex of buildings as the offices producing the record texts. Some are sign lists giving the names of such varied categories as fish, gods, and feasts; some are the earliest surviving Sumerian literary texts; and some are practice tablets. They served familiar, clearly very ancient, teaching methods based on repetition and the copying of standard exemplars by novice scribes. Because these tablets belong so early in the history of writing, modern comprehension of the economic and administrative vocabulary is circumscribed. Although the general meaning of the common signs and groups of signs in these early texts is understood,

Carved steatite bowl of the late prehistoric period found in a house of the Persian period, almost three thousand years later (see p.43)

their specific implication often is not, particularly when it involves the social standing and function of various officials or the correct equivalents of units of measure. Yet still they give us a unique glimpse of an increasingly complex society in operation in south Mesopotamia in the earlier third millennium B.C. regulating and distributing the agricultural land and production upon which its wealth and well-being rested. For the most part we are dealing with lists, relating commodities and people. Types of grain and small animals (sheep and goats) are deposited by named individuals, sometimes with a title or place of origin also given; rations are allocated in similar lists. Blocks of land are noted by size or description, with a personal name or rank; other texts record land allocation to individuals, by name or title, and to groups of people. Although most is learned about the regulation and direction of rural activities and personnel, there are isolated glimpses of the town organization with references to a palace and the first appearance of the term *lugal*, now usually rendered as 'king'.

Something more, though not a great deal, can be got from the seal-impressions found in the rubbish strata with the tablets. Here we have lumps of clay which were plastered over the stoppers of store-jars, round the stringing of bales, and perhaps sometimes on the bolts of store-houses, and then impressed with a design by rolling a small cylinder seal across it. Some of these small seals had one end also cut with a design, which might be stamped on or alongside the rolling. By this time the stamp seal, which the cylinder seal had begun to supersede in the Uruk period, had almost completely given way to the cylinder seal, which soon lost these last vestiges of the stamp seal and was only engraved on its curved surface. A hole was bored vertically down through the centre of the cylinder so that it could be mounted on a pin or in a small metal frame. Some of these cylinder seals bore pictographic signs—the conventionalized pictures which belong to the infancy of writing—and they are of particular interest. As very little is known at this time of the economic and political relations between the growing city-states of Sumer, great interest attaches to any clues. Some of the Ur sealings bear signs denoting one or other of seven towns, some of which seem to be paired off more regularly than pure chance would explain: Ur and Larsa; Larsa and Adab; Adab and Kesh. These 'collective' sealings may signify some kind of political league in which various Sumerian cities contributed to a common fund of goods for mutual sustenance or just to an economic relationship, some kind of common market, which linked up networks of production and distribution centres across southern Mesopotamia.

The majority of the seal-impressions are decorative, i.e., have mere patterns, more or less geometrical, patterns distinctive enough to identify ownership, or they are pictorial. The last are very interesting, for side by side with designs of birds and animals and what are clearly domestic scenes we find primitive versions of the religious scenes which were to be revived, or continued, in the art of later times. Thus we have the ritual banquet, with two seated figures one facing another and drinking through tubes; the scene of worship wherein the god is shown in the shrine, a naked

49

priest brings goats for sacrifice and carries the traditional jug for libations, and draped worshippers follow with their offerings; the god enthroned on a boat; the milking scene outside the byre as we have it on the temple at al-'Ubaid (p.108); the ritual dance, and erotic scenes.

Further Reading

The basic description of the rubbish tips covering the period from Uruk IV to Early Dynastic III at Ur is in C.L. Woolley, *Ur Excavations* IV (London, 1955), pp.23ff.; the account of excavation on the archaic temple platforms is in C.L. Woolley, *Ur Excavations* V (London, 1939), pp.1ff. The archaic seal-impressions were published in L. Legrain, *Ur Excavations* III (London, 1936); the early tablets in E.T. Burrows, *Ur Excavations: Texts*, II (London, 1935). Supplementary notes on the seal-impressions will be found in P.R.S. Moorey, 'Unpublished Early Dynastic Sealings from Ur in the British Museum', *Iraq* 41 (1979), pp.105ff.

An important new perspective for the first part of the Early Dynastic period at Ur is provided by H.T. Wright, *The Administration of Rural Production in an Early Mesopotamian Town* (Ann Arbor, 1969), which describes the excavation of a small village at Sakheri Sughir near Ur, with a reassessment of Woolley's excavations in contemporary levels at Ur and at Tell al-'Ubaid. A complementary study of the early tablets is provided by P. Charvát's 'Early Ur', *Archív Orientální* 47 (1979), 15–20.

The chronology of the 'Jamdat Nasr' period graves at Ur and the rubbish strata, particularly S.I.S. 8–4, is still a matter of debate among archaeologists. This discussion is complicated by Woolley's extension of the term 'Jamdat Nasr' in his final excavation report to cover pottery attributed by other archaeologists to the subsequent periods Early Dynastic I–II, *c.* 3000–2650 B.C. As these periods were not well represented in the excavations at Ur conducted by Woolley, further digging there will be required to resolve these differences; but see B.Abu Al-Soof, 'The Relevance of the Diyala Sequence to South Mesopotamian Sites', *Iraq* 29 (1967), pp.133ff.; G. Korbel and H. Youzan, 'Der sogenannte Gemdet-Nasr-Friedhof in Ur-eine Keramikanalyse', *Baghdader Mitteilungen* 10 (1979), pp.9ff.

The 'Royal' Tombs of
the Early Dynastic Period
c. 2600–2450 B.C.

The first thing that I did when, in 1922, we started the excavations at Ur, was to dig trial trenches which might give us some idea of the lay-out of the old city. The main purpose was to trace the line of the great wall with which Nebuchadnezzar enclosed the Temenos, or Sacred Area of Ur; Dr Hall had cleared a short stretch of it in 1919, but since within the Temenos would lie the principal temples of the city, it was necessary to establish as early as possible its exact limits as a guide to our future work. The trench designed to give us Nebuchadnezzar's south-east wall was laid down by guesswork, since there were no surface indications to help us, the ground here being badly denuded, and for most of its length our trench proved to lie actually inside the Temenos; at its south-west end two or three courses of the brick foundations of the wall were found, all the superstructure having been weathered away, but the rest of it produced no vestige of any building at all. The disappearance of the late Babylonian structures did not of course mean that there was nothing to be found underneath, so I deepened the trench, and at once things began to happen; there turned up, sometimes singly, sometimes apparently in groups, clay vases (nearly all broken), limestone bowls, small bronze objects, and quite a lot of beads made of glazed faience or stone; when the foreman spotted beads coming up, and either he or one of the staff took over the task of excavating, there might be gold beads as well, but none such were produced by our workmen.

It was easy enough to recover what had been stolen. The men worked in gangs of five, each under a pick-man, each in a defined plot of ground. On pay-day I announced that for every gold bead found by Hamoudi the foreman or by ourselves the gang working on the plot concerned was being paid a *baksheesh*; and the *baksheesh* was about three times what I thought the local goldsmiths would have paid. The announcement was greeted with astonishment and very obvious chagrin. This was a Saturday; on the Monday the trench-diggers produced a surprising harvest of gold beads—all of which had on the Sunday been bought back from the goldsmiths. So far so good; but the real difficulty was something quite different. The trench evidently ran across a cemetery which, judging by our finds, might well be a very rich one. Graves, if they are to produce the proper scientific results, have to be dug with the greatest care; we had been digging graves, but in scarcely a single case could we say that all its furniture had been recovered; most of the objects had been got out without any scientific context, and no one grave had been recorded as it should have been. We had a force of very wild Arab tribesmen, few of whom had ever handled tools before; they were completely ignorant, had no idea of what good workmanship was, were reckless, and of course dishonest. Moreover, we were ignorant too. The archaeology of Mesopotamia was in its infancy and there was no means of dating the small objects that come out of graves; the state of knowledge at that time is shown by the fact that when I asked expert opinion as to the date of things we had found, I was told that since they lay fairly close to the surface, they must be late Babylonian, about 700 B.C., whereas in truth they were Sargonid and dated to about 2300 B.C. Our object was to get history, not to fill museum cases with miscellaneous curios, and history could not be got unless both we and our men were duly trained. So I stopped work on the 'gold trench' and, in spite of the workmen's annual petition to return to it, waited until four years' experience had equipped us better for the task. The delay was fortunate, for the excavation of the 'gold trench' area, which was to take us a number of seasons, was not only of immense importance but one of the most difficult that I have ever undertaken; but conditions were now all in our favour, for we had secured an outline at least of Sumerian archaeology going back to the First Dynasty of Ur and, beyond that, to the al-'Ubaid period (though this was still isolated from its context) and we had a gang of thoroughly trained workmen, keen, well-disciplined, and altogether trust-worthy, while Hamoudi's two sons Yahia and Ibrahim, now junior fore-men, had developed a technical skill in digging which was to prove invaluable to us.

So, at the beginning of 1927, we started to dig the cemetery. As we found out, there were really two cemeteries, one above the other, belonging to different periods. The upper graves were dated by inscriptions on cylinder seals to the time of Sargon of Akkad and his dynasty; those will be described later. Below them, dug into the rubbish-mounds which lay outside the Sacred Area, was what we call 'The Royal Cemetery'.

We had started digging, as I have said, inside Nebuchadnezzar's Temenos, but this, we found, was very much larger than the Temenos of the early city. The Ziggurat and main temples of those days stood on a high walled terrace, the core of which must have been formed by the superimposed ruins of buildings going back to the first settlement of the al-'Ubaid people at Ur; south of the terrace there was an open space, free of

Royal Tombs and Death-pits

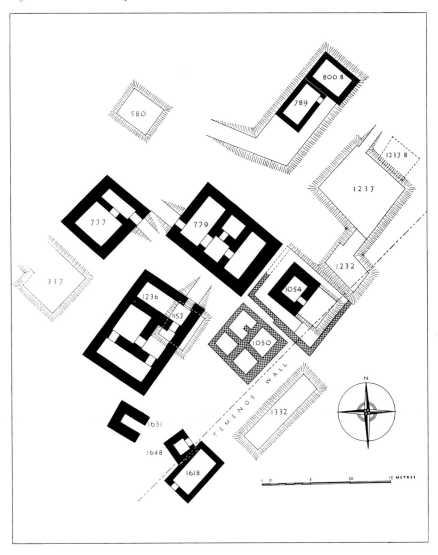

The unexcavated side of a trench (looking north-west, in 1929–30) showing the straight line of the Neo-Babylonian Temenos wall above the debris tiplines dipping from south-east to north-west over the Royal Cemetery

buildings, and here the people of Ur, with true Oriental *insouciance*, emptied their rubbish; in time this rose to form a rough *talus* sloping gently down from the walls of the Sacred Area. Granted that it was a rubbish-mound, none the less it did lie as near as might be to the holiest place in Ur, and it was an empty space; not unnaturally therefore men got into the way of burying their dead there.

The burials were of two sorts, the graves of the common folk and the tombs of rulers; of the former we cleared about two thousand, and of the latter sixteen were more or less preserved.

The ordinary grave consisted of a rectangular shaft, anything from 4 to 12 feet deep, in which the dead man was laid either wrapped in matting or enclosed in a coffin which might be of basket-work, of wood, or of clay; there was no rule regarding orientation and the head might be facing in any direction, but the attitude of the body was invariable; it lay on its side, the back straight or very slightly curved, the legs more or less flexed at hip and knee and the hands brought up in front of the breast almost to the level of the mouth; it is the attitude of a person asleep, and is wholly unlike the rigid straightness of the al-'Ubaid dead or the tightly contracted 'embryonic' position which marks the Jamdat Nasr graves. That this should be invariable, whereas so much else in the ritual of the burials seems casual and capricious, must mean that a special significance attached to it and that it reflected some religious belief. With the body there were placed such personal belongings as beads and ear-rings, a knife or dagger, the pin that fastened the dress or the shroud and perhaps the cylinder seal, the impression of which on a clay tablet was equivalent to the owner's signature. Outside the matting roll or the coffin were set what were more properly offerings to the dead, food and drink in vessels of clay, copper, or stone, weapons and tools, toilet articles, etc.; in most cases the bottom of the pit was lined with matting and mats were spread over the offerings to keep them from immediate contact with the earth which was thrown in to fill the shaft.

This provision made for the dead seems clearly to prove a belief in a future life of some sort, but there is nothing found which expressly defines such belief; in no single grave has there been any figure of a god, any symbol or ornament that strikes one as being of a religious nature; the dead man took with him what he might require for a journey to or for a sojourn in another world, but what he thought about the world to which he was going nothing tells us. The tomb furniture is intended to satisfy purely material needs and its quantity and quality merely reflect the social standing of the dead man and his family in this world. It was essentially a very simple form of burial and so far as we could tell there was nothing in the way of a tombstone. Generally the first sign that a workman had of a grave as he dug down into the mixed soil of the cemetery was a paper-thin wavy line of white powder, the edge of the reed matting that lined the original shaft, or else a few small holes set in a line and running down vertically into the earth, holes left by the decay of the wooden staves which strengthened the sides of a wooden or wickerwork coffin. It is a strange thing that in soil wherein so much that might be thought enduring rots away completely a fragile material such as wood or matting, though it lose all its substance, yet retains its appearance and its texture and can with care be exposed in such condition that a photograph of it looks like the real thing whereas it is but a film which a touch of the finger or even a breath obliterates more easily than it dislodges the plumage from the wing of a butterfly. There was one tragic instance of this. The cemetery site had been squared and poles set up as bench-marks from which measurements could be taken for plotting the position of the graves, and every now and then as work went deeper the poles would be left standing on pillars of earth too high up for convenient measuring and had to be re-set at a lower level. On one such occasion I told a workman to knock down a pillar and he, for fun, simply gave it a hard push. The upper part fell, as he expected, but with a clean diagonal break, and in a moment he was shouting to me to come. On the top of the column-stump, lying aslope, there was what looked like a wooden panel, and it was exquisitely carved with a procession of little figures in relief. Hurriedly I sent for the camera, and in the meantime began to make a measured sketch of the design, when, all of a sudden, down came one of the rare rainstorms of southern Iraq and, though the workmen did their inadequate best to shelter the monument with their cloaks, before I had more than outlined two or three figures, the 'panel' had disintegrated into featureless mud.

But the traces of matting and the impression made by wood were of the greatest help to us in the digging of the cemetery because they gave timely warning of things to come, so that we were not taken by surprise, the pickmen striking blindly into the earth only to ruin some delicate treasure; the pick could be dropped in due time and be replaced by the excavator's knife and brush and some member of the staff was always on the spot for the final clearing and recording of the grave. I must admit that with two thousand graves to be duly noted the necessary routine became wearisome at times, for there was a great deal of repetition and only too many of them contained nothing of very obvious interest, either because of their original poverty or because of subsequent plundering. At least two-thirds of the graves in the cemetery had been plundered or completely destroyed. While the cemetery was still in use, the men digging a new grave, if they hit upon one of earlier date—and in the overcrowded graveyard that was more likely to happen than not—could not resist the temptation to remove its more valuable contents. At a later date men, induced perhaps by chance discoveries, went in for deliberate tomb-robbing. They must have known—perhaps from the survival of surface monuments—the whereabouts of the old royal tombs, but feared to attack them openly, for we found circular shafts (one of them was dated by potsherds found in it to about the time of Sargon of Akkad) driven down vertically to the level of the tombs but at some distance from them and then turning horizontally to tunnel towards the tomb they proposed to plunder; in some cases they succeeded only too well, in one or two they missed their mark and abandoned the attempt in disgust. At Ur, as in Egypt, tomb-robbing is a very ancient profession, and the men who followed it did not work at random but had direct knowledge to guide them to what was most worthwhile. We found hundreds of untouched private graves whose contents were valuable indeed for scientific archaeology but of no interest for seekers after treasure; only by a stroke of unusual luck would we hit upon a grave at once rich and intact.

The finest of all such was the grave of Meskalamdug (PG 755), found in the season 1927–28; it was dug down into the shaft of one of the largest of the royal tombs but was itself an ordinary grave distinguished from countless others in the cemetery only by its wealth. The first indication we had of what was to come was a copper spear-head sticking straight up in the ground; following this down we found that it was attached to a golden haft, and below this was the hole left by the decay of the wooden shaft running down to a corner of the grave. Except for the fact that it was rather larger than usual, the grave was a normal one, a plain earth pit big enough to take a wooden coffin and to leave on three sides of this a free space for offerings. Along the head of the grave were stuck spears in a row, the blades downwards, and between these were vases of alabaster and clay; by the side of the coffin, lying on the remains of what may have been a bossed shield, were two gold-mounted daggers, copper daggers, chisels and other tools, some fifty copper bowls, many of them fluted, and other bowls of silver, copper jugs, and plates, and more vessels of stone and clay; at the foot of the grave again spears, and with them a set of arrows having chisel-edged points of chipped flint.

But it was when the earth from the coffin itself was removed that we had our great surprise. The body lay in normal fashion on its right side; round the waist was a broad belt of silver, now decayed, from which hung a gold dagger and a whetstone of lapis lazuli fixed on a gold ring; in front of the waist was a solid mass of lapis lazuli and gold beads, hundreds in all; between the hands was placed a bowl of heavy gold, a larger oval gold bowl lay close by, and near the elbow a gold lamp in the form of a shell, while yet another gold bowl stood behind the head. Against the right shoulder was a double axe-head of electrum, and an electrum axe-head of normal type was by the left shoulder; behind the body there were jumbled together in a heap a gold head-dress, bracelets, beads, and amulets, lunate ear-rings, and spiral rings of gold wire.

The bones were so far decayed that there was here none of the grimness of a skeleton, only a few strips of crumbling brown which served to show the attitude of the dead man, and the prevailing note was struck rather by the gold, clean as when it was put into the grave; and most of all was the eye taken by the helmet which still covered the rotten fragments of the skull.

It was a helmet of beaten gold made to fit low over the head with cheek-pieces to protect the face, and it was in the form of a wig, the locks of hair hammered up in relief, the individual hairs shown by delicate engraved lines. Parted down the middle, the hair covers the head in flat wavy tresses and is bound round with a twisted fillet; behind it is tied into a little chignon, and below the fillet hangs in rows of formal curls about the ears, which are rendered in high relief and are pierced so as not to interfere with hearing; similar curls on the cheek-pieces represent whiskers; round the edge of the metal are small holes for the laces which secured inside it a

Ground-plan of PG755, the grave of Meskalamdug, showing objects in position

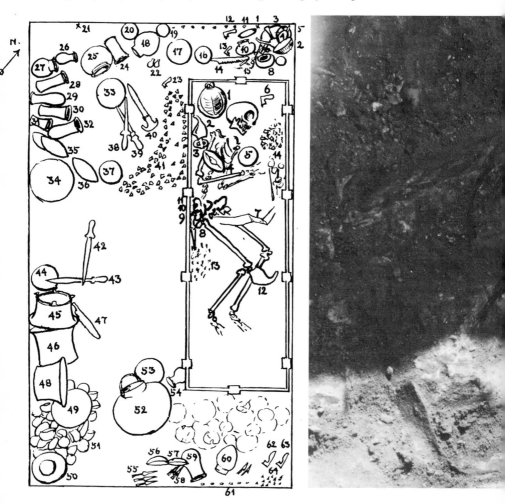

padded cap, of which some traces yet remained.

As an example of goldsmith's work this is the most beautiful thing we have found in the cemetery, finer than the gold daggers or the heads of bulls, and if there were nothing else by which the art of these ancient Sumerians could be judged, we should still, on the strength of it alone, accord them high rank in the roll of civilized races.

On two of the golden bowls and on the lamp was repeated the inscription 'Meskalamdug'. The name is the same as that found on the cylinder seal dedicated with the two gold daggers above the domed stone tomb of a

Grave PG 755, of Meskalamdug, with the gold wig in situ

*Sheet gold vessels,
two inscribed with his
name, from the tomb
of Meskalamdug*

queen (p.84), but the owner of the seal is called *lugal*: 'King', and here
there is no such title of royalty. One at least of the copper vessels in the
grave was inscribed for a lady named Ninbanda with the title *nin*: 'Queen'.
We shall have to return to them when considering what we know about
the people buried in the remarkable 'royal' tombs, to which we now turn.

There were sixteen 'royal' graves found in the cemetery, and although
no two of them were exactly alike, yet they all shared certain characteristics
which set them altogether apart from the ordinary graves. The dead was
laid not merely in a coffin but in a built tomb of stone or of stone and burnt
or mud-brick—it might be a single chamber or it might be a more
elaborate structure with several rooms. The ritual of burial included
human sacrifice; the number of victims might vary from a mere half-dozen
to seventy or eighty, but a certain number had to accompany the owner
of the tomb. The refilling of the tomb-shaft was not a simple matter of
throwing back the earth; it was a long-drawn ceremony involving elaborate
rites.

Owing to the destruction caused by plunderers and, to some extent, by
the diggers of later graves (only two royal tombs were intact), the evidence
for the ritual was not complete in every case; it had to be drawn impartially
from different graves on the assumption, which cannot always be proved,
that what was true of one was true of the rest also; it is a composite picture
that I give, but the description of a few graves will justify it.

The first of the royal tombs to be found told us, in effect, very little,
partly because it had been hopelessly wrecked by robbers and partly
because we had only just begun to excavate it (knowing nothing about
what it was to prove) on the last day of the 1926–27 season. Amongst a mass
of bronze weapons which did not at the time seem to be associated with any
burial we found the famous gold dagger of Ur, whose blade was of gold, its
hilt of blue lapis lazuli decorated with gold studs, and its sheath of gold
beautifully worked with an openwork design derived from plaited grass—
the material of which a commoner's dagger-sheath was sometimes made;

with it was another object, almost equally remarkable, a cone-shaped reticule of gold ornamented with a spiral pattern containing a set of little toilet instruments, tweezers, lancet, and pencil, also of gold. Nothing at all resembling these things had ever yet been unearthed in Mesopotamia; so novel were they that a recognized expert took them to be Arab work of the thirteenth century A.D., and no one could blame him for the error, for no one could have suspected such art in the third millennium before Christ. Returning to the spot at the beginning of the next season we were able to get more evidence as to the dagger's associations, but even so it had to be interpreted in the light of more complete discoveries.

In that season, 1927–28, digging in another part of the cemetery area, we came upon five bodies lying side by side in a sloping trench; except for the copper daggers at their waists and one or two small clay cups they had none of the normal furniture of a grave and the mere fact of there being a number thus together was unusual. Then, below them, a layer of matting was found, and tracing this along we came to another group of bodies, those of ten women carefully arranged in two rows; they wore head-dresses of gold, lapis lazuli, and carnelian, and elaborate bead necklaces, but they too possessed no regular tomb furnishings. At the end of the row lay the remains of a wonderful lyre, the wood of it decayed but its decoration intact, making its reconstruction only a matter of care; the upright wooden beam was capped with gold, and in it were fastened the gold-headed nails which secured the strings; the sounding-box was edged with a mosaic in red stone, lapis lazuli, and white shell, and from the front of it projected a splendid head of a bull wrought in gold with eyes and beard of lapis lazuli; across the ruins of the lyre lay the bones of the gold-crowned harpist.

By this time we had found the earth sides of the pit in which the women's bodies lay and could see that the bodies of the five men were on the ramp which led down to it. Following the pit along, we came upon more bones which at first puzzled us by being other than human, but the meaning of them soon became clear. A little way inside the entrance to the pit stood a wooden sledge chariot decorated with red, white, and blue mosaic along the edges of the framework and with golden heads of lions having manes of lapis lazuli and shell on its side-panels; along the top rail were smaller gold heads of lions and bulls, silver lionesses' heads adorned the front, and the position of the vanished swingle-tree was shown by a band of blue and white inlay and two smaller heads of lionesses in silver. In front of the chariot lay the crushed skeletons of two oxen with the bodies of the grooms by their heads, and on the top of the bones was the double ring, once attached to the pole, through which the reins had passed; it was of silver, and standing on it was a gold 'mascot' in the form of a donkey most beautifully and realistically modelled.

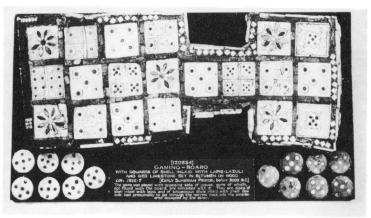

Inlaid gaming-board with its 'men'

Close to the chariot were an inlaid gaming-board and a collection of tools and weapons, including a set of chisels and a saw made of gold, big bowls of grey soapstone, copper vessels, a long tube of gold and lapis which was a drinking-tube for sucking up liquor from the bowls, more human bodies, and then the wreckage of a large wooden chest adorned with a figured mosaic in lapis lazuli and shell which was found empty but had perhaps contained such perishable things as clothes. Behind this box were more offerings, masses of vessels in copper, silver, stone (including exquisite examples in volcanic glass, lapis lazuli, alabaster, and marble), and gold; one set of silver vessels seemed to be in the nature of a ritual set, for there was a shallow tray or platter, a jug with a tall neck and long spout such as we know from carved stone reliefs to have been used in religious rites, and tall slender silver tumblers nested one inside another; a similar tumbler in gold, fluted and chased, with a fluted feeding-bowl, a chalice, and a plain oval bowl of gold lay piled together, and two magnificent lions' heads in silver, perhaps the ornaments of a throne, were amongst the treasures in the crowded pit. The perplexing thing was that with all this wealth of objects we had found no body so far distinguished from the rest as to be that of the person to whom all were dedicated; logically our discovery, however great, was incomplete.

The objects were removed and we started to clear away the remains of the wooden box, a chest some 6 feet long and 3 feet across, when under it we found burnt bricks. They were fallen, but at one end some were still in place and formed the ring-vault of a stone chamber (RT 789). The first and natural supposition was that here we had the tomb to which all the offerings belonged, but further search proved that the chamber was plundered, the roof had not fallen from decay but had been broken through, and the wooden box had been placed over the hole as if deliberately to hide it. Then, digging round the outside of the chamber, we found just such another pit as that 6 feet above. At the foot of the ramp lay six soldiers, orderly in two ranks, with copper spears by their sides and copper helmets crushed flat on the broken skulls; just inside, having evidently been backed down the slope, were two wooden four-wheeled wagons each drawn by three oxen—one of the latter so well preserved that we were able to lift the skeleton entire; the wagons were plain, but the reins were decorated with long beads of lapis and silver and passed through silver rings surmounted with mascots in the form of oxen; the grooms lay at the oxen's heads and the drivers in the bodies of the cars; of the cars themselves only the impression of the decayed wood remained in the soil, but so clear was this that a photograph showed the grain of the solid wooden wheel and the grey-white circle which had been the leather tyre.

Against the end of the stone chamber lay the bodies of nine women wearing the gala head-dress of lapis and carnelian beads from which hung golden pendants in the form of beech leaves, great lunate ear-rings of gold, silver 'combs' like the palm of a hand with three fingers tipped with flowers whose petals are inlaid with lapis, gold, and shell, and necklaces of lapis and gold; their heads were leaned against the masonry, their bodies extended on to the floor of the pit, and the whole space between them and the wagons was crowded with other dead, women and men, while the passage which led along the side of the chamber to its arched door was lined with soldiers carrying daggers, and with women. Of the soldiers in the central space one had a bundle of four spears with heads of gold, two had sets of four silver spears, and by another there was a remarkable relief in copper with a design of two lions trampling on the bodies of two fallen men which may have been the decoration of a shield.

On the top of the bodies of the 'court ladies' against the chamber wall had been placed a wooden lyre, of which there survived only the copper head of a bull and the shell plaques which had adorned the sounding-box; by the side wall of the pit, also set on the top of the bodies, was a second lyre with a wonderful bull's head in gold, its eyes, beard, and horn-tips of lapis, and a set of engraved shell plaques not less wonderful; there are four of them with grotesque scenes of animals playing the parts of men, and while the most striking feature about them is that sense of humour which is so rare in ancient art, the grace and balance of the design and the fineness of the drawing make these plaques one of the most instructive documents that we possess for the appreciation of the art of early Sumer.

Inside the tomb the robbers had left enough to show that it had contained bodies of several minor people as well as that of the chief person; overlooked against the wall we found two model boats, one of copper now hopelessly decayed, the other of silver wonderfully well preserved; some 2 feet long, it has high stern and prow, five seats, and amidships an arched support for the awning which would protect the passenger, and the leaf-bladed oars are still set in the thwarts; it is a testimony to the conservatism of the East that a boat of identical type is in use today on the marshes of the Lower Euphrates, some 50 miles from Ur (see p.154).

The tomb-chamber of RT789 lay at the far end of an open pit; continuing our search behind it we found a second stone chamber (RT800) built up against it either at the same time or, more probably, at a later period. This chamber, roofed like the king's with a vault of ring arches in burnt brick, was the tomb of the queen to whom belonged the upper pit with its chariot and other offerings: her name, Puabi, was given us by a fine cylinder seal of lapis lazuli which was found in the filling of the shaft a little above the roof of the chamber and had probably been thrown into the pit at the moment when the earth was being put back into it. The vault of the chamber had fallen in, but luckily this was due to the weight of earth above, not to the violence of tomb-robbers; the tomb itself was intact.

At one end, on the remains of a wooden bier, lay the body of the queen, a gold cup near her hand; the upper part of the body was entirely hidden by a mass of beads of gold, silver, lapis lazuli, carnelian, agate, and chalcedony,

RIGHT *Gold wig from Meskalamdug's grave (PG755): a remarkable replica in sheet gold of a man's hairstyle of the later Early Dynastic period*

long strings of which, hanging from a collar, had formed a cloak reaching to the waist and bordered below with a broad band of tubular beads of lapis, carnelian, and gold: against the right arm were three long gold pins with lapis heads and three amulets in the form of fish, two of gold and one of lapis, and a fourth in the form of two seated gazelles, also of gold.

The head-dress whose remains covered the crushed skull was a more elaborate edition of that worn by the court ladies: its basis was a broad gold ribbon festooned in loops round the hair—and the measurement of the curves showed that this was not the natural hair but a wig padded out to an almost grotesque size; over this came three wreaths, the lowest hanging down over the forehead, of plain gold ring pendants, the second of beech leaves, the third of long willow leaves in sets of three with gold flowers whose petals were of blue and white inlay; all these were strung on triple chains of lapis and carnelian beads. Fixed into the back of the hair was a golden 'Spanish comb' with five points ending in lapis-centred gold flowers. Heavy spiral rings of gold wire were twisted into the side curls of the wig, huge lunate ear-rings of gold hung down to the shoulders, and apparently from the hair also hung on each side a string of large square stone beads with, at the end of each, a lapis amulet, one shaped as a seated bull and the other as a calf. Complicated as the head-dress was, its different parts lay in such good order that it was possible to reconstruct the whole and exhibit the likeness of the queen with all her original finery in place.

For the purposes of exhibition a plaster cast was made from a well-preserved female skull of the period (the queen's own skull was too fragmentary to be used), and over this my wife modelled the features in wax, making this as thin as possible so as not to obliterate the bone structure; the face was passed by Sir Arthur Keith, who has made a special study of the Ur and al-'Ubaid skulls, as reproducing faithfully the character of the early Sumerians. On this head was put a wig of the correct dimensions in the fashion illustrated by terracotta figures which, though later in date, probably represent an old tradition. The gold hair-ribbon had been lifted from the tomb without disturbing the arrangement of the strands, these having been first fixed in position by strips of glued paper threaded in and out between them and by wires twisted round the gold; when the wig had been fitted on the head, the hair-ribbon was balanced on the top and the wires and paper bands were cut, and the ribbon fell

LEFT *Gold head of a bull, with eyes, beard, and horn tips of lapis lazuli, projecting from the sounding-box of a lyre found in the 'King's Grave'*

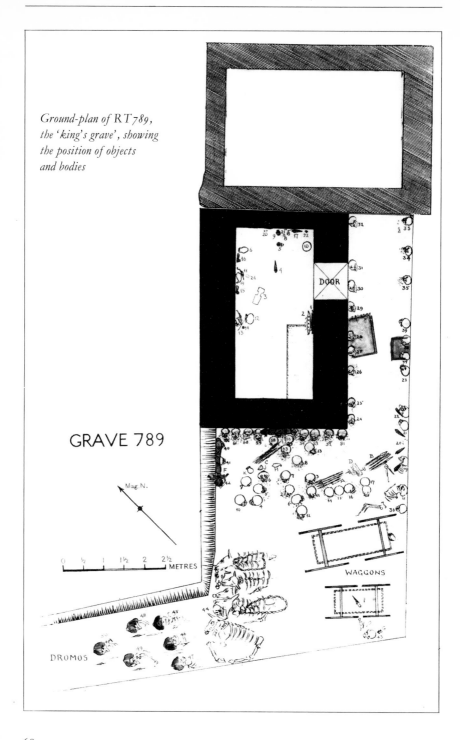

Ground-plan of RT 789, the 'king's grave', showing the position of objects and bodies

GRAVE 789

DOOR

Mag. N.

0   ½   1   1½   2   2½   METRES

WAGGONS

DROMOS

naturally into place and required no further arranging. The wreaths were re-strung and tied on in the order noted at the time of excavation. Though the face is not an actual portrait of the queen, it gives at least the type to which she must have conformed, and the whole reconstructed head presents us with the most accurate picture we are likely ever to possess of what she looked like in her lifetime (see p.77).[2]

By the side of the body lay a second head-dress of a novel sort. On to a diadem made apparently of a strip of soft white leather had been sewn thousands of minute lapis lazuli beads, and against this background of solid blue was set a row of exquisitely fashioned gold animals, stags, gazelles, bulls, and goats, with between them clusters of pomegranates, three fruits hanging together shielded by their leaves, and branches of some other tree with golden stems and fruit or pods of gold and carnelian, while gold rosettes were sewn on at intervals, and from the lower border of the diadem hung palmettes of twisted gold wire.

The bodies of two women attendants were crouched against the bier, one at its head and one at its foot, and all about the chamber lay strewn offerings of all sorts, another gold bowl, vessels of silver and copper, stone bowls, and clay jars for food, the head of a cow in silver, two silver tables for offerings, silver lamps, and a number of large cockle-shells containing green paint; such shells are nearly always found in women's graves, and the paint in them, presumably used as a cosmetic, may be white, black, or red, but the normal colour is green. Queen Puabi's shells were abnormally big, and with them were found two pairs of imitation shells, one in silver and one in gold, each with its green paint.

Modern plaster impression from a seal,
with hero and animal contest above a banquet scene,
from tomb RT 789

The discovery was now complete and our earlier difficulty was explained: RTs 789 and 800 were exactly alike, but whereas the former was all on one plane, the queen's tomb-chamber had been sunk below the general level of

Stone vaulting of the chambers in RT 789

her grave-pit. Probably they were husband and wife: the king had died first and been buried, and it had been the queen's wish to lie as close to him as might be; for this end the grave-diggers had reopened the king's shaft, going down in it until the top of the chamber vault appeared; then they had stopped work in the main shaft, but had dug down at the back of the chamber a pit in which the queen's stone tomb could be built. But the treasures known to lie in the king's grave were too great a temptation for the workmen; the outer pit where the bodies of the court ladies lay was protected by 6 feet of earth which they could not disturb without being detected, but the richer plunder in the royal chamber itself was separated from them only by the bricks of the vault; they broke through the arch, carried off their spoil, and placed the great clothes-chest of the queen over the hole to hide their sacrilege.

A reconstruction of the scene in the Death-pit of RT 789 (cf. p.74)

No other explanation than this would account for the plundered vault lying immediately below the unplundered grave of the queen. And on this showing we have two almost identical burials, the sole difference being that in the queen's case the tomb-chamber is below the level at which the other victims lie, and for this too the sentimental motive is sufficient. What the two graves tell us is quite clear so far as it goes.

To begin with, a more or less rectangular shaft was dug into the mixed soil of the rubbish-mounds to a depth of some 30 feet; at the top the shaft might measure as much as 45 feet by 30 feet; the earth walls were necessarily sloped but were kept as nearly vertical as might be, and on one side there was cut an entrance in the form of a steeply sloped or stepped passage running down from ground-level. On the bottom of the shaft, but occupying only a small part of its area, the tomb-chamber was built, with

71

stone walls and brick vaulted roof and a door in one of the longer sides. The royal body was carried down the sloping passage and laid in the chamber, sometimes, perhaps generally, inside a wooden coffin, though Queen Puabi lay upon an open wooden bier and another queen in the only other undisturbed burial was apparently stretched upon the floor of the tomb. Three or four of the personal attendants of the dead had their place with him or her in the tomb-chamber; thus, two were crouched by Puabi's bier and one lay a little apart and four shared the tomb of the other (nameless) queen; in the plundered tombs scattered bones betrayed the presence of more than one body. These attendants must have been killed, or drugged into insensibility, before the door of the tomb-chamber was walled up. The owner of the tomb was decked with all the finery befitting his station and with him in the chamber were set all such objects as we find in the graves of commoners, the only difference being that they are more numerous and of

Reins, covered for their whole length by date-shaped beads of lapis lazuli and silver, over bitumen cores, ending in a double rein-ring topped by a silver ox from a chariot in R T 789

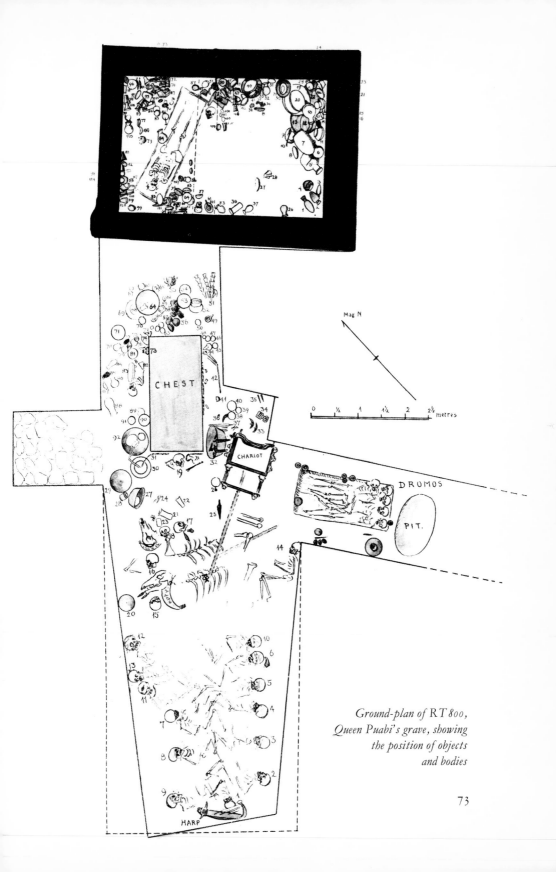

Ground-plan of RT 800, Queen Puabi's grave, showing the position of objects and bodies

Copper collar worn by one of the oxen in RT 800 drawing Queen Puabi's land sledge

more precious material—the vessels for food and drink may be of gold and silver instead of clay—the attendants, on the other hand, while they wear what we may call their court dresses, are not laid out properly as for burial but are in the attitudes of those who serve, and they are unprovided with any grave equipment of their own; they are part of the tomb furniture.

When the door had been blocked with stone and brick and smoothly plastered over, the first phase of the burial ceremony was complete. The second phase, as best illustrated by the tomb of Puabi and by RT 789, was more dramatic. Down into the open pit, with its mat-covered floor and mat-lined walls, empty and unfurnished, there comes a procession of people, the members of the dead ruler's court, soldiers, men-servants, and women, the latter in all their finery of brightly coloured garments and head-dresses of carnelian and lapis lazuli, silver and gold, officers with the insignia of their rank, musicians bearing harps or lyres, and then, driven or backed down the slope, the chariots drawn by oxen, the drivers in the cars, the grooms holding the heads of the draught animals, and all take up their allotted places at the bottom of the shaft and finally a guard of soldiers forms up at the entrance. Each man and woman brought a little cup of clay or stone or metal, the only equipment needed for the rite that was to follow. There would seem to have been some kind of service down there, at least it is certain that the musicians played up to the last, then each of them drank from their cups a potion which they had brought with them or found prepared for them on the spot—in one case we found in the middle of the pit a great copper pot into which they could have dipped—and they lay down and composed themselves for death. Somebody came down and killed the animals (we found their bones on the top of those of the grooms, so they must have died later) and perhaps saw to it that all was decently in order—thus, in the king's grave the lyres had been placed on the top of the

Queen Puabi's head-dress in situ *in grave R T 800; to the left a cylinder seal, pins, and other ornaments*

bodies of the women players, leant against the tomb wall—and when that was done, earth was flung in from above, over the unconscious victims, and the filling-in of the grave-shaft was begun.

Two modern plaster impressions of seals showing banquet scenes from RT 800; that on the right is inscribed 'Puabi, nin'

This account is based for the most part on the two tombs, RTs 789 and 800 (Puabi), which have been described in detail; the royal tombs, as I have said, differed a good deal one from another, but not to the extent that the account would not apply broadly to them all. Where the single built chamber was elaborated into a building containing several rooms and occupying the whole area of the shaft, one of these was clearly the monarch's actual burial-chamber and the others were for the members of his court, taking the place of the open death-pit which is invariably associated with the single-chamber tombs; in one case the sacrifice of the human victims took place before even the tomb was prepared for the great dead, for the stone chamber was built on the earth which covered the bodies lying at the bottom of the mat-lined shaft, but normally the rite must have followed the order described above. The best example of the death-pit was that of our royal grave RT 1237; the tomb-chamber had been completely destroyed by robbers, only one bit of ruined wall and a number of loose limestone blocks remaining from it, but the death-pit was intact, as indeed was always the case, for whereas it was a simple matter to tunnel down and enter a built chamber, only such wholesale excavation as we practised could get at individual bodies shrouded in the earth, and the old robbers dared not work thus openly. The pit measured, at the bottom, 27 feet by 24, and had the usual sloped approach and its sides had been mud-plastered and hung with matting. Six men-servants carrying knives or axes lay near the entrance, lined up against the wall; in front of them stood a great copper basin, and by it were the bodies of four women harpists, one with her hands still on the strings of her instrument. Over the rest of the

A modern reconstruction of Queen Puabi's head-dress

pit's area there lay in ordered rows the bodies of sixty-four ladies of the court. All of them wore some sort of ceremonial dress; a few threads and patches preserved by being in contact with stone or metal showed that this had included a short-sleeved coat of scarlet, the cuffs enriched with beadwork in lapis lazuli, carnelian, and gold, with sometimes a belt of white shell rings; it may have been fastened in front with a long pin of silver or copper; round the neck was worn a 'dog-collar' of lapis lazuli and gold together with other looser necklaces of gold, silver, lapis lazuli, and carnelian beads; in the ears were very large crescent-shaped ear-rings of

Gold vessels, one from the tomb of Queen Puabi, the other from the grave of Meskalamdug

gold or silver and twisted spirals of gold or silver wire kept in order the curls above the ears. The head-dress was much like that of Queen Puabi; a long ribbon of gold or silver was looped several times round the hair and, at any rate with those of higher rank, a triple band of gold, lapis lazuli, and carnelian beads was fastened below the ribbon with gold beech-leaf pendants hanging across the forehead. Twenty-eight of these court ladies wore golden hair-ribbons, the rest silver. Unfortunately silver is a metal which ill resists the action of the acids in the soil, and where it was but a thin strip and, being worn on the head, was directly affected by the corruption of the flesh, it generally disappears altogether, and at most there may be detected on the bone of the skull slight traces of a purplish colour which is silver chloride in a minutely powdered state: we could be certain that the ribbons were worn, but we could not produce material evidence of them.

But in one case we had better luck. The great gold ear-rings were in place, but not a sign of discoloration betrayed the existence of any silver head-dress, and this negative evidence was duly noted: then, as the body was cleared, there was found against it, about on the level of the waist, a flat disc a little more than 3 inches across of a grey substance which was certainly silver; it might have been a small circular box. Only when I was cleaning it in the house that evening, hoping to find something which would enable me to catalogue it more in detail, did its real nature come to light: it was a silver hair-ribbon, but it had never been worn—carried apparently in the woman's pocket, it was just as she had taken it from her room, done up in a tight coil with the ends brought over to prevent its coming undone; and since it formed thus a comparatively solid mass of metal and had been protected by the cloth of her dress, it was very well preserved and even the delicate edges of the ribbon were sharply distinct.

Why the owner had not put it on one could not say; perhaps she was late for the ceremony and had not time to dress properly, but her haste has in any case afforded us the only example of a silver hair-ribbon which we were able to preserve.

Another thing that perishes utterly in the earth is cloth, but occasionally on lifting a stone bowl which has lain inverted over a bit of stuff and has protected it from the soil one sees traces which, although only of fine dust, keep the texture of the material, or a copper vessel may by its

Lyre retrieved by running plaster into the cavities left by the decayed wooden parts, so that the inorganic fittings adhered to it in the correct positions. From the grave of Queen Puabi

corrosion preserve some fragment which was in contact with it. By such evidence we were able to prove that the women in the death-pit wore garments of bright red woollen stuff; and as many of them had at the wrists one or two cuffs made of beads which had been sewn on to cloth, it was tolerably certain that these were sleeved coats rather than cloaks. It must have been a very gaily dressed crowd that assembled in the open mat-lined pit for the royal obsequies, a blaze of colour with the crimson coats, the silver, and the gold; clearly these people were not wretched slaves killed as oxen might be killed, but persons held in honour, wearing their robes of office, and coming, one hopes, voluntarily to a rite which would in their belief be but a passing from one world to another, from the service of a god on earth to that of the same god in another sphere.

Obviously a great pit so crowded with objects could be cleared only a little at a time. The soil was removed until the bodies were almost exposed, covered only by the few inches of broken brick which had been the first of the filling thrown over the dead; here and there a pick driven too deep might bring to view a piece of gold ribbon or a golden beech leaf, showing that everywhere there were bodies richly adorned, but these would be quickly covered up again and left until more methodical work should reveal them in due course. Starting in one corner of the pit, we marked out squares such as might contain from five to six bodies, and all these were cleared, noted, and the objects belonging to them collected and removed before the next square was taken in hand.

It was slow work, and especially so in those cases where we decided to remove the entire skull with all its ornaments in position on it. The wreaths and chains and necklaces re-strung and arranged in a glass case may look very well, but it is more interesting to see them as they were actually found, and therefore a few heads on which the original order of the beads and gold work was best preserved were laboriously cleaned with small knives and brushes, the dirt being removed without disturbing any of the ornaments —a difficult matter as they are loose in the soil—and then boiling paraffin wax was poured over them, solidifying them in one mass. The lump of wax, earth, bone, and gold was then strengthened by waxed cloth pressed carefully over it, so that it could be lifted from the ground by undercutting. Mounted in plaster, with the superfluous wax cleaned off, these heads form an exhibit which is not only of interest in itself but proves the accuracy of the restorations which we have made of others.

In the furnishing of the royal graves one constant feature is the harp or lyre; in this great death-pit there were no less than four lyres. One of these was the most magnificent that we have yet found; its sounding-box was bordered with a broad edging of mosaic in red and white and blue, the two uprights were encrusted with shell and lapis lazuli and red stone arranged in zones separated by wide gold bands, the cross-bar was half of plain wood, half plated with silver, shell plaques engraved with animal scenes adorned the front, and above these projected a splendid head of a bearded bull wrought in heavy gold. A second lyre was all of silver with a silver cow's head in front of the sounding-box, which was decorated with a narrow blue and white border and with shell plaques. A third, also of silver, was in the form of a high-prowed boat on which stood a statue of a stag sculptured in the round. This hybrid instrument with the body of a harp, but also the two upright arms and the horizontal yoke of a lyre, is a mystery. Some musicologists have suggested that it is two separate instruments confused when we excavated the crushed remains. Two copper stag statuettes found nearby do not appear to be part of a lyre or a harp.

The commonest decoration of a harp or lyre is the head of an animal, and we now have the bearded bull, the cow, and, in an instrument of different form, the stag, though in this case the complete beast is shown; the difference is not, however, so great as might appear, because in the other cases the sounding-box itself represents, though in a highly conventional, not to say 'cubist' form, the body of the animal, resolved almost entirely into straight lines, but still recognizable as such.

Now, there is an inscription by a governor Gudea (it is true that he lived some centuries later, but tradition also is long-lived) in which he describes a harp he had presented to a temple; it was decorated with the head of a bull, and the sound of the instrument is compared to the bellowing of the beast. If there exists such a connection between the tone of the harp and the figure represented on it, might we not assume that our instruments are of three different sorts, the bull denoting the bass, the cow the tenor, and the stag perhaps the alto?

In a corner of the same pit there were lying two statues made of gold, lapis lazuli, and white shell; slightly different in size, they were otherwise a pair, the subject being the same in each case. On a small oblong base decorated with silver plate and mosaic in pink and white stands a goat, 'a ram of the goats', erect on its hind legs in front of a tree or bush to whose branches its front legs were bound with silver chains; the leaves and flowers of the golden tree stand out high on either side, and the beast's golden head with its horns and hair of lapis lazuli peers out between them. Undoubtedly the subject of the Sumerian sculpture had some religious significance; this and similar scenes are common in the artistic repertoire of the early period and probably illustrate some well-known legend, and there

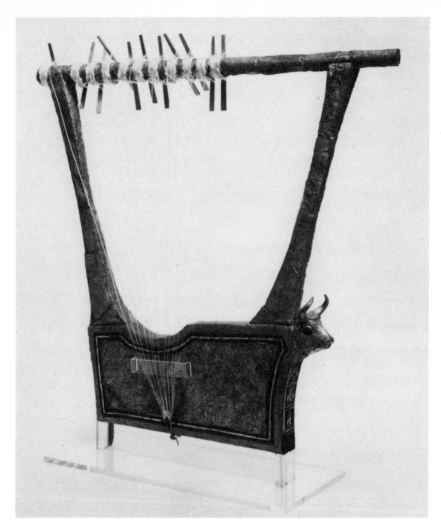

Silver lyre from the Great Death-pit as restored in the British Museum

is no reason to suppose that legend and illustration did not survive into a later time.

When the earth was thrown back into the death-pit and the tomb-chamber of the king and the bodies of the victims around it had been buried out of sight, the ritual of burial was far from being complete. Generally the upper soil of the cemetery has been so disturbed by later interments and by tomb-robbers that for a long time we failed to find any

*Shell plaques, engraved with
motifs common in Sumerian art,
decorating the front of the sounding-box
of a musical instrument with the head of
a bearded bull at the top*

evidence of the subsequent stages of the ceremony, but in the season 1928–29 we were more fortunate.

We had been digging a patch of ground where, near the surface, the graves of commoners lay unusually thick, and were surprised to find that the shaft of one of them, containing a clay coffin, had been cut into a stout mud-brick wall (RT 1054). Working against the face of this, we came upon a number of clay jars, an alabaster vase, and a rectangle of faint grey lines which represented a wooden box. Scraping away the surface soil, we discovered in the box, lying side by side, two daggers of which the blades were of gold and the hilts decorated with gold studs, and between them a white shell cylinder seal inscribed with the name 'Meskalamdug the King' (*lugal*). Next to the box was a wooden coffin containing the body of a man, but the furniture with it was by no means of the type which one would expect with a royal person, and the wall not only went further down into the soil, but as we followed it out, developed into a large square of which the coffin occupied only a humble corner; we felt sure that we had not yet found the king's grave.

A modern plaster impression of the seal inscribed for 'Meskalamdug, Lugal', found in RT 1054

Under the floor of beaten clay on which the coffin rested more clay vessels appeared forming a consistent layer over the whole area of the brick enclosure, and with these, but in another corner than that occupied by the coffin, was a second burial of a man with his weapons and vases of copper and stone. This clay floor was removed, and a fresh layer of pots and another burial came to light, and below this more layers of offerings alternating with layers of clay. Then came clean filling extending to the base of the brick walls, and at this level a single great clay bowl put upside-down in the earth sheltering two or three little food-bowls set out on a piece of matting—the meal spread for the god of the underworld.

We dug deeper down, and suddenly limestone blocks appeared bedded in green clay and forming a curve; we took it to be the end of a stone vault, and when the stones quickly dipped again, feared that the roof had been broken through by robbers; but another half-hour's work proved to our delight that the masonry continued and that what we had was a small dome absolutely intact. It was particularly exciting because the top of the dome had been built over a centring supported by stout beams which ran right through the stone-work, and the decay of these had left half a dozen holes in the roof through which one could glimpse parts of the dim interior and by the light of electric torches could even see on the floor below the shapes of green copper vessels and catch an occasional glint of gold (see p.90).

We cleared down to the level of the tops of the walls of the tomb-chamber, and at each corner, resting on the heavy clay which filled the space between the walls and the sides of the pit, found the ashes of fires and broken clay pots and animal bones. In front of the chamber door were laid the carcasses of three sheep. The stone blocking of the door was pulled away, and inside, beneath the remains of rotten wood fallen from the ceiling, lay five bodies, four of them were of men—servants, judging from their poor equipment, and the fifth was that of a woman; she had the golden head-dress of one of high rank, a long curved golden pin such as we had not seen before fastened her cloak, in her hands was a fluted and engraved tumbler of gold, and by her side a golden cylinder seal, the first we have ever found: this clearly was the queen.

Now the ritual of the interment could be understood. The royal body with its attendants, many or few, was laid in the tomb, and the door was sealed and sacrifice was made in the little court before the entrance, and then this was filled in until only the crown of the dome was left above ground. Round it fires were lit and a funeral feast was held, and libations to the dead were poured into the clay drain which ran down into the soil beside the tomb, and then more earth was thrown into the shaft. Next an offering to the underworld gods was set out and covered with a clay bowl to shield it from the fresh earth which buried it; and then, in the half-filled pit, there was constructed in mud-brick what was to be a subterranean building.

The filling-up of this building was done by degrees; clay was brought and trampled hard to make a floor over which offerings were spread and on which was laid the body of a human victim sacrificed in these later rites;

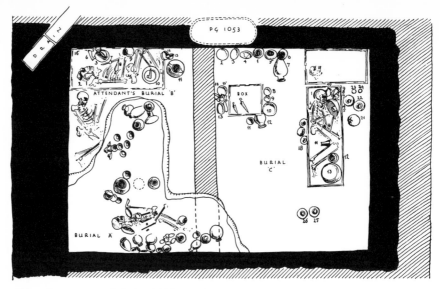

Plan of upper part of shaft of RT 1054 *showing brick walls and burials at different levels*

earth buried these, and another floor was made and more offerings placed in order and another victim did honour to the dead below, and this went on till the top of the walls was nearly reached; then half of the building was roofed in with a vault of mud-brick, and in this subsidiary tomb was put the coffin of one whom we may suppose to have been the chief sacrifice, and here King Meskalamdug dedicated to the unnamed queen his golden daggers and the seal bearing his title. Then this chamber too was buried under the filling of the shaft, and probably on the top of it all there was erected on the ground-surface some kind of funerary chapel which should perpetuate the sanctity of the spot.

The complexities of form and ritual found in all the sixteen 'royal' tombs were such that no single explanation of what we found carries complete conviction. It is all to a greater or lesser degree speculative. Although the reconstruction just given for the cutting and subsequent filling of the tomb-shaft we numbered RT 1054 is in accord with what we observed at the time, it is only one of a number of possible explanations of the original ceremonies. Indeed it is possible that the upper male grave was subsequent to the female burial in the lower stone-built chamber and is not to be directly associated with it. It was certainly over the tomb-chamber, but the sides of the shaft which we would have expected to have linked the two, if they were indeed part of a single extended burial rite, were not certainly detected running continuously downwards. As new information comes to hand, our interpretations will have to be critically assessed and, wherever possible, speculation replaced by certainty.

Fifty years later nothing like these tombs has yet been found in Mesopotamia. There is no archaeological parallel to the wealth, the architecture, and, above all, to the ritual which they display. Who then were the people who received such rites?

When the cemetery was dug, it was assumed that tombs differing so much from the common run must be those of kings and in the preliminary report this view was put forward. It was immediately challenged, and

Plan of tomb-chamber and court of RT 1054

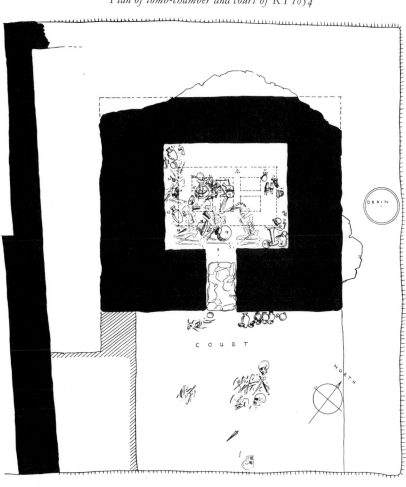

scholars are still not in agreement. The main alternative theory maintained that the primary burials were of priests and priestesses put to death after they had represented the chief god and goddess of Ur in a 'Sacred Marriage Ceremony' upon which the annual fertility of the land was believed to depend. Some scholars introduced a secondary hypothesis which sought to identify the participants as substitute kings and queens ritually slaughtered with their attendants once their brief reign was over. Neither view explains all the evidence revealed in our excavations. The textual sources for substitute kings, from Assyria, are very much later and from a different cultural background and even in their own cultural context they are not yet fully understood. Since, according to the Fertility Sacrifice theory, the occupants of the tombs should be the couple chosen to represent the deities in the 'sacred marriage', we should expect to find in each tomb a man and a woman buried together, but this is never the case—each tomb has only one principal occupant, a man or a woman. The bride chosen for the god would surely be a virgin, probably good-looking, certainly young; Puabi, however, was a woman of about forty years of age. The Fertility rite was, naturally, an annual affair; our cemetery, with its thousands of graves, superimposed sometimes five or six deep, must represent a considerable length of time (indeed we now know it to be over six hundred years), but there are only sixteen tombs of the kind in dispute; did then the ancient people of Ur celebrate only occasionally the rite that was to assure a good harvest and in most years leave the whole thing to chance? That is hard to believe.

For human sacrifice at a king's grave plenty of analogies can be quoted from other lands, most apposite being that of the pharaohs of the earliest dynasties in Egypt, a few hundred years before these tombs at Ur; what is even more important is that something of the sort seems to have persisted in Sumer itself right down to the end of the third millennium B.C. to judge by later multiple burials discussed on pp.131–2. But precisely what guide do we have to the identity of the people buried in these remarkable tombs? There is very little textual evidence. This discrepancy may not be wholly explained away by pointing out that these burials belong to an early stage in the use of writing for records. Such evidence as there is in the graves is provided by names, and occasionally titles, inscribed on cylinder seals: the distinctive form of seal rolled on clay by the Sumerians as a property mark or as a signature, for virtually all save the scribes were illiterate.

One royal grave had associated with it a seal inscribed for a priestess of Pabilsag, known from later texts as a brother of Nanna, the Moon-god. The famous burial of Puabi, already described in some detail, produced three inscribed seals. That found by the tomb-chamber bears the lady's name and the title *nin*; at Ur at this time this is normally taken as the feminine equivalent of *lugal*. When applied to deities they are now translated as 'lady' and 'lord'; when applied to mortals, 'queen' and 'king', though a king's wife was not necessarily honoured with this particular title, and, those who were, continued to hold it after their husband's death. In Puabi's case it is now almost always rendered 'queen', though the name of her husband remains uncertain. The name Abarage found on a seal loose in the pit of the queen's grave, need not, as was originally assumed, be that of a king; it is not even certainly known to be a male name. Another seal found in the same pit was for one Lugalsapada, whose name is not necessarily a royal one despite the element *lugal* in it. A further royal grave contained two seals each with the name of an untitled individual. Only one seal inscription from these tombs mentions both a king and his wife, and she is not titled *nin*. This inscription has been read to mean either: 'Akalamdug, king of Ur; Ashusikildigir is his wife' or 'To A., king of Ur, A., his wife, has dedicated this seal'. Most intriguing of all is the seal of a man named Meskalamdug, with the title *lugal*, but with no specific reference to Ur, in a royal tomb, where the primary burial is female (see pp.84–6).

It is reasonable to assume that this is the man also named, but without a title, on gold vessels in the very rich grave, without a pit and sacrificial victims, we have already discussed (pp.57–60). It was cut down into the shaft of one of the royal tombs and may fall at the very end of the series. In this grave we have seen there was also at least one copper vessel inscribed for a lady, Ninbanda, with the title *nin*, widely assumed to be king Meskalamdug's queen; but this was also the name of the wife of Mesanepada, first king of the First Dynasty of Ur in the Sumerian King-List. In excavations at Mari on the middle Euphrates in Syria, in the 1960s, a hoard of precious objects was found in a foundation deposit placed in a palace of the mid-third millennium B.C. Included in it was a fine votive bead, bearing a worn Sumerian inscription. It was immediately seen to contain the name of Mesanepada, king of Ur; but the rest of the reading has been disputed as it is difficult to read. A recent suggestion maintains that it also contains the name of Meskalamdug, and identifies him as the father of Mesanepada. If this is so and it is by no means certain, then there would be a direct link between the kings of Ur associated with the royal tombs, who do not appear to have exercised power much beyond Ur itself, and the First Dynasty rulers whose wider authority over Sumer earned them a place in the Sumerian King-List, which does not mention their predecessors.

If there is good reason to think that the Meskalamdug buried in a tomb lacking sacrificial victims was a king of Ur, why are they absent, if they really were indicators of a royal burial? Does it mean that not all rulers of Ur in Early Dynastic times were given such burials and, if not, why not? Might it be that kings of Ur were only rarely offered such human sacrifices and, if so, in what circumstances? Were the women in these graves invariably royal wives, or was there some other rank among the royal ladies that entitled them to burial with victims? Among the victims the large number of women is clear, and possibly a significant, clue to the special nature of the royal tombs.

Before looking a little further into this question it is useful for us to have clearly in mind what little we know about the rank and social role of the victims. In every case it seems to be only the immediate household staff of the buried dignitary. There is no evidence of children and no clear

Workmen revealing the top of the stone domed chamber in RT 1054

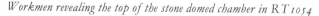

indication of the self-immolation of wives at their husband's funeral. Where men may be securely identified among the human victims they are usually either armed guards, grooms, or charioteers; the women, nearly always with a set of elaborate personal ornaments, including what we have called the gala head-dress, are either just in attendance without equipment or occasionally provided with lyres or harps. Distinctions of rank and function appear to have been retained in the mustering of the household in those graves where they took their positions down a ramp and into the pit outside the tomb-chamber. Within the chambers it has been assumed that the secondary burials of men and women were valets and personal maids. In the Great Death-pit (see pp.76ff), in all probability part of an elaborate female burial, the entrance was guarded by six armed men. All the bodies within the pit were female; four harpists and then sixty-four ladies-in-waiting lined up in orderly rows. The only marked distinction was between twenty-eight ladies with gold hair-ribbons and the remainder with silver. The court, as distinct from the personal household, that is the religious, military, and civil administrators in modern terms, were buried as they died in the simpler graves that clustered as close to the tomb of their patron as was possible.

The inscribed seals have already been considered; but what evidence for rank or social roles do their materials and designs offer us? Most of the seals in the royal tombs are of lapis lazuli, with a significant minority of shell; only two were of gold. One or other of two designs appears most often: contest scenes of animals and heroes, and animals with animals, or banquets, as on the famous 'Standard' (see p.97). Contests appear most often in association with men; in precious materials they may have been the prerogative of kings and senior male members of the royal family, whilst similar scenes in shell or calcite were the mark of lesser-ranking male members of the household. The 'banquet' seals, predominantly of lapis lazuli, are most closely connected with women and may denote affiliation to an institution or institutions predominantly for women.

The mystery of the royal burials is not yet resolved by any known reference in Sumerian literature. Professor Kramer has translated a possibly relevant passage in the *Epic of Gilgamesh*, but it only survives in fragmentary form and is tantalizingly obscure. It seems to describe a royal male burial:

> His beloved wife, his beloved son,
> The. ...-wife, his beloved concubine,
> His musician, his beloved entertainer,
> His beloved chief valet, his beloved. ....

His beloved household, the palace
attendants,
His beloved caretaker,
The purified palace. ... the heart of
Uruk—whoever lay with him in that place,
Gilgamesh, the son of Ninsun,
Weighed out their offerings to
Ereshkigal

Gilgamesh was an historical figure, the ruler of the city of Uruk at the time of the earliest royal tombs or a little before. After his death he passed into Sumerian tradition as the ruler of the underworld and the passage quoted above belongs to the great poem that grew up round his name over many centuries. At first glance it might be taken for the roll-call of exactly the royal household revealed in the best-preserved of our royal tombs. But a second reading raises doubts about exactly what the writer is describing. He seems to conceive of Gilgamesh at his death descending to the under-world as its king; but breaks in the text and uncertainties of translation still leave the crucial question open. Had the large retinue and family actually been buried with Gilgamesh at his death or did he go alone to present gifts they had offered in his tomb for the gods of the underworld?

Our finds might predispose us to the former explanation. But we have hesitated to identify actual members of the immediate family of the king, his wife and children, among the sacrificial victims. Indeed in the case of Puabi we have argued that her tomb was cut down close to her husband's, but some time after his death and in quite another burial ceremony in which she was also entitled to take with her part of her household. In short, the *Death of Gilgamesh* fragment does not allow us to suppose that Sumerian kings as a matter of course took their households with them in death-pits like those we found at Ur. The key to these may not lie so much with royal rank as we now conceive of it, as with a cult practice special to Ur, relating particularly to the god Nanna. And it is here that the many women in the graves may be the clue, if we regard them not so much as 'queens' but as 'high-priestesses' and their retinues.

Some centuries later the lady Enheduana, daughter of King Sargon and High-Priestess of Ur (see p.126), was an accomplished poetess, of whose works a long prayer in Sumerian to the goddess Inanna, daughter of Nanna, and a collection of hymns to the various major temples of southern Mesopotamia, have survived. Her prayer, now known as the 'Exaltation of Inanna', contains an enigmatic passage relevant to our present inquiry. In cursing a usurper in the city of Uruk, who threatened the rule of her nephew Naram-Sin, the High-Priestess wrote, addressing the goddess, in Professor Hallo's translation:

> In the place of sustenance   what am I,
> even I?
> (Uruk) is a malevolent rebel against your
> Nanna may An make it surrender!
> This city—may it be sundered by An!
> May it be cursed by Enlil!
> May its plaintive child not be placated
> by his mother!
> Oh lady, the (harp of) mourning
> is placed on the ground.
> One had verily beached your ship of
> mourning on a hostile shore.
> At (the sound of) my sacred song
>   they are ready to die.

The translator has suggested that this final line might be an allusion to the ritual involved in the royal tombs found at Ur. The imagery of the previous two lines could also be taken as a reminiscence of the musical instruments found with the ladies in the death-pits, and the model boats which were found in some of the tomb-chambers. There were silver and copper model boats in the 'king's grave' and two of bitumen in another royal tomb. They were to become more common in the private graves of the Sargonid period in this cemetery. Significantly, perhaps, later copies of this stanza replaced 'they are' in the final line with 'I am', possibly misunderstanding an allusion to a custom by then long forgotten though in Enheduana's time it would still have been a living memory at Ur, if no longer practised under her Akkadian-speaking rulers.

The answer to this intriguing problem of identity will only come from more information, both from excavated graves at Ur and from elsewhere in Sumer, and from an increasing knowledge of Sumerian texts. We still know too little of family relationships within Early Dynastic Sumerian ruling families, of the nature of their marriages and concubinage, of their lines of inheritance, of the distribution of ranks, titles, and religious offices, and, what is more important for this purpose, their precise ancient terminology, to allow us confidently to analyse the sociology of the 'royal' and associated tombs. For the men it may have been a question of the extent to which in life, or perhaps only in death, they assumed some divine or semi-divine status. For the women the case is more complex still and may have turned not so much on whether they were 'queens' in the modern sense, as on whether or not they had for some period of their lives been 'wives of Nanna' or some comparable ranking in the temple hierarchy of Ur. On this kind of interpretation the apparent predominance of women would be directly associated with the cult of Ur's city-god and may well not represent any general Sumerian custom.

As we worked towards the limits of the cemetery we came upon a group of graves which seemed to stand apart from the rest. They were all the graves of men, and they were poor graves, containing the bare minimum of tomb furniture, a cup or bowl and a clay pot was generally all that they could boast. But always there was a weapon with the body, a bronze dagger or spear-blade, and so striking was this uniformity that we concluded that this was the military quarter of the graveyard. And there was another thing. Every one of the bodies had a cylinder seal, but a seal of a special sort; carved in white shell, unusually large (about $1\frac{3}{4}$ inches long and $1\frac{1}{4}$ inches in diameter, which is nearly double the size of the normal cylinder) and with the same subject repeated in each case with only minor differences of treatment—the heroic hunter and the lion overthrowing the ibex or the bull. The figures on the seal certainly symbolize victory in battle, and I think it likely that these very splendid cylinders were in the nature of military medals distributed to the troops for service in the field—but instead of a medal you had something which would testify to your merits every time you put your name to a document. I can think of no other explanation that would account for the distinctiveness and the uniformity of seals found in what seem to be the graves of poor soldiers.

One of these graves, however, simple as its furniture was, contained something that made it unique in the whole cemetery; by the man's body there lay the statuette of a woman carved in white limestone. It was not the figure of a goddess (as has been remarked above, one of the curious features of the cemetery as a whole was the almost total lack of religious symbolism); she was an ordinary woman standing upright with her hands clasped in the attitude of prayer; however much we might value her, for she was the only human statue of the period that we found at Ur, we could not say that she was very beautiful, nor could we explain why one man of all the thousands buried in the cemetery should take a woman's image with him to the grave. Perhaps the sentimental explanation is the simplest and the most probable (see p.206).

While trying to give some idea of what the graves are like and describing some of the treasures they contain, I have said very little about the condition of the objects at the time of finding. It is true that no imagination was required to grasp the splendour of Meskalamdug's grave, because the objects in that were for the most part of gold, and gold is imperishable; a golden bowl may be crushed or dented, but its colour and its surface remain and every detail of its workmanship and decoration is as clear as when it was newly wrought; but other materials are less enduring—I have spoken of the way in which silver corrodes and even vanishes—and suffer both from internal decay and from the crushing weight of the 30 or 40 feet of earth below which they have lain buried for five thousand years. Often it is difficult to remove from the soil without further damage an object which it is essential to preserve; sometimes it is hard even to judge of the object's nature and importance; nearly always some measure of repair or restoration is required before the thing is fit for exhibition, and the restoration may be the most laborious task of all.

As an illustration of this I would take one of the two statues of goats found in the Great Death-pit. The figure was made as follows. The head and legs were carved in wood, the horns of lapis and the inlaid eyes being fixed in position by copper rivets driven through the head, and then gold, little thicker than gold leaf, was laid over them, a thin wash of bitumen acting as glue to fix the metal on to the wood. The head and legs were mortized into a rudimentary wooden body which was next rounded off into proper shape with plaster of paris and given a thick coat of bitumen; a thin silver plate was fixed over the belly, and into the bitumen covering back and sides were pressed the locks of hair, each carved separately from a piece of white shell, or, for the shoulders, in lapis lazuli; the tree was also of wood overlaid with gold leaf, the leaves and flowers made of double gold and fixed on after the trunk and branches were complete.

When we found them, both statues were in very sorry plight. The wood had decayed to nothing, the bitumen was dry powder, the plaster of paris reduced to irregular lumps and pellets; one figure was lying on its side, crushed absolutely flat so that the shell curls of the two flanks touched each other and the animal was a mere silhouette distorted by pressure, the other, standing upright, preserved some of its roundness but had been telescoped together and the legs had been broken off from the body, flattened and twisted. Nothing except the earth around them kept the fragments of lapis and shell inlay in position, and if that position were once lost, there would have been no guide at all for the restoration of the figure; the whole thing was therefore solidified with hot wax poured liberally on, and then bands of waxed muslin were applied to every exposed part until the ram was securely wrapped up as a mummy and could be lifted from the earth.

For restoration, the waxed wrappings were softened with heat sufficiently for the sides of the beast to be pressed apart and the dirt removed from

inside its body; then wax and bandages were applied to the interior, the outer bandages removed, and with gentle heating the body could be pushed out into its original shape, and that without dislodging the inlaid locks of the fleece now adhering to the inner coating of wax. The complete decay of the silver over the belly really facilitated the task, because it gave a chance to work at the body from the inside through a comparatively large opening. The legs were straightened, and with slender tools inserted down the tubes of them the dented gold was passed out again as much as possible, then copper wires were put down them and a boiling mixture of wax and bitumen was poured in to make all solid. The head presented greater difficulties, because the thin gold leaf was broken into eighteen small fragments and these were badly crushed and bent; each had to be unfolded, worked out to its original curve, and strengthened from the back, and then the joints had to be found and the various morsels brought together and fixed with due regard to the curves of their outer face. It was a jigsaw puzzle in three dimensions, but in time the head took shape and character. Plastic wood was used to fill the body and to secure the wires of the legs, the belly was painted with silver paint to replace the perished metal, and the statue was complete (see p.99).

Of course, methods of this kind cannot reproduce all the finesse of the original; to do that one would have to take the whole thing to pieces and re-create; but in so doing one loses something which is of sentimental if not always of scientific importance—the object as exhibited is really a copy, new throughout, of the old work, and no one can be quite certain of its faithfulness. In dealing with the antiquities from Ur we have preferred a restoration which implies the least possible interference with the object to a reconstruction which may give a better appearance but depends more on the modern hand.

Another instance will make the point clearer. In the largest of all the stone-built royal tombs, which had been entered by robbers and most thoroughly plundered, there remained only one corner of the last chamber to be cleared, and we had given up expectation of any 'finds' when suddenly a loose bit of shell inlay turned up, and the next minute the foreman's hand, carefully brushing away the earth, laid bare the corner of a mosaic in lapis lazuli and shell. This was the famous 'Standard' of Ur, but at the time we had very little idea of what it might be: the wooden background had perished entirely, and the tiny pieces of inlay, though they kept their

LEFT *One of the 'ram-caught-in-a-thicket' supports as first revealed during the excavation of RT1237* relative positions in the soil, were all quite loose; falling stones had bent and twisted the once flat panel, while as the wood decayed and the fragments sank back into the empty space behind, their different thickness made the surface of them rough and uneven. So delicate was the task of removing the dirt without further disturbing the mosaic that only about a square inch could be dealt with at a time—each section was waxed as soon as cleared, but so much of the surrounding dirt mingled with the hot wax that the face of the panel became invisible. When at last it could be lifted from the earth, I knew that we had found a very fine thing, but should have been hard put to it to say exactly what it was.

Now, it would have been perfectly feasible to take the mosaic to pieces, bit by bit, and re-make it on a new background, and the task might have been done as well as the modern craftsman as by the old, but the panels would have been the work of a modern craftsman.

What was done was this. The two sides of the panel were separated, and waxed cloth was fixed to the back of the inlay and the face of it was roughly cleaned; it was then laid face downwards on glass and warmed until the wax was soft, and it was pressed with the fingers from behind until by looking underneath one could be sure that each fragment of the inlay was in direct contact with the glass. The panel was now flat, but the pattern was much distorted; the edges of the mosaic fragments had lost contact in the ground and earth and powdered bitumen had filtered between them, and now wax as well, so that while some overlapped, others were widely apart. The next stage was to remove the cloth from the back, leaving the mosaic virtually loose on the glass, and to pick out all foreign matter, and then by sideways pressure with the fingers coax the pieces together. When this was done, fresh wax and cloth were applied behind and a proper backing fixed on.

The result of this is that the mosaic is not nearly so regular or smooth as the Sumerian artist made it, but what we possess is the work of that artist uninterfered with except by the accidents of time; the pieces of shell and lapis which he put together no one else has taken apart and re-set.

In the case of the 'Standard' the labour of restoration was at the same time a process of discovery; the work in the field had really been done in the dark, and it was only when the panels were cleaned and had begun to take shape in the laboratory that their importance could be recognized.

RIGHT *Restored support in the form of a rampant he-goat with its front legs in a small tree, from RT 1237*

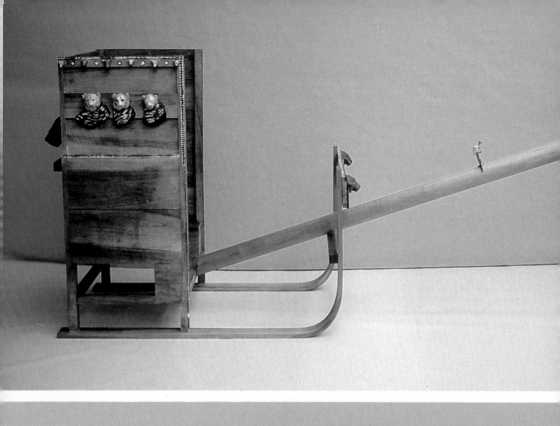

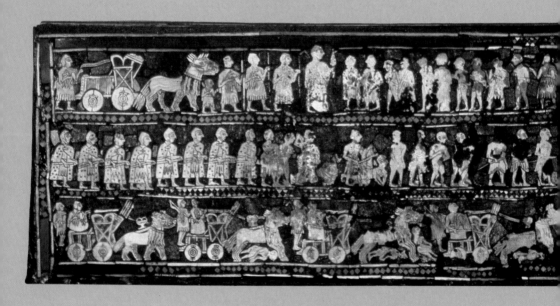

There are two main panels, rectangular and measuring 22 inches long by 9 inches high, and two triangular pieces which formed the ends; these were fixed together so that the larger sides sloped inwards and the whole thing was fastened on to the end of a pole, and would seem to have been carried in processions; we actually found it lying against the shoulder of a man who may have been the king's standard-bearer.[3]

The mosaic is composed of figures, silhouetted in shell with details engraved, which are set in a background of lapis lazuli relieved here and there with red. The triangular ends have mythological scenes of animals. On one side the king and the royal family are seen at feast. They sit in chairs, their costume consists of the old-fashioned sheepskin kilt or petti-coat and the upper part of the body is bare; servants wait on them, and at one end of the scene is a musician playing on a small harp, while by him a woman singer with her hands to her breasts sings to the accompaniment of the instrument.

These figures form the top row of the design; in two lower rows attendants are shown bringing in spoils captured from the enemy and food supplies for the banquet—one is driving a goat, another carries two fish, another is bent under the weight of a corded bale, and so on, several of the figures being repeated. On the other side, in the centre of the top row, stands the king, distinguished by his greater height, with behind him three attendants or members of his house, and a dwarf-like groom who holds the heads of the two asses which draw the monarch's empty chariot while the driver of it walks behind holding the reins; in front of the king soldiers are bringing up prisoners, naked and with their arms bound behind their backs, for him to decide their fate.

In the second row, at the back, comes the phalanx of the royal army, heavy-armed infantry in close order with copper helmets exactly like those found by us in the king's grave, and long cloaks of some stiff material which I take to be felt, just such cloaks as are worn by the shepherds of Turkey today, holding axes in their hands; in front of them are the light-armed infantry without cloaks, wielding axes or short spears, already engaged with an enemy whose naked warriors are either fleeing or being struck down. In the lowest row we have the chariotry of Sumer, each car

LEFT ABOVE *Reconstructed wooden land sledge decorated with mosaic and with golden lions' heads on the sides, from RT 800*
LEFT BELOW *So called 'Standard of Ur', with the mosaic inlays representing war scenes. It may have been the sounding-box of a musical instrument*

The 'Standard of Ur'. Side B shows a banquet, perhaps in celebration of victory, and a procession of spoils

drawn by two asses and carrying two men, of whom one is the driver and the other a warrior who flings light javelins, of which four are kept in a quiver tied to the front of the car.

Not the least surprising aspect of the civilization which the tombs illustrate is the advance it had made in architecture. The doorway of RT 789 was capped with a properly constructed brick arch, and its roof was formed by a brick barrel vault with apsidal ends; Puabi's (RT 800) tomb was similarly vaulted, others had vaults of limestone rubble masonry; we find a complete rubble dome built over a timber centring and supported by pendentives after the modern fashion. In these underground buildings no columns were required, but since the column was, as we shall see, freely used in the immediately succeeding period it must have been known in the cemetery age also. Summing this up, we can say that all the basic forms of architecture used today were familiar to the people of Ur in the early part of the third millennium before Christ.

Our royal cemetery dates, as I have said, to the latter part of the Early Dynastic period when Sumerian civilization properly so called is fully developed. It was an urban civilization of a highly evolved type; its artists, capable at times of a very vivid realism (as in the case of the donkey 'mascot' from Queen Puabi's chariot), followed for the most part standards and conventions whose excellence had been approved by many generations working before them; its craftsmen in metal possessed a knowledge of metallurgy and a technical skill which few ancient peoples have ever rivalled and which it must have taken long years to perfect; its merchants carried on a far-flung trade, its agriculture prospered, its armed forces were well organized, and men practised freely the art of writing.

Further Reading

The Royal Cemetery was published in two monumental volumes, one of text, one of plates: *Ur Excavations*, II: *The Royal Cemetery* (London, 1934). It was comprehensively re-examined by H. J. Nissen, *Zur Datierung des Königs-friedhofes von Ur* (Bonn, 1966).

Two articles have sought to extend interpretation of the finds through the evidence of seals in the graves: W.L. Rathje, 'New Tricks for Old Seals: A Progress Report' in *Seals and Sealings in the Ancient Near East* (ed. M. Gibson and R.D. Biggs, Undena Publications, Malibu, 1977), pp.25ff.; P.R.S. Moorey, 'What do we know about the people buried in the Royal Cemetery?' *Expedition* 20(1) (Fall, 1977), pp.24ff.

On the musical instruments see J. Rimmer, *Ancient Musical Instruments of Western Asia in the British Museum* (1969).

The three stone-built chambers of R T779, source of the 'Standard'

Al-'Ubaid and
the First Dynasty of Ur

In 1919 Dr Hall, working for the British Museum, visited about 4 miles to the north-west of the ruins of Ur proper a little mound where the surface indications promised remains of an unusual character; he therefore started excavations, and at once came upon a construction in plano-convex brick. He traced round three sides of a small rectangular structure and against the south-east face he found a hoard of objects lying under a mass of mud-brick.

There was a small stone statue of a man carved in the primitive and summary style already familiar to us from stray examples procured else-where, but with this were other monuments of a more novel sort. There was a great copper relief 7 feet 9 inches long and 3 feet 6 inches high, representing in heraldic fashion an eagle grasping two stags; there were bulls, the foreparts of lions, nearly life-size, made of copper hammered over bitumen and wood with inlaid eyes and white shell teeth through which protruded tongues of red stone; there were fragments of wooden columns incrusted with mother-of-pearl, red stone, and black shale; clay flowers with inlaid petals of white, black, and red, and more heads of animals in copper but on a smaller scale. Altogether it was a most important discovery, and since the excavation was left unfinished by Dr Hall, it was the obvious duty of the Joint Expedition to complete it as soon as possible. In the season 1923–24, therefore, a branch camp was set up at al-'Ubaid (such is the name of the little mound), and the work was restarted with the hope that more light would be thrown on the nature of the building and that there might yet be objects awaiting discovery.

Dr Hall's work had given us a warning. The copper statues found by him had suffered terribly through corrosion and breakage, and, important as they were, were but ghosts of the originals; of the lions' heads little more remained than the bitumen cores with the inlay of eyes and mouth, of the columns only the loose fragments of the incrustation could be collected and brought home, and the great copper relief, of which only one stag's head was recovered intact, had to be reconstructed from fragments, and in several respects the reconstruction was open to doubt. If, then, we should encounter any further objects of the kind we had to be sure that our resources would be adequate to the delicate task of their removal and transport.

The work of excavation which had produced the original hoard of statuary had begun at one corner of the building and had been carried on not quite to its central point, when the diggers had encountered and partly cut into a solid mass of mud-brick. We started at this point and, following up the brickwork—with some difficulty, for it showed no true face—found that it was one side of a staircase projecting at right-angles from the main structure; the treads, of which a number were preserved at the stairs' foot, were great slabs of white limestone, the first example of the use of stone for building that had been noted in the south of Mesopotamia except for a similar flight of stairs leading up to the staged tower of Abu Shahrein, a ruin about 12 miles south of Ur. Further examination proved that the structure itself was a solid mass of brick, a platform approached by the flight of steps, and only the substructure of a building which itself had completely disappeared.

Working round the stairway and following the wall between it and the far corner of the platform we found, under a mass of mud-brick of a later period (a new platform laid down over the ruins of the old), a second hoard of objects in part similar to those which had rewarded Dr Hall and in part different. In the angle between the stairs and the wall there lay two ten-foot columns of wood encrusted with mother-of-pearl, shale, and red stone, and other palm-log columns and beams overlaid with sheets of copper; piled in one heap there were four copper statues of bulls standing upright with their heads turned outwards over their shoulders; in a line along the wall were copper reliefs of reclining cattle, and mixed with these, sections of mosaic friezes in which figures silhouetted in white limestone or in shell were set against a background of black shale and framed with strips of copper; and everywhere we found fragments or complete examples of the inlaid clay flowers with cone-like stems which had figured in the earlier excavations.

One day a workman unearthed before my eyes, near the south corner of the stairway ramp, a white marble plano-convex shaped tablet with a sharply convex reverse and a depression in the centre just like the baked clay bricks of this shape. On the obverse it was inscribed: 'Aanepada King of Ur, son of Mesanepada King of Ur, has built this for his lady Ninkhur-sag'. It was the foundation-tablet of our building and the most important of our discoveries. When one of the copper bulls found by Dr Hall was being cleaned in the British Museum, a duplicate of this text was recognized on a copper panel hammered into its flank. It was welcome confirmation of our assumption that the elaborate fittings we had found were indeed from the temple erected by Aanepada. Among Dr Hall's finds there was a further, non-royal, inscription. It had been cut into the back of the torso of a limestone statue of a man. It read: 'Ekur, keeper of the granaries of Uruk, had this statue carved for Damgalnun [i.e., Ninkhursag] in the year in which the temple was built'. Ekur was presumably a high official of Aanepada, then also ruling over Uruk, who had wished to bring himself honour by presenting his statue, in an attitude of prayer, to his royal master's new temple for Ninkhursag.

At first reading the foundation text does not sound very exciting. Only a list of rather unpronounceable names, but we were excited enough. The first name was unknown to us or anyone, but the second was familiar as that of the first king of the First Dynasty of Ur according to the Sumerian King-List. I have, in the introduction to this book, explained the extra-ordinary importance of the discovery of the tablet as establishing the historic character of a dynasty which had been regarded as mythical only, but because it belonged to the al-'Ubaid temple it did something more than prove the accuracy of the King-List: it dated the building, so that the objects associated with it could be considered in their proper place in the development of Mesopotamian art, and that again meant that 'the First Dynasty of Ur' would not be merely an isolated fact but would have a content of its own; the phrase would denote a period in history whose character we could judge in the light of actual remains.

But the objects to which so much extra interest was lent by the finding of the foundation-tablet gave us a very anxious time; they lay so thickly in the ground that there might be half a dozen of them all exposed at one time and all calling for special care in their removal; and their condition was quite as bad as we had feared.

The uppermost of the four copper bulls was barely recognizable, only part of one leg and a mass of green powder betraying its existence. The second looked more promising, but the metal was broken into a thousand pieces and was so soft that it crumbled to dust at a touch (I spent three weeks preparing it and then when we lifted it, the whole thing collapsed in atoms); with the next two we had better success and they are now in the British Museum and at Philadelphia, battered and distorted figures but still figures of bulls showing something of the fine quality of the originals and remarkable as being the oldest copper statues preserved to us. The copper reliefs were less difficult to manage and only one was rejected as too fragmentary for removal; even then the head, cast in metal, more solid than the hammered sheets which formed the body, remained a first-class object.

The inlaid columns were crushed flat and the wood had perished, but most of the tesserae were approximately in position, only those along the edges having been dislodged and scattered. They were removed in sections, sacking being waxed onto the tesserae that lay face upwards and glued on to the backs of those which belonged to the lower face of the shafts: lifted thus in sheets, the decoration could be fixed onto a new core (it was found that circular petrol-drums were of exactly the right diameter, and these served our turn) without any disturbance of the individual bits of stone and mother-of-pearl, while other sheets and the loose tesserae collected from the earth were kept with a view to more drastic reconstruction.

Plan of the excavated area at Tell al-'Ubaid to show the temple platform and oval enclosure revealed by later excavations (see pp.110–11)

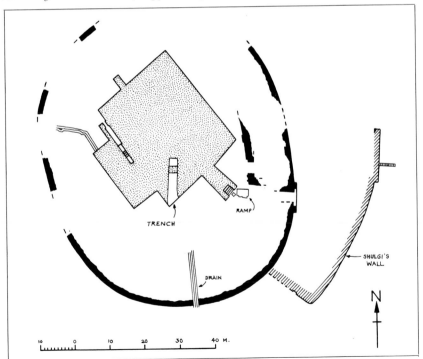

The mosaic friezes were held together with wax and muslin for such treatment as the British Museum authorities might choose to give them. The friezes were two in number. One was simple, a row of birds, probably doves, rather roughly cut in white limestone (which I think was originally painted in colour) against a black ground. The other was much more elaborate and showed much finer workmanship. It consisted for most of its length of a procession of cows carved in limestone, probably once painted, or in shell, which was probably left white, but in the centre there was a scene in which human figures are introduced; on one side of a reed-built byre, from the door of which two calves are seen issuing, men seated on low stools are milking cattle; the man sits under the cow's tail milking her from behind; the calves, duly muzzled, are roped to the cow's head-stalls so as to encourage them to give milk. On the other side of the byre two men, shaven and wearing the fleece petticoat which in later times seems to survive as the official dress of priests and priest-kings, are pouring milk through a strainer into a vessel set on the ground, while two others are collecting the strained liquid in great store-jars (see p. 240).

It is a typical scene of pastoral life, but the costume of the actors makes it likely that it is something more than this. There were in later days at least sacred farms attached to the temples, and here we may have priests preparing the milk of the Mother-goddess Ninkhursag which was the nourishment of kings. That the very domestic-looking picture of milking had a religious bearing is made more likely by the fact that in the same frieze there was introduced between the figures of walking cattle a small panel of a curiously incongruous character; it shows a bearded bull rampant in hilly country, on whose back is perched a lion-headed eagle apparently attacking him and tearing at his rump; this is certainly an illustration of some mythological legend and its presence here cannot but affect our view of the frieze as a whole.

It was obvious that all the objects found by us, and by Dr Hall previously, on either side of the stair-ramp leading on to the platform had belonged originally to a temple set on the platform or to the upper part of the platform itself. The flowers of baked clay, each with corolla and petals of red, white, and black stone, had once been set into a mud-brick wall with their colourful heads projecting, probably on the exterior of a structure. All were found close to the platform wall and apparently loose. But a complete statue of a man and an inscribed torso fragment had presumably been votives placed, as in other contemporary temples, within the shrine. What then of the great copper relief, the large copper lions and bulls, and the wooden columns covered with sheet copper or mosaic, were they from the interior of a temple or from the exterior? Later texts and finds indicate that the lions at least might have been set outside it, for the rest there is no way of knowing for certain, save that it must be doubted, for example, whether the mosaic-covered columns would have survived the rigours of exposure in an external position. The disposition of the objects as found does not suggest the chaos of collapse from positions just above where they were excavated.[4] The copper relief, for instance, was found the right way up, in an almost vertical position facing outwards; the lions were set side by side and the bulls were piled one on top of another. This looks more like an assembly point, near the staircase, for fittings both from the interior and the exterior of a temple. But that was not the whole story.

The temple had not been disintegrated by gradual decay. It had been suddenly and violently overthrown; that was clear enough. The walls had been undermined and then pushed over from the inside, so that in front of the platform there lay, sloped downwards, great blocks of intact mud-brick walling to the lower face of which the fragments of the friezes were still attached—we had to cut away the brickwork to get at the back of the frieze. Where, as did happen, bits of two friezes occurred on the same mud-brick block, we were given the order and the exact distance between the two; the relative position of the row of heifers and the shell mosaic of cattle was thus fixed. How are we to explain all this?

The answer probably lies in the subsequent history of the site as revealed by our excavations, though erosion was so extensive that all conclusions must necessarily be very provisional. As we have already noticed in studying the temple terrace at Ur, and the even more striking series of ancient temples at Eridu, it was customary in Mesopotamia, when rebuilding a temple, to incorporate the earlier one within the core of the platform upon which its successor was to be set. This often meant largely dismantling it. Thus objects and structures devoted to worship could not be plundered and profaned by having bricks and fittings cannibalized for subsequent use in secular structures elsewhere, as they would be securely sealed for ever within the mud-brick platform. Inscribed bricks indicate that Shulgi, king of Ur, c. 2094–2047 B.C., was responsible for some building high on the al-'Ubaid platform; but it is not clear whether it was he or some earlier ruler who was responsible for sealing the Early Dynastic platform within a series of terraces ready for fresh building. Erosion had reduced these to the merest trace; but it was sufficient to indicate that the most likely explanation for the well-ordered, if drastic, demolition of the Early Dynastic temple is to be found in a royal builder's piety. He wished to erect a new temple on the site, furnished in the style of his own day, but

The ruins of the temple platform at Tell al-'Ubaid

in doing so he had no wish to offend the gods by profaning an earlier shrine. In the traditional Sumerian manner he carefully dismembered it, both structure and furnishings, and entombed them in the base of his new structure, thus preserving for posterity the most representative series of Early Dynastic temple fittings yet discovered. It is our loss that his tidy workmen left so few clues from which to reconstruct the shrine he so scrupulously destroyed.

Our excavations at al-'Ubaid in the temple area were by no means exhaustive, as was shown in 1937 when Dr Delougaz of Chicago University briefly reopened excavations there to test a specific hypothesis about the setting of the Early Dynastic temple platform we and Dr Hall had discovered. During his excavations at Khafajah in the Diyala valley in 1931–32 Dr Delougaz had found a square structure not unlike the al-'Ubaid platform, also built of plano-convex bricks and dating to the final phase of the Early Dynastic period. It was set within an oval enclosure. Certain clues suggested that the same might also be true at al-'Ubaid, and so indeed it proved. Fresh excavation showed that the platform there was indeed a little off centre in an oval enclosure, some 80 metres long and 65 metres wide. Only part of the outer face of the artificial oval terrace, on which the platform had been built, was traced by the American team, but its form was clearly defined. There was an entrance opposite to the bottom of the stair-ramp on to the platform and, as again at Khafajah, there were traces of rooms on the inside of the oval enclosure wall; but they remain to be excavated. The asymmetrically placed stair-ramp onto the platform, and the relation of the whole platform to the entrance, suggest that platform and enclosure were not planned simultaneously. An earlier building may have been more symmetrically placed in the enclosure. Under the Early Dynastic platform was a line of foundations in red sandstone, running at an angle of 45 degrees to the platform itself. This was the late prehistoric shrine whose presence had earlier been indicated by baked clay cones for wall mosaics and very small rectangular bricks, with circular holes into which ornamental rosettes could be fixed, scattered higher in the debris.

If Khafajah helps us with the lay-out of the al-'Ubaid temple complex as a whole, does it also indicate what kind of temple had stood on the platform? Unfortunately in both places the platform surface was so eroded that no trace of foundations remained. At Khafajah an attempt was made to reconstruct the type of temple from the placing of the stairway and by an analogy with other contemporary local temples; but the temple on the platform we have been discussing is still isolated among finds in the south at this period and its two stairways, one oddly angled, are no clear guide to the location of entrances. It must remain a ghost, known only from its dismembered decoration and fittings.

Al-'Ubaid gave us yet another discovery, not so remarkable but none the less useful to us. In a second and smaller mound which lay close to the temple we found a number of graves. This cemetery had been much damaged by erosion and disturbance, so bones were variably preserved. Examination of the skeletons indicated a robust population with relatively long heads and prominent noses, some of whom had lived to be over sixty: a great age at this time. Graves dating from the Jamdat Nasr period . through to the time of the First Dynasty of Ur were excavated; but the main group belonged to the earlier part of the Early Dynastic period, before the temple built by Aanepada and before the time of the 'royal tombs' at Ur. In marked contrast to the tombs at Ur there were no features in the manner of burial, nor in the grave equipment, to suggest significant social distinctions between the people buried there. Simple copper axes and daggers, vessels and possibly also fish-hooks, accompanied a range of plain buff pottery. This was the burial ground of an ordinary rural community providing us with useful comparisons for the richly varied social range of graves at Ur, extending as they did over much of the subsequent part of the third millennium B.C.

At Ur, in the southern part of the Royal Cemetery area, there was spread over the tops of the grave-shafts a mass of rubbish forming three fairly distinct strata, the middle one being of a dark colour, burnt brick earth and charcoal, the upper and lower strata of a light grey, lime rubble plentifully mixed with potsherds, seal-impressions, and tablets; the three together seem to represent temple store-rooms which had been burnt and razed to the ground. The buildings must have been later in date than the cemetery, since their ruins lay above the shafts, but they need not have been much later, for when they were destroyed, the ground-surface from which the last graves had been dug was still exposed, not hidden by any such accumulation of rubbish as time would inevitably have produced. It is not impossible that they were chapels connected with the old royal graves, but of this no one can be certain; but in any case they must have been, or included, store-rooms in which were kept offerings made by kings, for the seal-impressions came for the most part from the stoppers of big jars and two of them bear the name of Mesanepada, king of Ur and founder of the First Dynasty, while loose in the rubbish we found the actual seal, a lapis lazuli cylinder, of the wife of Mesanepada and mother, as we may suppose, of the Aanepada who built the temple at al-'Ubaid. Here too then, in the capital of the state, the First Dynasty comes to life, but apart from the written record not very much of the period survives. We know that after the Jamdat Nasr period the temple terrace and its related religious struc-tures were rebuilt, and of these we have recovered the ground-plans; in the case of a number of other temples there have been found remains of plano-convex brick construction proving that the foundation at least went back to Early Dynastic times, but we cannot connect any of them definitely with the First Dynasty. Although that dynasty is in the Sumerian King-List put immediately after the First Dynasty of Uruk and on that showing might be placed early in the Early Dynastic period, it is archaeologically certain that it did in fact come relatively late in that period. That is proved by evidence gathered from many sites, but even at Ur we can see that the Royal Cemetery, which is Early Dynastic, antedates the First Dynasty—it may well be that the prosperous reigns of such local kings as Meskalamdug and Akalamdug enabled Mesanepada to establish his hegemony over the whole of Sumer and so to figure in the King-List. The buildings at Ur therefore, which for the sake of convenience in reference we have called 'First Dynasty', may be, and sometimes certainly are, of earlier foundation, though they may have been standing in the days of Mesanepada and his son. But there is one important exception.

The main Early Dynastic temple is completely buried inside the Ziggurat of Ur-Nammu, and we made no attempt to excavate it; all that we can say is that it was a good deal smaller than the Third Dynasty Ziggurat which stands today, but was none the less of imposing size, the main block, without the staircase, measuring about 150 by 120 feet at ground-level. It stood well back on a raised terrace enclosed by a heavily buttressed wall and partly occupied by religious buildings; these we were able to excavate and they told us a great deal. In the first place, we had to deal not with one building but with two. I have already described how the temple complex of the Jamdat Nasr time had been deliberately destroyed and how the new walls had been constructed with a certain admixture of flat bricks below and with plano-convex bricks above ground-level. These walls necessarily belonged to the very beginning of the Early Dynastic period, and they were sufficiently well preserved for us to trace out the whole of their ground-plan. But at a later time within the 'plano-convex brick period', i.e., well within the Early Dynastic period, the whole thing had been rebuilt on almost identical lines, the new walls resting on the stumps of the old; there was here no violent destruction by iconoclasts, no new religious departure requiring a different type of temple; it looked, quite simply, as if the original building had in the course of years fallen into disrepair and had to be rebuilt, but rebuilt with a pious conformity to tradition. We can have no certain assurance, but it is tempting and I think reasonable to assume that the costly work of reconstructing the central shrine of Ur was taken in hand by Mesanepada when he ceased to be a vassal city-king and became the sovereign lord of Sumer. A Sumerian king was regarded as the regent of his capital's patron god and his rise to power really meant that the city's god had become the chief of the pantheon of Sumerian gods; the new divine ruler would naturally require a house suited to his supreme dignity. For this reason I do not hesitate to call the buildings I am about to describe the main temple buildings of the First Dynasty of Ur.

The wall surrounding the terrace was a colossal structure no less than 36 feet thick, its outer face was relieved by shallow buttresses and—an extraordinary feature in this stoneless land—the mud-brickwork rested on a foundation of coursed limestone rubble masonry rising to a height of nearly 4 feet. The First Dynasty temple at al-'Ubaid has limestone foundations, but they are no more than a single course of stone laid at or below ground-level, and we have found other examples of the same thing in Early Dynastic buildings at Ur, but there is nothing at all like this terrace wall with its six or seven courses of rough unshaped blocks. And the curious point about it was that it was a sham; the stonework did not go back into the wall but was a mere skin one stone thick. The wall had been built of mud-bricks only—laid, in the initial stages, against the face of the First Early Dynasty wall, which was still standing to some height—and when they had got up to 4 feet, the builders set the stones against the smooth mud-brick face, levelled the top with mud mortar, and then carried on with their brickwork, bringing it forward to line up flush with the stone; it was a rather naïve method of construction, but an easy one for workmen not accustomed to building in stone and obliged to make economical use of an expensive material. A stone facing of this sort, not bonded into the brickwork behind, gave no additional strength but on the contrary was a source of weakness, and since it was plastered with mud like the upper part of the wall, it did not aim at spectacular effect; I can only suppose that it is a survival of a genuine constructional system (a temple of the Uruk period at Uruk has real stone foundations) now reduced to a religious formula.

The entrance of the terrace had been in the middle of the north-east wall; the gateway was a double one, for there was here an interior wall, so that the visitor passed through an entrance-lobby about 20 feet deep, in the side-walls of which were doors giving on to store- or service-chambers built against the inner face of the terrace wall. Once through the inner gate one probably had the temple directly in front and, on either side, subsidiary buildings occupying the north and east corners of the terrace. The builders of the Third Dynasty Ziggurat, remodelling the terrace and raising it level, had had to destroy the old buildings, but the stumps of the walls remained underneath their higher pavement and we could recover at least the ground-plan of them. If one can judge by the analogy of later times, the building in the north corner should, by its position, have been the special shrine of the Moon-god, Nanna, the patron deity of Ur to whom the Ziggurat of Ur was dedicated; so it may have been, but its arrangements do not correspond to those of a normal temple. Access was by a small and unpretentious door at the south-west end and from it one went by a bitumen-covered 'causeway' across a lobby into what must have been an unroofed central court; this had a floor of clay only, and against its north-west wall there was a raised brick and bitumen tank with shallow runnels on either side which reminds one of a scullery sink and was probably used for the preparation of food or for the washing of utensils— we found in it half a dozen clay cups and a few small animal bones and fish scales. Two doorways in the north-east wall led to two, small square chambers, behind each of which was a very narrow passage-like room; each of the main

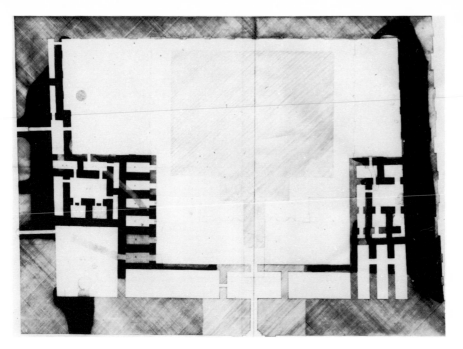

Buildings of the first half of the third millennium B.C. in the area of the later Ziggurat. The black areas represent existing Archaic I walls

chambers was entirely taken up by a great fireplace, square in the one case, circular in the other; they were filled with ashes and cinders, the brickwork of the edging was reddened by heat, and that they were in constant use was shown by the fact that the floor of the square furnace had been relaid no less than twelve times. A door in the south-west side of the open court led into a series of narrow rooms, virtually a passage, which in turn may have led (of the end wall only the foundations remained, so that it was impossible to say whether there had been a doorway or not) to three large store-rooms lying at the back of the building proper, in the north angle of the terrace wall.

There is nothing here that suggests a temple; the obvious term to apply to such a building is 'kitchen'. Now the sacrifices that men offered to the gods were in fact the food of the gods; the flesh of the votive animal had to be cooked, whether it was roast with fire or seethed in the pot, and the cakes and the bread had to be baked, so that a kitchen was an important part of a temple; we have an admirable illustration of this in the Larsa period. In the present instance we have a kitchen and no temple. The explanation is, I think, that the temple, the real house of the god, was in the centre of the platform.

The building in the east corner of the terrace was very similar in character. The main block here too was entered by a small door in the south-west end, and there was the lobby, the central court with side-chambers, and, facing the entrance, two rooms entirely taken up by big furnaces or fireplaces, one square and one circular. Behind the building there was, instead of store-chambers, a large open court entered by a passage through the terrace wall from which a paved causeway led to the north-easternmost of a range of small cells built against the side of the main block, and through this one could pass on to the platform. In the open court there was a circular base of burnt bricks set in and overlaid with bitumen, against which was a more or less rectangular brick platform, also remains of a second similar base, and, sunk in the floor, a circular basin of burnt bricks and bitumen. A third circular brick base lay in the open area south-west of the building, close to a row of service-chambers or store-rooms built against the inner face of the terrace wall, and here was a second narrow passage through the terrace wall itself, giving access from outside to the temple platform.

Woolley paying his workmen

Here then we have a second 'kitchen', complicated by a range of small cells all opening on to the platform; and again later analogies can be invoked in explanation. In all later periods there stood on the south-west side of the Ziggurat terrace a temple dedicated to Ningal, the wife of the Moon-god, and for one such at least we have written evidence that the temple served also for those minor deities who formed as it were the court of the supreme god and his consort. The small cells (with the exception of the one that, having doors at both ends, was no more than a passage) were probably chapels containing the statues of those minor gods; Ningal herself may have had her shrine in the centre of the platform. In the central court of the building we found a few fragments of just such inlay as was used for the mosaic frieze of the temple at al-'Ubaid and of wigs and beards carved in stone which came from opposite statues, and of gold objects; other pieces of gold came from the central chapel; it was enough to show that some part at least of the building had been decorated in such fashion as becomes a temple. Where nothing more survives than a few tattered mud-brick foundations it is not easy to conjure up anything of splendour; but with the analogy of al-'Ubaid before us we may be sure that these few fragments do witness to a structure whose very richness would account for its utter destruction. Actually one discovery did hint at the wealth of its contents. In the middle of the big open court lying in front of the 'kitchen' there was a clay pot sunk below the pavement in which were quantities of beads, two miniature toilet-vases of white limestone, two seals of coloured alabaster in the form of lion's heads, and stone figures of a man, a squatting bull, a calf, and a dog; they must have been offerings dedicated by the faithful.

Under the foundations of a house attached to one of the temples another discovery was made. The ground here had been terraced for the building, and tumbled together in the filling behind the terrace wall was a group of objects of First Dynasty date. Two of these were a pair, limestone figures of rams, only the heads and foreparts carved in the round, the rest left rough; they seem to be supports for a throne, probably the seat of some statue of a god whose sacred emblem was the ram. With them was a small relief in alabaster carved on both sides; it was badly weathered and only half of it was preserved, but it was curiously interesting. It represented a high-prowed boat made of reeds tied together and having an arched cabin or canopy amidships—a boat not unlike the silver model found in royal tomb 789; on one side a man was shown standing in the stern and a sow in the cabin, on the other two fish took the place of the man and a goose that of the sow. Probably the little object was dedicated in a temple by one of the marsh folk and pictures the sort of life he led, for fish, wild geese, and wild boar are the staple products of the marshland.

In spite of all the destruction that had been done by later builders working upon the same site our excavation of the terrace did yield more information than we might have expected regarding the lay-out of the Moon-god's shrine in the time of the First Dynasty; and it also threw an interesting light on what one might call political conditions. I have remarked above on the fantastic thickness of the wall enclosing the terrace, a thickness of 36 feet; it suggests a fortress rather than a temple. The south-east wall, between the eastern 'kitchen' building and the corner of the terrace, was double (as too was the north-east wall) where a gate passage led through from the city; the passage ended in a guardroom, and beyond this there were two narrow store-chambers between the parallel walls; here there were found a number of jar-stoppers bearing seal-impressions, but also many sling-bolts of baked clay and clay balls, some of them quite large, missiles for use, perhaps, with some kind of catapult. The store-room had in fact served as an armoury.

The city was dominated by the temple of its patron god. But since the god was really the king, it was quite natural that his temple should be the core of the city's defence as well as the centre of its worship. We can safely assume that the town was walled. Inside the town there was, then as later, the Temenos, or Sacred Area, which again was enclosed by walls: it was the second line of defence. Lastly, in a corner of the Temenos, rose the temple of the city god which, with its fortified terrace, corresponded to the keep of the medieval castle; here the fighting men of Ur would make their last stand against a victorious enemy. The city-states of old Sumer were constantly at war with one another; the long succession of dynasties recorded in the King-List reflects the instability of things as one vassal ruler after another rebelled against his overlord, overcame his neighbours, and made his own city for a time the capital of the land, his own city god becoming by right of conquest the temporary head of the Sumerian pantheon.

Further light on the religious observances of the time was thrown by a discovery in another part of the field. On the line of the south-west wall of Nebuchadnezzar's Temenos there was a low mound in which years before Taylor had done some excavation, finding little, but making worse confounded one of the most confused sites I have ever dug. Under the Babylonian wall there was a tangle of broken and scanty remains of buildings of different dates amongst which we were able to identify a temple set up by Shulgi, king of the Third Dynasty of Ur, of which, however, little was left. Later houses had complicated the site with their successive ruins, and house drains, driven down deeply into the soil, had made havoc of everything beneath. Consequently when we did come to the Early

Dynastic levels, we found walls and floors, but all so fragmentary that no coherent plan of them could be drawn up. But in three cases we found underneath the foundations of these walls 'foundation-deposits' of a sort we had never encountered before. When the old builders had cut the trenches for the foundations of the proposed building—probably it was a temple, the prototype of Shulgi's *Dim-tab-ba* Temple—but before they started to lay bricks, they would dig here and there on the wall line a square pit about 3 feet deep and on the bottom of it spread a mat, the 'table' of the desert banquet. On this were put small clay vessels containing foodstuffs; an ox rib showed that these must have been the god's portion of the consecration sacrifice. Then over the spread table there was inverted a great bell-shaped heavily ribbed bowl of clay and the pit was filled up with earth and the wall built across it. Under the floor of Shulgi's temple we found terracotta cylinders containing animal bones which clearly echo this primitive rite of consecration.

The site, as I have said, was terribly cut up by the drains which had served the houses of Larsa and later dates, but as we dug deeper, we found precisely similar drains connected with the Early Dynastic buildings. The nature of the drains is this. You begin by sinking a circular shaft about 5 feet in diameter to a depth of 30 or 40 feet; then in it you pile one on another your drainpipes, terracotta rings about 3 feet across with a heavy collar at one end (this to give a better balance) and small holes pierced through its sides, and as you put each in one place, you fill the space round it with broken potsherds, and so on up to floor-level, when you cap it with a pierced lid or leave a hole in the tiled pavement for the intake. As the water poured down the drain runs out through the holes in the sides (kept clear by the potsherd packing) and so seeps away into the subsoil, the drain will be effective for a very long time.

We had not known that the system had been introduced so early, but what did surprise and puzzle us was the number of drains in a single prehistoric building; it seemed quite illogical that there should be two contemporary drains in a tiny chamber measuring only 15 feet by 3, and in the next room two more; neither a house nor a temple could require sanitation on that scale. Then as we dug deeper and came to the lowest rings of the drains (which of course we had had to destroy as we went down), we had another surprise. At the bottom of each there were quantities of small clay vessels of the two types which we knew to have been regularly used for religious offerings—for instance, on the 'tables of the gods' which I have just described—and terracotta model boats. They had been dropped down the drains, but not by accident, for in a single drain we

Woolley and his wife measuring drains made of baked clay segments

might find as many as forty intact vases as well as fragments of as many more broken by the fall. I have occasionally found potsherds, and once a complete pot, in what were definitely domestic drains—accidents of course will happen; but this is something different.

If there is some kind of ritual act involved here, we might look for it in the cult of Ea (the Sumerian Enki), god of wisdom and lord of the sweet water ocean under the earth known as *Apsu* (Sumerian *Abzu*); the word also used to describe the ritual basin in a temple which symbolized it. An inscription of unknown origin has survived in which Elili, one of the later kings of the First Dynasty of Ur, recorded his construction of an *apsu* for Ea. Now there is nothing strange in the idea of pouring libations to such a god into a pit, a hole in the ground, or a well—in this way your offering goes more directly to the god, and the practice is common to many peoples.

Despite our excavations the first two kings of the First Dynasty of Ur, Mesanepada and his son Aanepada, remain shadowy figures; but even they have slightly more substance as a result of our discoveries than their successors. The third king of the line, Meskiaganuna, perhaps a brother of Aanepada, is little more than a name; but we did find an inscription of his time that is of very particular interest. It was incised on part of a calcite bowl dedicated for him by his wife. This is the oldest text certainly written in the Akkadian language and not in Sumerian as we might have anticipated at Ur at this early date. It shows how cautious we must be in drawing any sharp distinctions between the peoples speaking these two languages, when the Semitic, intrusive one is already apparent by about 2450 B.C. at Ur in a written text—and may have been spoken by some of the population even earlier.

Further Reading

The excavations at Tell al-'Ubaid were fully published in H.R. Hall and C.L. Woolley, *Ur Excavations* I: *Al-'Ubaid* (Oxford, 1927). The re-investigation by P. Delougaz has only been published in an article: 'A Short Investigation of the Temple at Al'Ubaid' in *Iraq* 5 (1938), pp. 1ff. and as part of a general commentary on Early Dynastic temple 'ovals' in *The Temple Oval at Khafajah* (Chicago, 1940), pp. 140ff. The account given here accepts the criticisms of Woolley's original reconstruction provided by Delougaz. The Early Dynastic levels under the later Ziggurat at Ur were discussed by C.L. Woolley, *Ur Excavations* V: *The Ziggurat and its Surroundings* (London, 1939), pp. 7ff. Woolley believed there was already a Ziggurat at Ur in the Early Dynastic period; but there is no proof of this and it is assumed in this revision that a temple on a high platform is more likely in the light of evidence from other contemporary sites.

Limestone tablet from Tell al-'Ubaid inscribed:
'Ninkhursag; Aanepada, king of Ur, son of Mesanepada, king of Ur,
for Ninkhursag, has built a temple' (see pp. 105–6)

From the First to
the Third Dynasty of Ur
c. 2450–2100 B.C.

The next stage in the history of Ur involves the ancient city-state of Lagash, some way to the north of Ur. One of its most important suburbs, ancient Girsu, has been excavated by the French, beginning in the 1870s, at the modern site of Tello. This work revealed the contemporary records and monuments of a local line of rulers who do not appear in the Sumerian King-List. The first of these rulers was named Ur-Nanshe. At Ur we found a small inscribed granite stela carved with a scene in which a king worships a seated deity; the subsequently defaced name of Ur-Nanshe may just be made out. We still do not know how to place Ur-Nanshe in relation to the kings of the First Dynasty of Ur described in the previous chapter. It is unlikely that he was earlier than Mesanepada and his son. He may well have been a contemporary and his supremacy at Ur, if that is what the presence of his stela implies, would have involved a struggle and brief victory over one or other of these two rulers. Wide supremacy over Sumer was certainly achieved by his grandson Eanatum. On his famous 'Vulture Stela' (so-called from the birds of prey shown devouring the dead bodies), found at Tello and now in the Louvre, he invokes the Moon-god as witness to his solemn denunciation of the neighbouring city of Umma, which he had defeated in a boundary war, and devotes two doves to the god's shrine at Ur. It is in his reign that we first encounter the dynastic and administrative union of Ur with both Uruk and Lagash that was to have a long and important role in the fortunes of Ur.

In an outlying part of the site at Ur we found an inscribed fragment of a clay cone, a sort of foundation deposit, which recorded the restoration of two shrines, which may not have been at Ur, by Enanatum I of Lagash, Eanatum's successor. He was in turn succeeded by Entemena, who left a much more notable monument for us to find at Ur. When we were clearing the area behind the Ziggurat, on the pavement of a gateway through the encircling wall built by Nebuchadnezzar in the seventh century B.C., we found a large headless diorite statue of a man wearing the conventional Sumerian garment of sheepskin and bearing incised on its back and shoulders a long inscription in six columns describing the pious works of Entemena. The bulk of this text enumerates work carried out in the temples at Lagash; two short columns are devoted to particulars of a grant of lands made by the king and his father Enanatum I to the god Enlil. There is no mention here of Ur. How the statue came there is a mystery. However that may be, its later fate may be more reliably guessed at. It looks as if the ancient and headless image had been set up in the gateway where we found it by the Neo-Babylonian builders nearly two thousand years later. The break at the neck is worn smooth, as if by the pressure of numerous passing hands. King Nabonidus (*c.* 555–539 B.C.), we know (p.233), made something of a collection of antiquities at Ur and this may well have been one of them. It is also possible that this venerable fragment was placed here for the same purpose as carved or modelled lions, dogs and minor deities, to secure the gateway against evil spirits (see p.124).

It is impossible to say how we are to interpret these scattered inscribed objects in historical terms, for the evidence is so meagre; but we are able to place Entemena in relation to the Second Dynasty of Ur as recorded in the Sumerian King-List. We know from other sources that Entemena made an alliance with Lugalkinishedudu, who is named as the first ruler of the Second Dynasty of Ur. His name was found by us on inscribed stone vase fragments from below *Enunmakh*. A merchant had made the dedication of the vase mentioning in the inscription both Lugalkinishedudu and his son, Lugalkisalsi. Other texts tell us that Lugalkinishedudu rose from being ruler over the city of Umma, to be ruler first over Uruk and then over Ur. The same course was followed a generation or so later by a man called Lugalzagesi, the last Sumerian ruler before Sargon of Akkad.

In this period, known to archaeologists as Early Dynastic IIIb, we may date an unusual limestone relief found in a room on the north-east side of the *Giparu*. It is a plaque about 10 inches square with a hole in the centre for a peg, probably to fix it to a temple wall. On it are carved two scenes in low relief: above, a male figure, ritually naked, pours a libation before the seated image of the god; he is followed by three smaller figures wearing heavy cloaks; in the lower scene we have the same figure pouring a libation, but instead of the god's statue or image there is the façade of a temple, and behind come three figures of which the leader is a woman shown standing full-face. This is how enthroned goddesses are shown at this period; but here the identity of the lady may be otherwise. It has been

LEFT *Headless statue of Entemena, ruler of Lagash*

RIGHT *Limestone plaque once fixed to a temple wall, by a peg through the centre, showing scenes of worship before a seated god (above) and a temple façade (below)*

plausibly suggested that this is the High-Priestess wearing mitre and long cloak; she is followed by two servants, one carrying a kid for sacrifice, and the other what may be a wreath or necklace. Later analogies may be used to extend this explanation. The man making the sacrifice would be the king, denoted as such by his greater stature; the High-Priestess was a close female relative of the king, maybe a daughter. As we have already seen (p.92), the position of High-Priestess of the Moon-god at Ur was so important as to merit this royal appointment.

We may indeed have the name of one of the earliest of these High-Priestesses. She was a lady named Ninmetabarri, daughter of king AN.BU of Mari, mentioned on a calcite vase fragment found on the *Ekhursag* site just south-east of the *Giparu*, the official dwelling of the priestess. Although this building is best known in its later form (see p.183), there is some archaeological evidence to suggest that it had existed in the Early Dynastic period. Mari was a city on the Middle Euphrates, now in Syria, where French excavations in the last fifty years have revealed a large and flourishing city of this period. Through communication along the river, it was subject to strong Sumerian cultural influence. This king of Mari

conquered large parts of Sumer, perhaps about the time of Eanatum of Lagash, and may have sought to stabilize his hold over Ur (as did later rulers) by appointing his daughter to this prestigious office in the temple hierarchy there. Mari's supremacy, like that of many cities at this time, depended on the enterprise of individual rulers and is very unlikely to have outlasted the short few years of his energetic campaigning. Even when one king captured the city of another, it is likely that the ruler would have survived in some lesser role until an opportunity came for him to regain his authority.

We also found another interesting sculpture of similar form, though sadly only the left-hand bottom corner of a plaque; it may be a generation or two earlier than the one just described. It shows an empty two-wheeled 'straddle-car' for one driver, of a type common in Sumer at this time, followed by a groom and a bearer. Most remarkably this scene may be convincingly completed from excavations at Khafajah in the Diyala valley, where one of these plaques was found with just this corner missing. The Ur fragment fits the scene as a whole so well as to suggest that closely similar or identical plaques of this type were set up in temples throughout

Mesopotamia. The completed plaque shows a feast in the upper register with a procession of animals, supplies, and chariots below; either the celebration of a victory, with the spoils of conquest displayed, or some kind of religious festival and ritual feasting.

The independence of Lagash was ended by a ruler of their old enemy, the city of Umma. By about 2330 B.C. Lugalzagesi had established himself by force of arms as ruler over all the most important cities of Sumer, notably Ur and Uruk, and claimed in his inscriptions to have campaigned far beyond its boundaries. He made special mention of his concern for the status of Ur. His eventual defeat at the hands of Sargon of Akkad is taken to mark one of the climactic events in early Mesopotamian history. During the later Early Dynastic period the personal names of private individuals, and of a handful of gods and rulers, as well as occasional inscriptions, indicate a progressive infiltration of Sumer by Semitic Akkadian-speaking peoples from the north. Sargon, a man of forceful character, rising to power at Kish, gave these people a political identity and supremacy. He established a new capital at Akkad on an unknown site in the vicinity of Babylon, and by force of arms in a long reign created a vast domain. During the Akkadian period (c. 2334–2154 B.C.) there are no original inscriptions of any local kings at Ur, though the last king of the Second Dynasty was apparently contemporary with Sargon's successor Rimush. Sargon claims to have captured Ur, dismantling its fortifications. To the city's gods he paid due respect, no doubt as much from the political need to secure the allegiance of its Sumerian-speaking inhabitants, as from personal piety. His main act in the city, to which monuments bear witness, was deeply political in purpose. In a room of the *Giparu* we found a sadly battered alabaster disc on one side of which was carved in relief just such a scene of worship by the High-Priestess as we have identified on the earlier limestone plaque from the same building. In this case, happily, an inscription on the back tells us that the principal figure with her flounced dress and high conical hat is none other than Enheduana, daughter of King Sargon of Akkad.

Her own dedication is not the only memorial we have of Enheduana's life at Ur; from the cemetery come two cylinder seals, one of Adda, the steward of her household, one of another member of her establishment, and an impression on clay from the seal of her scribe. The finding of these seals enabled us to date with accuracy the cemetery which overlies the royal tombs and the minor graves of Early Dynastic III times. The graves of the Akkadian and immediately following period lay above those of Early Dynastic III, and were quite distinct from them not only by stratification

Alabaster disc showing Enheduana, daughter of King Sargon, High-Priestess of the Moon-God Nanna (2nd figure from left), participating in a libation ceremony; LEFT *as found and* RIGHT *as restored for exhibition in the University Museum, Philadelphia*

but also by the nature of their contents. The grave itself, and the ritual of burial, show no change; but the pottery is quite different. There is a whole new range of shapes and the vessels are much more carefully made and very often are rendered more attractive by being covered with a wash of red paint and then burnished brightly. It is perhaps a sign of diminished wealth among those now being buried in this part of Ur, for it is when men cannot afford cups and dishes of stone or of metal that the humble art of the potter comes into its own. Certainly the graves are nothing like so rich as those associated with the royal tombs. There are no vessels of gold or silver and even stone is rare. We still find beads of lapis lazuli and carnelian, and to those are added materials unknown or uncommon in the old days, haematite, agate, and chalcedony; but when gold is used, we generally find, instead of solid metal, the thinnest gold foil placed over a copper core. Rudimentary axes of hammered copper or bronze which begin to appear in graves in the Early Dynastic period are now commoner. Although very few analyses have yet been made, it seems likely that the substitution of the thin hammered type of axe for the solid cast one was due either to a falling-off in the general supply of metals like copper and the rarer tin or to the lower social status of the people whose graves we were now uncovering. Ur was no longer the great political and commercial centre she had been before the axis of power swung to the northern region of Akkad.

Since we cleared more than four hundred graves of the Akkadian period, we were able to collect plenty of material for establishing characteristic features of the period, and the most striking was a change in the fashion of head-dress. In the Early Dynastic III graves men wore round their heads a ring of gold or silver chains and long 'bugle' beads of lapis lazuli or carnelian which, like the *agêhl* of the present-day Arab, kept the head-cloth in place, and the women, at least those connected with the court, had an elaborate garniture of broad gold or silver ribbon, wreaths of gold and stone beads with pendant leaves and rings of gold, hair-rings of coiled gold wire, and enormous moon-shaped ear-rings of gold. The men of the later period have nothing but a small oval frontlet of thin gold foil tied across the forehead, and the women have a similar frontlet (worn, as with the men, across the forehead, not in the hair), and ear-rings of gold, moon-shaped but very small, and a lock of hair starting from just above either ear was plaited and spirally bound with a very narrow gold ribbon and pinned in position above the forehead. Granted that these are relatively poor graves which could not be expected to rival the exuberant splendour of the royal tombs, nonetheless so radical a change in fashion is significant.

And change is apparent in the cylinder seals also; indeed they provide one of the best criteria for distinguishing the graves of various periods. The crowding-together of figures which in the Early Dynastic seals make the composition so intricate and confused is abandoned, and instead the seal-cutter has learned how to space out his design so that each figure, isolated against a clear background, may gain in significance. This use of space as an essential part of design is an innovation of Akkadian times and one of its leading characteristics both in major and in minor art. There is also now much more emphasis on individual power, human, animal, and divine, with a stress on bulging muscles and scenes of exaggerated action. But above all, for it led to an enormous expansion of the seal-cutters' repertory, there was a marked concern for the vivid and intelligible illustration of divine activity. Mythological scenes now become for a brief period one of the glories of this miniature art. Sadly, secure identification of the scenes depicted is not possible in the absence of any direct links between the texts telling us the ancient myths, many of them known only from later editions, and these little illustrations. The best we are able to do at present is to isolate motifs and symbols involving a series of the more major deities: Shamash, the Sun-god, identified by his saw and the rays emanating from his shoulders; Ea, the Water-god, who bears a vase from which two streams flow over his shoulders, sometimes with fishes in them; and anonymous gods of vegetation, associated with sprouting grain, or a god whose lower body is that of a snake. We can also see old themes disappearing and new ones emerging. Banquet scenes linger on, but disappear after a time. In these later scenes the feasting figures are occasionally identified as deities by their horned crowns, whereas before the character of the participants remains undetermined. A favourite scene of later periods, minor gods introducing worshippers to major deities, now appears for the first time. Although inscriptions had appeared before on seals, they now become steadily commoner and some provide evidence for the profession of their owners.

During the reign of Sargon's successors Ur continued to enjoy the favour of her alien rulers, in spite of a rebellion which broke out on Sargon's death, for not only was a princess of the royal house again installed as High-Priestess of Nanna at Ur, but the city's temples were regularly honoured. In the ruins of *Enunmakh*, the store-house of Ningal, the divine wife of Nanna, we found under a later pavement an enormous mass of fragments of stone vases which had been dedicated to the temple and kept in its treasury; when the Third Dynasty of Ur (*c.* 2112–2004 B.C.) crashed and the Elamite forces broke into the city, they sacked the temples and wantonly destroyed the offerings of ancient kings that were stored there. The temples were rebuilt, but with the broken stone *ex votos* nothing could be done, so the fragments were collected and, because they were holy and so could not be treated as mere rubbish, buried under the new pavements of the shrines to which they had belonged. There we found them. Stone mace-heads and vases of steatite, limestone, and alabaster, many of them bore inscriptions recording the name of the donor; they were of different dates, coming right down to the last days of the Third Dynasty, but amongst them not a few belonged to the dynasty of Sargon of Akkad. One mace-head may have been the gift of Sargon himself, many vases had been dedicated by his son Rimush, treasure selected from the king's share of 'the booty of Elam' after 'the king of all had smitten Elam and Barakhsi'. One steatite bowl, very curiously carved with a demon and animal figures, is in a style which may be native to Elam or some other part of south-west Iran. Here then was evidence enough of the pious regard paid to the temples of Ur by kings of the Akkadian dynasty, but it is all the evidence that we found. Nowhere was there any record of buildings erected by them. A copy made on clay by a later scribe records the inscription on the base of a statue set up by Manishtushu, Rimush's successor, at Ur and dedicated to the god Enlil. Even the last great king of the dynasty, Naram-Sin, is only evidenced at Ur by similar later copies of statue inscriptions, and by vessel and mace-head fragments bearing his name.

This dynasty ended in a period of political chaos. 'Who was king? Who was not king?' plaintively writes the compiler of the King-List. The fall of the Akkadian dynasty came to mark the end of an age in Mesopotamian tradition much as the 'Flood' marked the beginning of the dynastic period in literary tradition. Foreign elements, among whom the Gutians (from the region of the Lower Zab river in north-east Mesopotamia) were the most disruptive according to the surviving records, took advantage of internal dissension to penetrate much of southern Mesopotamia. In this political uncertainty the ancient Sumerian city-states reasserted their independence, with Lagash playing a particularly important role in the evidence available to us. Among other things the close connection between Lagash and Ur that had existed in the Early Dynastic period was now revived. Ur-Bau, founder of the line of rulers at Lagash, had sufficient control over Ur to appoint his daughter, under the cult name Enanepada, High-Priestess of the Moon-god Nanna. Among the fragments of votive stone vases found under the pavement of *Enunmakh* no less than four bore her name and parentage. Ur-Bau was succeeded in turn by three sons-in-law, of whom the most significant was Gudea. He is the most familiar of all the Sumerian rulers today on account of the striking series of statues of him revealed by the French excavators at Tello. He maintained the connection Ur-Bau had established with Ur, where we found a few inscriptions bearing his name.

When the excavations of the Royal Cemetery area were first published in 1934 one particular group of graves was attributed to the 'Second Dynasty of Ur', which, as we have seen, was contemporary with the later Early Dynastic III and early Akkadian periods. This was a rough-and-ready way of distinguishing graves which were intermediate between the First and Third dynasties of Ur and was not at all insisting on a connection with the relatively unknown Second Dynasty. A number of these graves contained cylinder seals. Advances in our understanding of their classification and chronology in the last fifty years now clearly indicate that the main graves in this group are to be dated after the time of the dynasty of Akkad, but before the building of Shulgi's wing of the Mausolea of the Third Dynasty, since it overlapped the shaft of one of them. This embraces about half a century for the Gutian intrusions and perhaps up to some sixty years of the Third Dynasty.

There were originally fifteen graves in the classification of this 'Second Dynasty' group. It may now be seen that four of these are earlier, covering a period from Early Dynastic IIIb to the later Akkadian dynasty. Of the remainder six are normal and distinguished only by their contents, which are most akin to the graves of the later Akkadian period, and five are shaft graves containing multiple burials which recall in their arrangement one or two of the royal tombs of Early Dynastic IIIa. None of them can compare in wealth with the old royal tombs, but they are richer than any of the Akkadian period graves. In the pottery, the metal vessels, and the tools and weapons alike there are many types peculiar to this group; there are fairly numerous survivals from the earlier period but a greater number that are shared in common with the Sargonid; and the head-dresses of both men and women are all in the Sargonid fashion. The best of the single graves had a mud-brick-lined shaft in which there was a gable-topped wooden coffin containing the body of a man. Outside the coffin were placed numerous clay pots, several of them red-painted and burnished, a large ribbed tray of copper on which rested copper bowls and vases, a knife and an arrow-head, and the complete bodies of two sheep; against the head of the coffin a row of spears had been planted upright, as they were in the grave of Meskalamdug in the earlier cemetery. On the man's head there were six gold fillets arranged in tiers overlapping one another, a small gold ear-ring, and a twisted gold ribbon originally wound round a lock of hair; four necklaces were round the neck, made of beads of various coloured stones, carnelian, agate, jasper, chalcedony sard, and of gold, to one of which was attached an amulet in the form of a standing goat, a fine lively little figure solid-cast in gold. On the right shoulder was a silver toggle-pin that had fastened the cloak and on the arms were bracelets, a plain gold band on the right arm and on the left three of gold and two of silver, with which was a large lapis lazuli cylinder seal; by the waist was a gold-mounted copper dagger and a silver axe-head; other weapons of copper lay beside the body. Two gold ear-rings and a spirally-coiled gold hair-ring were put in front of the head (they were not worn) and various copper and clay vessels completed the furniture of the coffin.

The multiple graves might contain anything up to twenty bodies. The stratification showed that all these were of one period and had been buried at the same time; the principal bodies were in coffins, and their furniture was much the same as that described in the single grave above; the others were not all together in a death-pit, as in the old royal graves, but lay separate, generally wrapped in matting, not necessarily at the same level but at different stages in the filling-in of the tomb-shaft; but although they thus obtained what seemed to be a more individual status, yet for the most part the bodies, often richly decked with personal ornaments of gold and semi-precious stone, still had none of the grave furniture considered essential for the dead—no such vessels for food and drink as the traveller to another world requires. All the offerings were with the principal burials. To this extent the graves of the group do seem to carry on, with certain modifications, the tradition of the royal tombs of the older cemetery and to link those up with the Mausolea of the Third Dynasty which I shall describe later.

One object of quite extraordinary interest was found in the upper filling of one of the multiple graves; here there had been some disturbance and it was difficult to be sure whether the object in question belonged to the grave or must be associated with the later rubbish introduced at the time of the disturbance. Even in this case it is not likely to be later than the time of the Third Dynasty (c. 2112-2000 B.C.). The unusual object was a worn white-coated, circular steatite seal engraved with the figure of a bull with an inscription above it in the distinctive script of the Indus Valley cities. We had had evidence of contacts between Ur and the Indian sub-continent at an earlier date, for in the Early Dynastic III graves we had found beads of carnelian, with etched geometrical patterns exactly corresponding to examples from the great Indus Valley site of Mohenjo-Daro in modern Pakistan. It was inconceivable that the invention of this special technique for decorating carnelian beads should have been made independently in the two countries at more or less the same time; at Ur we only find such beads very rarely in any later setting, but in India the craft has been practised right down to the present day. Little things like beads can, of course, be carried far afield, passed from hand to hand, and their occurrence does not necessarily mean direct contact between the two countries concerned. But it is a different thing with so strictly personal an object as a seal; and, when we find, as we do, that from the Akkadian period on quite a number of them occur at Ur, and elsewhere in Babylonia, including at least one impression on a clay tag, sometimes real imports from the Indus Valley, sometimes imitations of Indus seals made by Sumerian seal-cutters, then the conclusion is clear. By the time of the Akkadian dynasty, if not before, trade between Sumer and the Indus Valley had attained such proportions that there may have been agents from that distant region resident in Mesopotamia.

RIGHT *'Dagger of Ur' from RT580, the blade of gold, with hilt of lapis lazuli decorated with gold studs, and the sheath of gold with an openwork design (see pp.60-1)*

Since the excavations at Ur discoveries on islands in the Gulf, notably on Failaka, south-west of the mouth of the Tigris and Euphrates, and Bahrein (identified with ancient *Dilmun*) off the middle of the south-western shore, have allowed us to recognize another group of imported seals at Ur which have an important bearing on its trading activities up the Gulf to Oman, source of copper, and beyond. These seals are closely similar in shape, all are of steatite, and all were probably once white-coated like the Indus seals. They are circular, with low domed backs cut with three grooves and four evenly spaced dot-in-circle devices. These 'Gulf Seals', dating into the second millennium B.C., extend the archaeological evidence for a trade clearly revealed in texts from Ur that will be considered in a later chapter (pp.204, 213).

Little more than a generation elapsed between the last of the kings of the Akkadian dynasty and Ur-Nammu, first ruler of the Third Dynasty of Ur (*c.* 2112–2095 B.C.). After the overlordship of the various rulers of Lagash, Uruk briefly superseded them in control of Ur, as we know from an important fragmentary inscription on a stela which we found: 'For Ningal the beloved wife of Sin, his lady, for the life of Utehegal, the mighty man, the king of Uruk, the king of the four regions, Ur-Nammu, the military governor of Ur....' Ur-Nammu is acting here as servant of the king of Uruk, and he is making offerings or building temples to secure the prosperity of his overlord, Utehegal, who was largely preoccupied in a brief reign of little more than seven years with expelling the Guti from Sumer. At Utehegal's death, if not before, Ur-Nammu asserted his independence. As ruler of Ur he inherited a long tradition of administrative union with both Uruk and Lagash, whose last independent governor he defeated and whose monuments he defaced. It is possible that Ur-Nammu was a close relative of Utehegal and was for this reason his governor of Ur, much as the military governors at Uruk and elsewhere during the Third Dynasty were drawn from the king's extended family. Ur-Nammu first rebuilt the walls of Ur, marking in traditional fashion his bid for supreme power. Initially he was known just as 'mighty man and king of Ur'. In this role he built the temples of his personal gods, the great terrace, and the walls of the Temenos at Ur. Only when he was firmly established as 'King of Sumer and Akkad' did he begin the construction of great monuments to the patron deities of Ur, the network of irrigation canals round the city, and the temple of Enlil at Nippur. His coronation was thrice celebrated; in

LEFT *Electrum rein-ring topped by a donkey, from Puabi's grave, RT800 (see p.62)*

Nippur, as the religious centre of his new realm, at Ur, as his political capital, and at Uruk, the ancestral home of his dynasty.

Further Reading

Basic information on the periods covered in this chapter is given in C.L. Woolley, *Ur Excavations* IV: *The Early Periods* (London, 1955), pp.49ff.; and *Ur Excavations* II: *The Royal Cemetery* (London, 1934), pp.482ff. for the so-called 'Second Dynasty Graves'. Their correct dating was first established by B.W. Buchanan, 'The Date of the So-called Second Dynasty Graves of the Royal Cemetery at Ur', *Journal of the American Oriental Society* 74 (1954), pp.147ff. The historical inscriptions relevant to this period and to the Early Dynastic III graves are conveniently listed by E. Sollberger, 'Notes on the Early Inscriptions from Ur and el-'Obed', *Iraq* 22 (1960), pp.69ff.

The Indus Valley and related seals were first studied by C.J. Gadd, 'Seals of Ancient Indian Style found at Ur', *Proceedings of the British Academy* XVIII (1932), pp.191ff.; and extended by W.W. Hallo and Briggs Buchanan, 'A "Persian Gulf" Seal on an Old Babylonian Mercantile Agreement', *Studies in Honor of Benno Landsberger* (Chicago, 1965), pp.19ff. For the etched carnelian beads see J.E. Reade, *Early Etched Beads and the Indus–Mesopotamian Trade* (British Museum, Occasional Paper No. 2, 1979).

Woolley holding the plaster 'skeleton'
of one of a number of musical instruments from graves in
the Royal Cemetery recovered in this way

The Third Dynasty of Ur

c. 2100—2000 B.C.

For a hundred years, from 2112 to 2004 B.C., under the five kings of the Third Dynasty, Ur was the capital of a great empire and its rulers were at pains to make it a centre worthy of its political pre-eminence. We very seldom excavated the ruins of a temple without finding some record of that period; either it had originally been founded or it had been restored by some king of the Third Dynasty. Ur-Nammu, the first of his line, was particularly active as a builder. His reign was not a long one, some sixteen years, and did not suffice for the programme on which he embarked; in some cases either haste or economy led him to construct in mud-brick only and it was left to his successors to pull down the rather shoddy walls and rebuild in baked brick. Certainly by the time the Third Dynasty was drawing to its close the city of Ur was crowded with magnificent monuments testifying to the wealth and piety of its kings; it was but natural that when Ibbi-Sin, the last of Ur-Nammu's line, was defeated by an alien enemy, those monuments should be specially signalled out for destruction. With the exception of the Ziggurat there are very few Third Dynasty buildings of which the walls still stand up above ground-level; when the time came to restore the ruined temples, it was a case not of patching but of pulling down all the old work and rebuilding; it is only in the foundations that we find the stamped bricks bearing the names of the Third Dynasty founders.

The inscriptions tell us that Ur-Nammu built the walls of Ur. The walled city was in shape an irregular oval, measuring about 1130 yards in length by 750 yards in width, and was surrounded by a wall and rampart. The rampart was of mud-brick built with a steeply sloping outer face; the lower part of it was in fact a revetment against the side of the mound formed by the ruins of the older town, but the upper part of it extended inland over the top of the ruins to make a solid platform from 25 to 35 yards wide rising

26 feet above the level of the ground at the rampart's foot while its back stood only 5 feet above the ground-level inside the city. Along the top of this ran the wall proper, built of burnt bricks; where the rampart was narrowest one had simply the wall with a berm in front of it and behind it a passage for the manoeuvring of troops; where it broadened out it was because here there was a temple or other public building standing on the rampart; such might be incorporated in the system of defence, its outer wall linking up with the city wall and its roof serving as a tower. This massive fortification was further strengthened by the fact that the river Euphrates (as can be seen from the sunken line of its old bed) washed the foot of the western rampart while 50 yards from the foot of the eastern rampart there had been dug a broad canal which left the river immediately above the north end of the town, so that on three sides Ur was ringed with a moat and only from the south could be approached by dry land. It was a colossal work and must have seemed to the builder impregnable, but it was to fall in the end; the rampart, backed by a solid mass of earth, could not be violently overthrown and although in places wind and rain have weathered it almost all away, yet we seldom failed to find at least the lower part of its worn and battered face; but of Ur-Nammu's wall not a trace remained. We would come on examples of the very large bricks, specially moulded and inscribed with the king's name and titles, re-used in some later building, but none of them was *in situ*; just because the defences of Ur had been so strong the victorious enemy had dismantled them systematically, leaving not one brick upon another.

With the Ziggurat it was very different. Of all the great staged towers which characterized the cities of Sumer that of Ur is the best preserved, and it is for the most part the original work of Ur-Nammu. Here a few words of explanation are called for. The Ziggurat is a peculiar feature of Mesopotamian architecture, also found in ancient Elam. It is still not certain whether the ziggurats of the Ur III period were the expression of a new religious concept or whether such buildings raised by Ur-Nammu in various of his cities were merely the final stage of a long architectural development, as seems most likely. Over the centuries, in the course of the renewal of the older temples on a high platform, the main shrine was slowly raised ever higher, as each temple was encased in a terrace for the new one. There is some scattered evidence for true ziggurats, rather than temples on high terraces, in later Early Dynastic and Akkadian times; but the best surviving evidence for their widespread occurrence appears with the Third Dynasty of Ur. Their meaning and purpose has been much debated. The names by which they were known suggest that they were conceived as 'mountains', though little credence is now given to the idea that this must indicate builders who originally came from a mountainous region. This apparently simple description embraces a complex religious concept evoking the cosmic mountain of Sumerian mythology which symbolized life-giving forces and was the setting in which superhuman powers were made manifest. In this context men and gods were brought into closest contact.

It is commonly accepted that a shrine stood on the top of each ziggurat on the evidence of the description of the ziggurat at Babylon in the fifth century B.C. given by Herodotus. None survives to that height. There was also a major temple at the foot of each ziggurat in a way there had not previously been a 'lower' temple corresponding to each of the temples on a high terrace. The question of function turns on the relative significance of these two temples: which was now regarded as the 'house' of the god, the upper or the lower one? Was the 'high temple' merely a resting place for the deity on his journey from heaven to his residence in the 'lower' temple, with the tiers of the ziggurat providing, as it were, a ladder to and from heaven, or was the ziggurat a gigantic tiered altar with cult practised as much in the 'upper' as in the 'lower' temple? To this question no clear answer has yet emerged, though the 'lower' temple certainly seems to have been the one regarded in most cities as the god's primary residence. At Babylon, Herodotus tells us, the upper shrine was equipped 'with a fine couch in it, richly covered, and beside it a golden table. . . . The Chaldaeans also say (though I do not believe them) that the god enters the temple in person and takes his rest upon the couch'.

The site of the Ziggurat of Ur was fixed by ancient tradition. I have spoken already of the temple platforms of the Jamdat Nasr and Early Dynastic periods; what Ur-Nammu did was to build over these, probably incorporating their remains in the core of his new structure. The site was in the west corner of the Temenos (the Sacred Area of the city); the king rebuilt the enclosing wall of the Temenos (which formed the second line of the defences of Ur) and although very little of that wall survives, we found traces of it sufficient to give its outline and the proof that it was indeed the work of Ur-Nammu. The Sacred Area as a whole was dedicated to the Moon-god Nanna and his wife Ningal—at least, this seems to be the case, for Ur-Nammu expressly states on his brick-stamps that he built it for Ningal, while other inscriptions of the Third Dynasty speak of it as belonging to Nanna; presumably the two deities shared it in common. But the north-east end was the peculiar property of the Moon-god; here, in the west corner, rose the terrace on which the Ziggurat stood, and in front of the terrace, to the north-east, occupying about two-thirds of the terrace length and extending to the far wall of the Sacred Area, was the Great Court of Nanna; the great court was low-lying, actually sunk somewhat below the general level of the Temenos, and there must have been a flight of steps in the monumental gateway that gave access from it to the terrace, for the latter was raised 3 feet above Temenos level. The terrace was surrounded by a massive double wall of mud-brick with intramural chambers; much of it had gone, but on the north-west side it was well preserved, standing still to a height of $5\frac{1}{2}$ feet. It was of mud-brick, built against the core of the old First Dynasty terrace wall; the front sloped steeply back (the angle was 35 in 100) and was relieved by shallow buttresses 16 feet wide and little more than a foot deep which must be considered decorative rather than constructional, since they can have added nothing to the building's strength. The face of the wall was smoothly rendered with mud plaster; much of this had fallen away and we very soon cleared off the rest, for beneath the plaster there was a dramatic discovery to be made. At regular intervals of 2 feet there appeared the small rounded heads of clay 'nails' driven into the mud mortar between the brick courses; these were 'foundation-cones' and on the 'nail's' stem was the inscription 'For Nanna the strong bull of Heaven, most glorious son of Enlil, his King, has Ur-Nammu the mighty man, King of Ur, built his temple, *Etemennigur*'. Such cones were familiar enough as objects on museum shelves, but now for the first time we saw them in position just as the builders had set them four thousand years before. That they should be found *in situ* is of course most important scientifically, for we not only learn that a particular king built a particular temple, but they positively identify a building which we have excavated and they give it a positive date; but at the same time one felt a quite unscientific thrill at seeing those ordered rows of cream-coloured knobs which even the people of Ur had not seen when once the terrace wall was finished and plastered.

The excavation of the Ziggurat itself was a formidable task. In the middle of the last century Mr J.E. Taylor, then British Consul at Basra, was engaged by the British Museum to investigate some of the ancient sites of southern Mesopotamia, and amongst others he visited Ur, in those days a place difficult and dangerous of access. Struck by the obvious importance of one mound, which from its height, overshadowing all the other ruins, he rightly judged to be the Ziggurat, he attacked it from above, cutting down into the brickwork of the four corners. The science of field archaeology had not then been devised and the excavator's object was to find things that might enrich the cases of a museum, while the preservation of buildings on the spot was little considered. To the greatest monument of

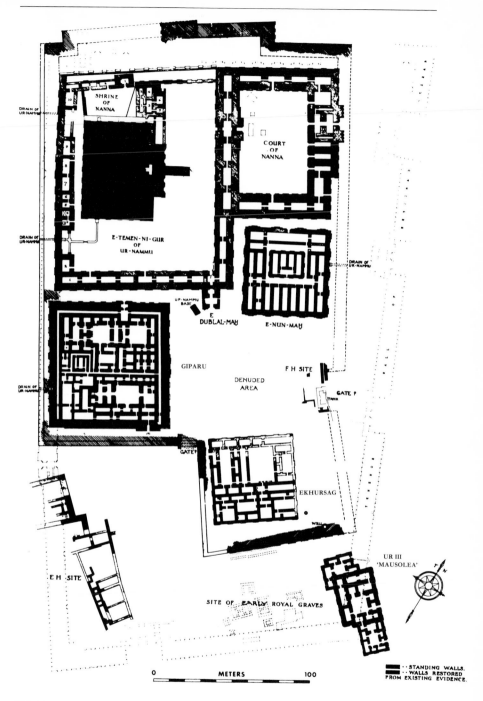

SHRINE
OF
NANNA

COURT
OF
NANNA

E-TEMEN-NI-GUR
OF
UR-NAMMU

DRAIN OF
UR-NAMMU

DRAIN OF
UR-NAMMU

DRAIN OF
UR-NAMMU

DRAIN OF
UR-NAMMU

UR-NAMMU
BASE

E
DUBLAL-MAH

E-NUN-MAH

GIPARU

DENUDED
AREA

F H SITE

GATE P

TANK

GATE F

GATE F

EKHURSAG

WELL

E H SITE

UR III
'MAUSOLEA'

N

SITE OF EARLY ROYAL GRAVES

STANDING WALLS.
WALLS RESTORED
FROM EXISTING EVIDENCE.

0   METERS   100

The Temenos at the time of the Third Dynasty of Ur

Ur, Taylor did damage which we cannot but deplore today, but he succeeded in his purpose and at least made clear the importance of the site whose later excavation has so well repaid us. Hidden in the brickwork of the top stage of the tower he found, at each angle of it, cylinders of baked clay on which were long inscriptions giving the history of the building. The texts date from about 550 B.C., from the time of Nabonidus, the last of the kings of Babylon, and state that the tower, founded by Ur-Nammu and his son Shulgi, but left unfinished by them and not completed by any later king, he had restored and finished. These inscriptions not only gave us the first information obtained about the Ziggurat itself, but identified the site, called by the Arabs el-Mukayyar, the 'Mound of Pitch', as ancient Ur.

Taylor's excavations did not go very far. Those were the days when in the north of Mesopotamia Layard and others were unearthing the colossal human-headed bulls and pictured wall-slabs which now enrich the British Museum, and, dazzled by such discoveries, people could not realize the value of the odds and ends which alone rewarded the explorer in the south, and the work at Ur was therefore abandoned. Towards the close of the century an American expedition again attacked the top of the mound and exposed some of the brickwork, but apart from that apparently fruitless attempt at excavation the site was deserted and what showed of the upper stages of the Ziggurat was left to the mercies of the weather and of Arab builders in search of cheap ready-made bricks; when British troops advanced to el-Mukayyar in 1915, only a few ragged bricks could be seen protruding from the top of a huge mound of undisturbed sand and rubble up whose gently sloping sides a man could ride on horseback. In 1919 Dr H.R. Hall initiated the real excavation of the monument and cleared part of the south-east end down to the level of the terrace floor, and discovered that the lower part of the brick casing, protected by the rubbish heaped against it, was wonderfully well preserved. It was manifest that the work begun by Hall must be continued by the Joint Expedition, and we started on it almost at once, but it was a task that could not be completed in a hurry.

The amount of rubbish which had to be removed was very great, running into thousands of tons, all of which had to be lifted in small baskets and then carried by our light railway to a safe distance where it would not hamper later operations. In this mass of fallen brick and wind-blown sand there were no objects of any sort to be found, so that, until we were down to floor level, the job was mere navvy work unimpeded by any considerations of archaeological method, and actually the end of our 1923–24 season saw the great building standing free of the rubbish which

Clearing debris from the Ziggurat

had shrouded it for so many centuries. Of course a vast amount remained to be done on the surrounding buildings, but I fondly imagined that our work on the tower itself was finished, and taking advantage of the assistance of Mr F.G. Newton, the most experienced of archaeological architects, ventured to reconstruct on paper the Ziggurat as it had originally been.

The reconstruction was wrong. Because of all the ziggurats in Iraq that of Ur seemed to be the best preserved the government had very properly seen to its protection and we had been instructed that on no account were we to move any of the brickwork remaining *in situ*. The cylinders found by Taylor told us that Ur-Nammu and his son Shulgi had between them built the staged tower and that Nabonidus had restored and finished it, but they did not say that other kings too had worked upon it. A fair proportion of the burnt bricks of Ur-Nammu bore his stamp, and so did some of Nabonidus's bricks, but the vast majority of the bricks bore no name. We were in our early days at Ur and had still everything to learn; for us a plain brick was just a brick, and we had not got the experience to decide by its measurements and proportions to which period of history it ought to be assigned. Consequently when, high up on the Ziggurat, we brushed the surface of the bricks which we might not move (and the stamps were most often on the under side!), we assumed, or I assumed, that what did not belong to Nabonidus necessarily belonged to the Third Dynasty, and when it came to working out the reconstruction of the Third Dynasty building some of the evidence on which I relied was brickwork of an entirely different period. Later on, of course, I recognized that this first attempt was premature and we returned to the study of the Ziggurat fortified by all that we had learned in the meantime about Sumerian and Babylonian brick-work and able to eliminate all that was not of Ur-Nammu's date, and in 1933 could put forward a new version of the Ziggurat reconstruction which in all essentials is demonstrably correct.

In form the Ziggurat is a stepped pyramid having three stages. The whole thing is solid. The core is of mud-brick (probably laid round and over the remains of the First Dynasty temple-platform) and the face is a skin of burnt bricks set in bitumen mortar, about 8 feet thick. The lowest stage, which alone is well preserved, measures at ground-level a little more than 200 feet in length by 150 feet in width and is about 50 feet high; from this rose the upper stages, each smaller than the one below, leaving broad passages along the main sides and wider terraces at either end; on the topmost stage stood the little one-roomed shrine of the Moon-god, the most sacred building in Ur, for whose setting the whole of this vast substructure had been planned.

On three sides the walls rose sheer to the level of the first terrace, but on the north-east face fronting the Nanna temple was the approach to the shrine. Three brick stairways, each of a hundred steps, led upwards, one projecting out at right-angles from the building, two leaning against its wall, and all converging in a great gateway between the first and the second terrace; from this gate flights of stairs ran straight up to the second terrace and to the door of the shrine, while lateral passages with descending flights of stairs gave access to the lower terraces at either end of the tower; the angles formed by the three main stairways were filled in with solid, flat-topped buttress-towers.

When first we started the work of drawing out the plan and elevations of the Ziggurat, we were puzzled to find that the different measurements never seemed to agree; then it was discovered that in the whole building there is not a single straight line. The walls not only slope inwards, but the line from top to bottom is slightly convex; on the ground-plan the wall-line from corner to corner of the building has a distinct outward bend, so that sighting along it one can see only as far as the centre. It was originally suggested that these variations were intended by the architect as an optical illusion akin to that which the Greek builders of the Parthenon at Athens were to achieve many centuries afterwards, the curves being so slight as not to be apparent, yet enough to give to the eye an appearance of strength where a straight line might by contrast with the mass behind it have seemed incurved and weak. This now seems an unwarranted assumption. The variations are better accounted for by settling. A monument of such mass built of a pliable material like mud-bricks would be particularly vulnerable to such displacement.

Yet, the whole design of the building is a masterpiece. It would have been so easy to pile rectangle of brickwork above rectangle, and the effect would have been soulless and ugly; as it is, the heights of the different stages are skilfully calculated, the slope of the walls leads the eye upwards and inwards to the centre, the sharper slope of the triple staircase accentuates that of the walls and fixes the attention on the shrine above, which was the religious focus of the whole structure, while across these converging lines cut the horizontal planes of the terraces.

No one looking at the Ziggurat can fail to notice the tall and narrow slits which at regular intervals and in rows one above another pierce the brickwork of the walls; they run clean through the burnt-brick casing and deep into the mud-brick of the core, where they are loosely filled with broken pottery. These are 'weeper-holes' intended to drain the interior, a necessary precaution, for with damp the mud-brick would swell and make the outer walls bulge if it did not burst them altogether.

This is the obvious and correct explanation and for a long time it satisfied us; but then the difficulty arose, how was the damp likely to get into the core? There was no real danger at the time of construction, for though there would then be plenty of water in the mud mortar used for the crude bricks, this would dry—indeed, with so vast an area to build over, one course would be virtually dry before the next was laid above it—and the tendency of the core would be to shrink rather than expand. It is true that torrential rains fall in Mesopotamia, but in the days of the Third Dynasty it was usual to lay pavements of burnt brick two, three, or even five courses thick set in bitumen mortar, and no surface water could penetrate this and do harm below. If there had been such a pavement, the precaution was needless; and if there was not such, why not? And further, at each end of the tower there is in one of the buttresses a deep recess in the brickwork running from the edge of the first terrace to the ground, and at the bottom of this there is what engineers call an 'apron', a mass of brick waterproofed with bitumen and built with its top at a slant calculated to carry off smoothly and without splash water falling from above: evidently there was water on the terrace.

There seems to be only one explanation. The terraces of Ur-Nammu's staged tower were not paved with brick but were covered with soil, and in this trees were planted; the long recesses in the buttresses may have carried off the waters of a violent storm, but they may equally have served as water-hoists for the irrigation of the terrace; and what made possible the swelling of the core of the tower and therefore necessitated the weeper-holes in its facing was just this irrigation—the water poured at the roots of the trees would percolate through the top soil into the crude brick, and if it had no outlet, would really endanger the building.

Thus we have to imagine trees clothing every terrace with greenery, hanging gardens which brought more vividly to mind the original conception of the Ziggurat as the Mountain of God, and we shall recognize how much better the sloping outer walls harmonize with this conception, rising as they do like the abrupt bare sides of some pine-topped crag, than if they had been uncompromisingly vertical, the walls of a house of man's building.

The lowest stage stands today to its original height, the tops of its walls indeed being weathered away but fragments of paving against the foot of the second stage sufficing to give its true level. Of the second stage just enough remains to give its outline, and of the third stage the lower part of the mud-brick core, bereft of its facing, gave both the measurements of this stage and the approximate level of the second-stage floor. Of the three flights of stairs the two built against the sides of the Ziggurat still had

Ur-Nammu's wall supporting the Ziggurat terrace

much of their burnt-brick treads, though these were not original but restored by Nabonidus in the sixth century B.C.; the central stairs had suffered more severely, but the solid staircase survived although its upper surface had perished. The gate-tower under which the three flights converge is frankly a restoration; it had been ruined away almost to its foundations, but those massive piers remained; the four doorways (of which the jambs could be distinguished) were of course essential to the plan and while a pointed corbelled arch is likely enough, we do possess evidence that the round (true) arch was used under the Third Dynasty and a little roofed cistern of Ur-Nammu's date on the Ziggurat terrace gives us a contemporary analogy for the suggested dome. We found the start of the stair-flight going up to the second stage, and part of the stairs going down to the main floor of the first stage; the topmost stair-flight and the actual shrine to which it led are frankly restorations.

The building is absolutely symmetrical except for one thing. At its south-east end, on the lowest platform, there was a small building leant up against the wall of the second stage which had no counterpart at the north-west end. Only enough of this remained for us to say that it did exist and had its entrance at the south-west end, as shown in the restored drawing; there was nothing found in it to explain its use.

On the north-west side of the Ziggurat, between it and the terrace wall, there was a building, many times repaired by later rulers, of which the foundation went back to Ur-Nammu; scanty as the remains of the original were, they can be restored in the light of the later reconstructions and bear a striking resemblance to the First Dynasty building on the same site. Undoubtedly the character of the building is the same and we have here the 'kitchen' in which the food of the gods was prepared. Next to it, in the thickness of the chambered wall of the terrace, there is a small room whose unusually solid walls suggest that it was a building of considerable height and a niche in one wall seems to mark it out as a shrine; we called it 'the shrine of Nanna' and it may well be such; associated with the 'kitchen' it may have been the shrine in which were offered the prepared foods that were in due course to be allotted to Nanna's priests. We had arrived at this conclusion when a further discovery confirmed it in a very gratifying manner. In the back wall of the 'kitchen' block and again in the angle wall of one of its rooms we found brick boxes containing big inscribed copper cylinders; three of them bore the name of Nur-Adad, king of Larsa (1865–1850 B.C.) and one that of Marduknadinahhe of Babylon (1099–1082 B.C.); apart from the difference of names the texts were practically duplicates, and they speak of the 'great cooking-pot' and of the preparation of 'the evening and the morning meals' of the gods. Evidently Nur-Adad had repaired Ur-Nammu's building and duly recorded the fact; centuries afterwards the Babylonian king carrying out similar repairs had discovered Nur-Adad's four cylinders and had piously replaced three of them, but for the fourth substituted a copy bearing his own name.

The Ziggurat of Ur-Nammu restored

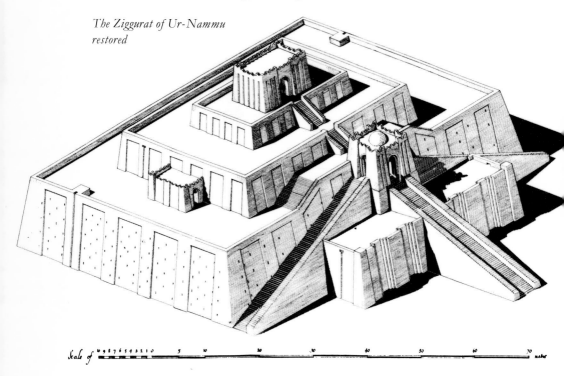

Scale of ... nahor

Whether or not there was a second kitchen building to the south-east of the Ziggurat in the Third Dynasty time as there had been in the time of the First Dynasty it is impossible to say, for only a single meaningless fragment of Ur-Nammu walling was left, and in later times this area was occupied not by a kitchen but by a regular temple of Ningal the Moon-goddess. That something stood here in the days of Ur-Nammu seems to be certain, for the angle taken by the Ziggurat drain was apparently dictated by the presence of some building, and we did find here a well originally made by Ur-Nammu (it had been restored by a whole succession of later rulers) and a four-compartment cistern of burnt brick and bitumen also his work.

It is probable also that there were buildings in front of the Ziggurat, though again nothing really survives, and although Ur-Nammu's Ziggurat at Uruk has a pair of temples flanking the central staircase and at Ur such temples do occur in Late Babylonian times, we should not be justified in attempting any reconstruction. Instead, our problems are complicated by the presence here of a most peculiar feature. In the floor of the terrace there had been very neatly made a rectangular hollow measuring about 15 feet by 11 and 3 feet deep. In this were laid three courses of large untrimmed limestone blocks, above which, filling the pit, was very clean reddish burnt earth. There was nothing underneath to explain this, so that the reason for it must have been something above, presumably rectangular in shape and (in view of the loose burnt earth) not very heavy; the size suggests an altar and the pit comes precisely below the site of the altar of the Late Babylonian shrine.

The Ziggurat terrace was entered from the Sacred Area by a single gate-way in its east corner where there was a solidly built gate-tower in which a flight of steps led up from the lower level outside; as built by Ur-Nammu it was merely an entrance, but under later rulers 'the Great Gate' was, as we shall see, destined to assume an importance of a different sort. The other entrance to the terrace was in its north-east wall where, again with a double flight of steps under a massive tower, one passed into the Great Court of Nanna occupying the rest of the north-west end of the Sacred Area. This was a very large open court, brick-paved, with chambers all round it and a monumental doorway facing the terrace doorway which gave on the outer town; its only internal feature of interest was a brick altar-like structure set immediately in front of the door leading to the upper terrace, this being a reconstruction of a similar but smaller 'altar' dating back to before the Third Dynasty period. Inscriptions on clay tablets found here made clear the purpose of the building; it was a store-house into which were brought the offerings made to Nanna and the dues paid to him. The tenant farmers who tilled the temple lands would bring their rent in kind, cattle and sheep, grain and cheese; the merchants would bring the tithes of their stock-in-trade, the pious would bring their free-will offerings; all would be duly recorded by the priests in charge who would weigh the goods and issue receipts in the form of clay tablets, the duplicates of which were filed in the temple archive; the great court with its score of magazines can have been none too large for all the business to be conducted there. The 'receipt of customs' was not the least important part of Nanna's establishment.

Actually of the 'Great Store-house' built by Ur-Nammu very little survived, and it would have been impossible to understand the tattered remnants of his walls but for the fact that after its destruction by the Elamite invaders later kings had rebuilt on a somewhat larger scale but on almost identical lines. Ur-Nammu himself had not, apparently, lived long enough to finish the building which, like several other of his works, was completed by his son Shulgi. His grandson Amar-Sin found the main structure complete and in good condition and so did no more than add a second 'altar'; and then the whole thing was razed to the ground by the Elamites. The thoroughness of their destruction is intelligible enough if one glances at the plan with its huge walls, the flat roofs of the intramural chambers giving plenty of room for the manoeuvres of defending troops; for a victorious enemy to dismantle such fortifications was an obvious precaution.

When the rulers of Isin and Larsa considered that their position was secure, they could afford to rebuild at Ur even these semi-military works; the Great Court was not only reconstructed but it was actually enlarged at the expense of the Ziggurat terrace, the front of which was cut back some 24 feet, and its north-east wall was thickened and the gate-tower apparently heightened. Further, the inner face of the south-west wall through which ran the passage leading to the Ziggurat terrace and the outer faces of the other three walls were all decorated with an elaborate system of attached half-columns divided down the middle by double T-shaped niches; carried out in brick this is an extremely effective form of ornament, relying as it does not on applied colour but on the varying depth of shadow cast by the sun; it set the pattern for temple-builders for many centuries to come.

The first record that we found of these repairs dated to about sixty years after the fall of Ur, when Ishme-Dagan was king of Isin (1953–1935 B.C.). Reverting to old tradition he had made his daughter Enanatuma High-Priestess of Nanna at Ur, and naturally the High-Priestess was active in rebuilding her temples; we find her name on bricks in the Great Court, but it may well be that essential repairs had been done by other Isin authorities before her. Of the Larsa kings several have left their mark—and their names—on the Great Court. One of them, Siniddinam, also worked on the north-west retaining-wall of the Ziggurat terrace. There Ur-Nammu's buttresses wall had been of mud-brick, and with time it had suffered severely; Siniddinam added to it a revetment of burnt brick, following exactly the pattern of the old work. Centuries later a Kassite king, Kurigalzu, added another skin of burnt brick, again on the same lines though with a less pronounced slope; when we excavated the site, we

RIGHT *General view of the site of Ur as it appears today*
OVERLEAF *The Ziggurat of Ur*

found the three constructions of such different dates one behind the other, archaeological strata arranged vertically instead of horizontally.

But the most striking work in this area was done by Warad-Sin, last king but one of the Larsa Dynasty (1834–1823 B.C.). He probably found but little to do in the Great Court itself (though we did find there broken foundation-cones both of him and of his father Kudur-Mabuk), but he made great changes in the terrace adjoining it. On the north-west side of the terrace he threw out a brick bastion corresponding in width to the interval between the wall of the Great Court and the front line of the Ziggurat; it was a huge gate-tower giving a new access to the Ziggurat terrace. The whole of the lower part of the tower was solid brickwork except for the gate-passage running through the middle of it and a staircase leading up to the guard-chamber over the gate; in the heart of the brickwork, carefully arranged in lines parallel with the frontage, we found *in situ* numbers of clay foundation-cones inscribed with the dedication of the building (see p.181).

It certainly was a splendid building. The entire façade was decorated with half-columns divided down the middle by double T-shaped grooves. In the re-entrant angles of the porch, flanking the lower of two flights of steps that led up to the terrace, there were slender free-standing columns built of mud-bricks specially moulded and producing on the surface a pattern of triangles in shallow relief to imitate the effect of palm-tree trunks. Strikingly similar decoration was used later on the Old Assyrian temple and ziggurat façades at Tell al-Rimah in northern Iraq. In both places the surface of the moulded mud-brick had been covered with plaster, coloured grey or green. If the materials had been available, there may be little doubt columns would have played as conspicuous a part in Mesopotamian architecture as they did elsewhere in the ancient world. The date-palm, as the only tree native to Sumer, is all that was available. Its products as a living tree were too valuable, and its wood too fibrous, to encourage its use architecturally; but still it served as an inspiration. The moulded brick columns both at Ur and at Tell al-Rimah imitate frond scars in various stylized patterns which represent different methods of trimming the palm trunk. Earlier, as we have seen, not only were the columns at Tell al-'Ubaid built round a palm-tree core, but their mosaic inlays reproduced the same designs.

LEFT ABOVE *Model boat of silver, from the 'King's Grave' (RT789)*
LEFT BELOW *Present-day boat of the same form used by the Marsh Arabs of Southern Iraq*

The other building operation in which Kudur-Mabuk and his son Warad-Sin were associated was the terrace entrance in the east corner, known as *Dublamakh*. Ur-Nammu had built it simply as the gateway leading to the terrace of the Ziggurat and his building was of mud-brick, except for the floors which were of burnt bricks set in bitumen; it was invoked as 'great exalted gate'. The first change was made by Amar-Sin, Ur-Nammu's grandson, and was not inconsistent with the original purpose of the structure. The Great Gate led into the area peculiarly sacred to Nanna; as one mounted the steps, one was passing on to holy ground, and it would seem natural enough that there should be there a statue of the god to which one could pay reverence before entering his domain. Again, it is the immemorial custom of the East that 'the judge sat in the gate to give judgement'; it might be the gate of the city, but the gate of the Holy Place would confer a special sanction on the judgements pronounced there, and so it came about that the Great Gate served also as a court of law. An inscribed door-socket stone told us just how these ideas took shape in the course of time.

> To Nanna his beloved King; *Dublamakh*, from of old an enclosure where daily offerings were laid before his heavenly emblem, this house had not been built. Amar-Sin . . . the king of Ur, the king of the four quarters of the world, *Dublamakh*, the House, the wonder of the land, the place of his judgements, his net from which the enemy of Amar-Sin does not escape, this house he built for him, he completed, he adorned with gold and silver and lapis lazuli . . .

Amar-Sin had in fact pulled down his grandfather's mud-brick gatehouse and rebuilt it in good burnt brick, and he added a fore-chamber where perhaps there had been the unroofed enclosure to which his inscription refers; he made it a real shrine and a law-court. The Elamites, when they sacked Ur, destroyed *Dublamakh* and carried off the statue of Nanna to Anshan (modern Tepe Malyan in Iran), their own city, but as soon as the dynasty of Isin was established, its kings took the work of repair in hand. We found two door-sockets of Shu-Ilishu, the second king of the dynasty (1984–1975 B.C.), the inscriptions on which state that 'Shu-Ilishu the mighty hero, king of Ur, when he had brought Nanna from Anshan to Ur built for him *Dublamakh*, his place of judgement', and the name of Ishme-Dagan (1953–1935 B.C.) appears on some of the bricks in the walls. Then,

RIGHT ABOVE *The Ziggurat of Ur-Nammu; front view with access ramps*
RIGHT BELOW *The Ziggurat of Ur-Nammu; back view*

according to the brick-stamps, Siniddinam of Larsa (1849–1843 B.C.) did a certain amount of rebuilding, and finally (of the Larsa kings) Kudur-Mabuk. Of these, Ishme-Dagan made a radical change which his successors followed; he walled up the doorway at the back of the gate-tower so that the building could serve as a gate no longer but became simply a shrine, and a new entrance to the Ziggurat platform was made by cutting a doorway through the enclosing wall against the south-east side of the Great Court. Such was the building which Kudur-Mabuk in his turn restored, the city's law-court and the 'House of Tablets'.

Under the pavement of a Larsa annexe to *Dublamakh* we found a mass of clay tablets which had belonged to the business archives of Nanna's temple. They were of unbaked clay and were in very bad condition, reduced by infiltered moisture to the constituency of mud and impregnated with salts, and many had been broken or chipped when they fell from the shelves on which they had been stored; we had to lift them with the earth still about them and bake them in an extemporized furnace before any cleaning could be attempted, but in this way we did salvage several hundreds of interesting documents of the Third Dynasty.

It was no polite fiction that made Nanna the King of Ur. He controlled its destinies more effectually than did his mortal representative and he must therefore have his ministers and his court; he was a great landowner and therefore needed stewards to manage his estates; apart from the High-Priest and his clerical associates we read of the Sacristan and the Choir-master, the Treasurer, the Ministers of War and of Justice, of Agriculture and of Housing, a Controller of the Household, a Master of the Harem, and Directors of Livestock, Dairy Work, Fishing, and Donkey transport. All these carried on their duties in the temple precincts, and so the temple is not a single building like the self-contained temples of Greece and Rome, but a huge complex which is at once temple and palace, government offices and stores and factories. Something of this sort has already been assumed in our description of the ruins and is proved by the plans here published; fortunately just as our plans grow more complete and more complicated, the tablets turn up to throw light upon the use of those many courts and chambers.

As landowner the god received as well as tithes either rent or a part share in the produce of the soil, and since money was unknown, these were all paid in kind; and since the temple was also a fortress, enormous quantities of foodstuffs were stored within it, ready to meet the normal requirements of the temple staff but also to act as a reserve in case of war. For everything that was brought in a receipt was given, a small tablet carefully dated recording that so-and-so has paid in six pounds of the best butter, so much oil, sheep, cattle, or what not; and every month a full balance-sheet of all returns was drawn up in parallel columns showing each farmer's contribution under separate headings. While farmers and cowmen paid in country produce, the townsfolk used another currency; there are receipts for all sorts of hides, for gold and silver from the jewellers, for copper from the smiths; in one room we found a smelting-furnace, and in other rooms big jars full of scrap copper and ingots of the metal presumably of some standard weight; evidence that this quarter of the building served a special department of the temple affairs.

But if the revenues are scrupulously recorded, the outgoings are not less carefully checked, and these are just as illuminating for the life of the time. Naturally the temple officials drew their rations from the stores, and the issue vouchers were all preserved in the registry; every man had his regular allowance of foodstuffs, flour and oil, etc., for which he or his servants had to sign, and special issues were authorized in case of sickness—thus a man may draw an extra quarter-pint of best oil as liniment for his headache. But the most interesting records deal with the industrial side of the establishment. Numbers of women devotees were attached to the temple, and these were employed in regular factories inside the precincts; there were slaves similarly employed, and piece-work was given out to private contractors who had small factories outside the temple area: all these had to be supplied with the raw materials which had been brought in as tithe, and with the food which was their wage.

The main temple industry, fascinatingly illustrated by the tablets found this season, was weaving. In one building alone 165 women and girls were kept at work, and we have the accounts made out for the month, quarter, and year of the quantity of woollen thread supplied to each and of the amount of cloth produced, each sort distinguished by quality and weight, with due allowance for the wastage of thread in weaving. The rations are in proportion to the output, the older women receiving less than the young ones (who would have larger appetites but did more work)—no more in fact than did the youngest children; thus if four pints of oil a day was the standard allowance for adults, children of different ages got two pints, one and a half, or one, and the really old woman one also. For the sick there were special rates: if any one died, her name was kept on the books until the end of the financial year, but the date of her death was recorded and an entry made against the name to the effect that henceforth no rations were drawn, or were drawn only for an accredited substitute. The whole system was coldbloodedly businesslike, but the records of it are not without their dramatic side and go far to re-create the life which was lived within the temple walls.

Some seventy years after Kudur-Mabuk's death the House of Tablets was again destroyed, and again after that was rebuilt in a somewhat altered form. Those later vicissitudes do not concern us here and will be described in their proper place, but it is worthwhile noting that even in the four-teenth century B.C. Kurigalzu calls it *Dublamakh*, but also *Kagalmakh*, the Great Gate, the Ancient One. Just as the names of the gates of London have long outlived their reality, so Ur-Nammu's gateway preserved its identity through the ages.

All the rulers of the Third Dynasty of Ur were active builders and we found few temples which did not owe their foundation to one or other of them. But in most cases the remains were scanty. To restore a temple was a work of piety which ensured the favour of the gods, and the temples therefore were constantly and thoroughly repaired by later kings who often pulled down in order to rebuild; the city was sacked and its monu-ments destroyed first by the Elamites, at the close of the Third Dynasty, then by Hammurabi of Babylon, and again by his son Samsuiluna as a result of the city's revolt against the Babylonian yoke; it is not surprising that little of the Third Dynasty work was left, and such traces as survived were intelligible only because the later builders piously reproduced the original plan, even using the footings of the old walls as a foundation for their own. Most of these buildings therefore such as *Enunmakh* and the *Giparu* will be described hereafter under the heading of the period to which the best-preserved of their ruins belong; but there are two exceptions, two Third Dynasty structures which were never touched in after generations and so should be described here.

The first of these is *Ekhursag*. It was a large square building lying within the Sacred Area but distinct from the other buildings of the Temenos in that it occupied a salient projecting from the south-east side; either it was there before the Temenos wall of Ur-Nammu was built, and the wall had to be specially deflected in order to enclose it, or else the salient was designed specially with a view to the erection of *Ekhursag* as a thing apart. The building, which measures 190 feet square, was orientated, as usual, with its angles to the four points of the compass; the whole of the north corner, comprising about a third of the ground-plan, is completely destroyed, but can be fairly confidently restored.

Now there are generally three ways in which the authorship and charac-ter of a Sumerian temple can be identified—by the brick-stamps, by the door-sockets, and by the foundation-deposits. The Sumerian door consisted of a wooden leaf fixed to a pole rather higher than itself; the projecting top end was held by and revolved in a metal ring attached to the lintel, the lower end was shod with metal and went down through a hole in the pavement to rest and turn on the hinge-stone. This was a boulder of (imported) hard stone, limestone or diorite, in which a cup-shaped hollow had been cut to take the pole-shoe, and generally one part of it had been smoothed and inscribed with the name of the king who dedicated the building and of the god in whose honour he built it. Door-sockets then can give us all the information we require; but they have to be used with caution because imported stones were valuable and an old stone would often be taken away and re-used for some building other than that for which it had first been intended, so that the old inscription no longer applies. In the case of *Ekhursag* all the hinge-stones were in position, but they bore no inscriptions at all.

Foundation-deposits are found in the corner of buildings. Built into the wall-foundations there is a small box of burnt bricks, lined with matting and waterproofed with bitumen; in it is set a copper figure of the king modestly represented as a labourer carrying on his head a basket of mortar; at his feet is a stone tablet in the form of a plano-convex brick; on the brick and on the king's skirt is an inscription recording his name and that of the temple. In two of the angles of *Ekhursag* (the only two preserved) the boxes duly came to light, but figures and tablets alike were plain and uninscribed. In every other way they resemble inscribed deposits of Shulgi and should probably be dated to his reign (2094–2047 B.C.). The walls of the building were built of bricks stamped with an Ur-Nammu text mentioning the temple of Nanna. The pavement, by contrast, was of bricks bearing the name of his son Shulgi, who seems likely to have been responsible for the building, using bricks left over from his father's time. All seven of Shulgi's peg foundation-deposits in the Inanna Temple at Nippur were also uninscribed, so this anomaly at Ur may not be used to argue that *Ekhursag* was a palace in which such inscriptions would have been inappropriate. Shulgi calls it 'his beloved house or temple'. As we have a Sumerian hymn dedicated to the temple of the deified king Shulgi at Ur called *Ekhursag*, there may be little doubt that this building, in part at least, was a shrine dedicated to the cult of the ruling king.

The *Ekhursag* was of one storey only. It was very well built, all its walls of burnt brick,[5] the outer face of the external walls was decorated with shallow buttresses resembling those of the Ziggurat, its corners were rounded; all the rooms were paved with burnt bricks set in bitumen and two rooms (26 and 27 on the plan) had immensely solid floors raising them

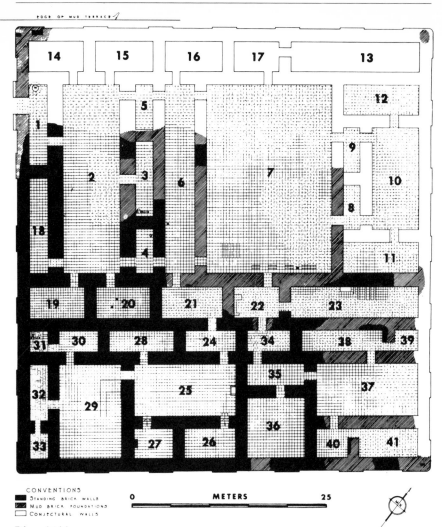

EDGE OF MUD TERRACE

CONVENTIONS
■ STANDING BRICK WALLS
▨ MUD BRICK FOUNDATIONS
□ CONJECTURAL WALLS

0   METERS   25

Plan of Ekhursag

above the general level and approached by steps in the doorways. The ground-plan shows a building which may be described as falling into two distinct parts. In the upper, or north-western, part of the plan there is an inner and an outer court, immediately inside the entrance, and along the two sides are rows of long, narrow rooms. The group of three rooms in front of a long narrow room (nos. 3–5, and 6) separating the two courts formed a reception suite of a type standard in later Mesopotamian palaces. Beyond it, across the inner court, is a group of rooms (nos. 8–12) which

162

look as if they constituted a shrine, with room no. 10 as its focus (the *cella*), though its doors are not niched as is usual with religious buildings. Doorways from rooms 21 and 22 lead into two similar, but not quite identical, complexes, which are divided by a wall and have no direct communication with each other. Each consists of a large room which must have been an open court or light-well and seven or (in the larger complex) nine other chambers. These were probably domestic quarters, more likely for priests or priestesses, than for any major royal household. Dr Hall, who was the first to excavate in this building, found two interesting fragments of sculpture; both are of the Ur III period. One is the cheek and eye of a diorite statue, probably male; the other is the ear and much of the finely plaited hair of a female statue. Such finds are more likely in a religious than in a secular building. The main palace of the Ur III kings may have been at Uruk or Nippur rather than at Ur; even if there, it is unlikely to have been on the Temenos platform.

The other undisturbed Third Dynasty building was a tight-knit group of structures which we called the 'Mausolea of the Third Dynasty kings'. This lay just outside the Temenos, to the south-east, close to the great wall holding up the terrace on which *Ekhursag* stood. This was the site of the old Royal Cemetery and the traditions of four hundred years earlier may have still held good. As is shown by the ground-plan, there were three distinct buildings forming a single block. The largest one, in the centre, is built with bricks bearing the name of Shulgi; at the north-east end of this, communicating with it by a single doorway, there is a smaller building almost identical in plan, and at the south-west end there is a third building awkwardly tacked on to the west corner of the first (with which it has no communication) and less symmetrically arranged; both the last two buildings are constructed with bricks bearing the name of Amar-Sin, Shulgi's successor. The order in time of the three parts is clear—the Shulgi building is the earliest, as is shown by the others being built up against it, and it is obvious that the builder of the north-east wing had the choice of sites and took the better, while the builder of the south-west extension had to make shift with the only site left to him. As nothing like these buildings have yet been found elsewhere in Mesopotamia, I shall describe them at some length, but an account of the Shulgi building will go far to explain the others.

The building consists of two parts, the underground chambers which were constructed first, and the superstructure which only took its final form after the lower chambers had been filled in. The latter is a building measuring 125 feet by 85; its walls, of burnt brick set in bitumen mortar,

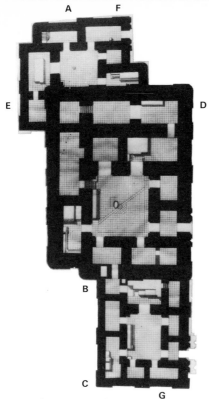

A F

E D

B

C

G

LEFT *Plan of the 'Mausolea' of the kings of the Third Dynasty of Ur*

RIGHT *Sections through the 'Mausolea' of the Ur III kings to show the burial vaults*

are no less than 8 feet thick so that the structure, though only one storey high, must have been very lofty; the walls, relieved by shallow buttresses, are battered, having a pronounced inward slope, like the walls of the Ziggurat, and further resemble the Ziggurat walls in not being straight but having a slight outward curve; the corners are not square but rounded, and where on the south-east side there is a salient, that too is rounded.

On the north-east side is the entrance, its buttress jambs decorated with T-shaped grooves; through an entrance lobby in which was a drain one passed into a paved central courtyard open to the sky. The pavement sloped down to the centre, as did tiled surface drains meant to carry rainwater from the roof, to a sump-pit lined with terracotta rings; by this was a terracotta bitumen-lined bath for ablutions. In every wall were doorways leading to the rooms which surrounded the court, on three sides a single range but a double range on the north-west; in the doorways we would find, amongst the ashes of the woodwork, fragments of gold foil showing that the doors had been overlaid with gold. Between the doors in the south-west wall were the remains of a brick altar with bitumen runnels in front of it exactly like the altar in room 5, and in the angle of the door-jamb

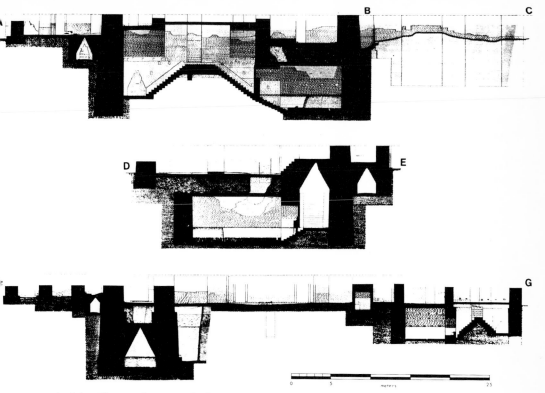

a brick pillar such as we find in the chapels of private houses in the Larsa period.

Most of the rooms do not call for detailed description, but in room 3, in the ashes covering the floor, there were stone hammers on whose striking surface could be seen traces of gold; they had been used by the despoilers of the building for breaking up the precious metal for loot. In rooms 5 and 8 were fragments of wall decoration, fairly thick sheet gold cut into open-work patterns with shield-shaped holes into which were set inlays of agate or lapis lazuli; in room 9 tiny stars and sun's rays in gold and lapis lazuli may have come from the ceiling; in any case there had been here a wealth of ornament which amply rewarded the plunderers, and the few traces of it that remain suffice to give us a very different idea of the appearance of the building from that which we get by looking at the stripped walls of bare brick.

Room 4. In the doorway we found fragments of an inscribed alabaster vase of Shulgi. In the south-east wall was a doorway leading out of the building into that of Amar-Sin: it was peculiar in having no reveals and might be thought therefore not to have been part of the original plan, but there was no visible sign of alteration, and if indeed the door had been cut through the wall, the jambs had been refaced with a very clever imitation of the old brickwork. Close to the door there was in the thickness of the wall a low corbel-vaulted chamber which certainly was original. On the outside it was closed by a mere skin of brick which had been damaged when the wall of Amar-Sin's annexe was built up against it; on the inside it had been closed by a similar skin only one brick thick, and to mask this every alternate brick in the corners of the jambs had been chipped back so that the new brickwork might show no break of bond, a trick employed several times in the Shulgi building. Possibly the chamber had been intended for a foundation-deposit; in any case it had been broken open and looted by the Elamites. When we found it, the entrance had been very roughly blocked up again with mixed bricks projecting beyond the wall-face, and inside were two bodies and a number of clay pots of the Larsa period. Some Larsa householder digging into the ruins below his foundations must have found the little chamber and re-used it as a burial vault.

Room 5 was the most interesting in the building. The whole of the north-west end was occupied by a raised brick base divided into three parts, a lower ledge along the front, a low platform along the north-east wall, and a higher platform in the west corner; the back was destroyed by plunderers who had dug through it into the tomb below, but the front was almost intact. The brickwork was overlaid with bitumen, and sticking to this were found fragments of gold leaf, so that the whole must have been gilded. In the top of the front ledge were six channels running parallel with the front and arranged two deep. Starting as shallow depressions they deepened as they ran and then, turning outwards at right-angles, came to the edge and were continued as grooves down the front of the platform, emptying into six small brick compartments which formed a row on the floor in front of the platform; in these compartments we found wood ashes. On the top of the lower platform in the north corner there were the remains of one and apparently of two similar channels running down into brick compartments. Along the south-east half of the south-west wall and along the south-east wall was a low bench of brick covered with bitumen in which again there were long channels starting in front of a raised base which faced the door of the room, but these ended not in brick compartments but in cup-like hollows in the top of the bench.

The explanation which suggested itself for the channels, etc., in the west corner was that over each runnel there would be set a porous (or pierced) vase containing scented oil which, escaping from the vase, would run along the channel and trickle down into a fire made in the brick compartment below, and so would go up as incense before a statue placed on the high base behind. Remains of similar altars were found in room 8 and, as I have said, in the central court, and there were others in the Amar-Sin buildings; in every case they had been dug through to floor-level. Evidently some votive object of intrinsic value was embedded in the brickwork and the Elamites, well informed as to where treasure might be found, overlooked nothing.

The long runnels in the wall benches must have been for liquid offerings and the raised pedestal for solid foods. This was clearly the dining-room of the dead king, and while the smoke of the incense rose into his nostrils, his more material needs were satisfied with the food and drink passing ceaselessly before him; very properly, the dining-room was directly above the tomb in which the king lay.

There was a flight of steps in the doorway of room 6 and the floor of the room was about 6 feet higher than that of the central court; below this high pavement lay the approach to the underground chamber. The pavement had been pulled up and plunderers had dug down for a little way below it, but stopped, seeing that their fellows had found a quicker way of getting at the spoil; we soon came on clean and undisturbed earth filling. The massive brick walls went steadily down. Between rooms 6 and 7 there was a doorway which had been bricked up and carefully camouflaged; below floor-level the blocking was undisguised and at length we found the foot of a flight of steps in the door passage and, in front of it, a landing from which stairs ran down to left and right into the earth; now the pit which we were digging had walls on either side, to north-east and south-west, but at either end there was a high corbelled vault built of bricks and bitumen, and it was into the earth filling those vaults that the stairs descended. The vaults had been built over a timber centring which had of course decayed away and we could not by any means be sure that they would not collapse when once the earth filling had been removed; so work had to be interrupted until we had shored up the brickwork—which we did on the same lines, using the old joist-holes for the brackets that supported the sloping roof-beams. Clearing a little at a time and adding fresh centring as the work went forward (it was a ticklish job, for the bitumen mortar had dried and lost all its cohesive qualities so that the bricks were virtually loose) we were at last able to empty out all the filling and expose the bricked-up doors of the lower chambers. There were two of these. The north-west stairs ended in a landing with a doorway on the right; under the blocking-wall more steps went down into a corbel-vaulted chamber 34 feet long and running under rooms 11 and 10 of the superstructure; the south-east stairs ran up against a block-wall directly facing one and, continuing through the doorway passage, ended in a 30 foot chamber similarly corbelled, lying under room 5. Both chambers had been broken into from above, through the floors of the superstructure, and their roofs were in a dangerous condition, so that more reinforcement work was needed before any clearing could be done; when it was done, we discovered, as indeed we had expected, that our robber predecessors had done their job most thoroughly and, apart from human bones and fragments of clay pots, there was nothing left for us to glean (see frontispiece).

One curious and almost comic point about these chambers was this—when we entered them for the first time, we were frankly disappointed by their mean proportions; the bones and pot-fragments lay on a floor of mud-brick which was about on the level of the springers of the arches—the chamber was long indeed but so low that only in the middle could one stand upright. Then we noticed that the stairs in the doorway ran down below the floor; we made a hole in the floor, which was many courses thick, and then came on burnt bricks set on edge with open spaces between them; there were two courses of these, and then the real pavement of the chamber, five courses of burnt brick set in bitumen and bonded in to the side-walls. The explanation was that Shulgi's architect had been too ambitious and had put his underground chambers too deep down—nearly 30 feet below ground level, and that when the river Euphrates washed the city walls—with the result that when the chambers were to be used, they were awash with infiltered water and the only thing that could be done at the short notice was to raise the floors by 5 or 6 feet at the sacrifice of the proportions of the building.

In Shulgi's building, as in one of the buildings of Amar-Sin's, there were two chambers; both chambers were closed at the same time and neither of them could afterwards be reopened. The underground chambers, though designed as part of a plan which was to be completed later, were the *raison d'être* of the building and were constructed first, together with a superstructure, some of which was purely temporary, but some was to be incorporated in the later building. To judge by existing remains, the temporary superstructure may have been confined to the area overlying the chambers proper; slight changes of line in the brickwork of the pit walls may indicate that even the temporary building was not strictly contemporary with the

RIGHT ABOVE '*Shulgi's Mausoleum*'; *the offering-tables in room 5*
RIGHT BELOW '*Amar-Sin's Mausoleum*'; *the stairways leading to the tomb-chambers*

vault construction but was added. In any case the presence of the building suggests that the rites which it served lasted for a considerable time. The two vaults were occupied at the same moment and their doors were walled up, but the staircase to the doors remained open and the presence of the door in the superstructure wall implies that people came down the upper flight of steps to perform ceremonies in front of the doors or on the central platform and on wooden galleries which prolonged it above the tomb entrance—evidence for such galleries was given by the holes in the side masonry which took the supporting beams.

Then the superstructure as we know it was built, and when it was virtually complete, with its floors at a higher level than those of the temporary building, the doors of the latter were bricked up, the galleries in the stair-pit dismantled, and the pit itself filled in and paved over. At this moment a dramatic incident occurred. When we dug away the filling, we found that in the upper part of the blocking of the door of each of the tomb-chambers there had been made a small breach just large enough for a man to get through; the dislodged bricks were lying in front of the door covered by the clean earth imported for the filling. The vaults had been robbed and, obviously, robbed just as the earth was about to be put in; nobody would have dared to rob them when the pit was still in use, nor, if such sacrilege had been done, would the bricks have been left scattered on the floor and the breach unfilled; the robbers must have chosen their moment when the inviolable earth would at once hide all traces of their crime and they could afford to be careless.

The south-east Amar-Sin building is, though on a smaller scale, so nearly a replica of that of Shulgi that no description of it is required. The entrance to the two chambers was under the pavement of room 5 and the chambers themselves underlay rooms 6 and 4 respectively. The north-west building was less regular in that it had no rooms opening off the south-east side of the central court where it was built up against the external wall of Shulgi's building; also it contained three burial chambers instead of two; one underlay room 5, its approach being under room 4, one was below room 6 and one in the middle of the courtyard; but all alike had been made, and occupied, before the superstructure was erected. In this last building, as also in Shulgi's, we found inscribed tablets bearing dates which took us up to the last year of the reign of Ibbi-Sin, the last king of Ur-Nammu's

RIGHT ABOVE *Gold goat pendant from 'Second Dynasty' shaft grave (see p.131)*
RIGHT BELOW *Gold bowl from the grave of Queen Puabi (see pp.64ff)*

dynasty, who was defeated and carried off prisoner by the Elamites; they prove clearly enough to whom the destruction of the building was due. After the destruction the site was deserted for a century or more, and when at length it was reoccupied, it was by private houses of the Larsa period.

How are we to explain the function of this complex? To what extent is the description 'mausolea' a meaningful one? That Shulgi was not building a mortuary temple for himself is evident from the fact that the underground chambers had to be occupied and filled in before the building proper could be erected. The same is true of the others, and we should therefore have expected to find a third royal name on the bricks of the south-west wing, if indeed the obvious solution is the right one: that we have here Shulgi building a tomb for his father Ur-Nammu, killed in battle after a short reign, Amar-Sin for his father Shulgi, perhaps assassinated after a long reign, and Shu-Sin for his brother Amar-Sin, who may have died of some kind of foot infection. Yet, if the king was in one chamber, who was in the second? Not, it would appear, the queen mother, for she is known in certain cases to have lived on into the next reign. Then, by contrast, the south-west wing covers three rather than two subterranean vaults. Indeed its uncanonical plan may be explained not so much by an inadequate site as by the need to accommodate the above-ground building to three, rather than just two, ready-made vaults. There is, as yet, no independent evidence, documentary or archaeological, that the kings of the Third Dynasty of Ur were actually buried at Ur, rather than at Nippur, holy city of Sumer, or at Uruk, home of the family. Later evidence also suggests that kings in Assyria and Babylonia were buried in or adjacent to, their main residential palace in the funerary city of any particular dynasty, not in special buildings in the Sacred Area. On accession the Ur III kings were crowned in three separate ceremonies, one at each of these cities. They might well have been buried in any one of the three, with cenotaphs or libation places provided for their cult at the other two.

There is one indication that these mausolea may not be simply explained. We have already described the five shaft graves, containing simultaneous multiple burials of men, women, and children, which lay just to the north-west of the mausolea and may date through into Shulgi's reign (see p.131). They suggest that some privileged individuals, not kings, were already buried in special tombs with sacrificial victims at the time of the earlier Ur III rulers. Is it then possible that these fine brick structures continued an

LEFT *Modern reconstruction of the head-dress of one of Queen Puabi's attendant ladies* existing trend, but gave it a more enduring and spectacular architectural setting? In short, that it is not the nature of the burials and the rank of the occupants which are new to Ur at this time, but only the more impressive above-ground setting and the brick-built vaults replacing the earlier gabled coffins of wicker and wood? Shulgi, we know, was the first ruler of the dynasty to be deified during his lifetime and to erect a temple for the cult of the living, but divine, king just to the north-west of the Royal Cemetery on the Temenos: the building *Ekhursag*. If the people entitled to burial with victims at Ur, perhaps a Sumerian revival of customs illustrated by the earlier royal tombs (see pp.6off), were high-ranking priests and priestesses of the cult of Nanna and Ningal, with which members of the royal family were intimately associated, might it not be they, rather than the kings themselves, who lay here before the Elamites plundered and sacked both shrines and vaults? Only more evidence, not necessarily from Ur, will resolve this fascinating question.

When we were clearing the ruins lying under the shadow of the Ziggurat on its north-west side, we found, re-used as hinge-sockets in a late doorway, two fragments of limestone carved in relief. A hundred and fifty yards away, in the courtyard in front of *Dublamakh*, many more carved fragments appeared which actually fitted on to the first two, and another fragment apparently belonging to the same monument turned up in the ruins of *Enunmakh*. These widely scattered bits made up a considerable part of a round-topped stela almost 5 feet across and 10 feet high, sculptured on both sides, which in pictorial and written form commemorated the achievements of Ur-Nammu. Sadly incomplete as it is, it is none the less the most important piece of sculpture found by us at Ur; it has been restored, so far as possible, in the University Museum in Philadelphia.

On both sides the topmost register of the stela, with its curving upper edge, is the same. Under the crescent of the Moon-god the king Ur-Nammu is received and instructed by the gods. Only the lower part of Ningal's seated figure is now preserved. Above the duplicated figures of Ur-Nammu, as it were in the sky, are goddesses pouring life-giving water from vases which they hold in their hands. On a broad band on the reverse between the registers, there is an inscription giving a list of the canals in the neighbourhood of Ur built by the king's orders, and this text explains this scene: Ur-Nammu has been responsible for the actual work of digging the canals, but it is the gods who grant the blessed gift of water and bring fertility to the land.

RIGHT *The front of the Ur-Nammu stela; restored in the University Museum, Philadelphia*

The second scene on the front of the stela is the best preserved. At the two ends of the register are the enthroned figures of Ningal and Nanna, whilst Ur-Nammu, introduced by his personal goddess, makes a libation to each, pouring water into a vase from which plants grow, symbolizing the fruits of the earth. In this scene Nanna holds a rod and a ring, as do many of the 'Great Gods' in Mesopotamian art. These have been explained as a measuring rod and a line, or tape, and this gesture as a command to Ur-Nammu to build a house for the god Nanna, as indeed seems to be happening in the next register down. Be that as it may, whatever their original identity and practical purpose, these objects became standard symbols of divine power or lordship. In the register beneath, in the corner that remains intact, we see Ur-Nammu, behind the figure of Nanna (distinguished by his horned head-dress of divinity), bearing on his shoulders the tools of the builder, axe and compasses and mortar or brick basket, while a clean-shaven priest helps with the load. Of the two remaining registers only scattered fragments have survived; but they showed the actual building in progress. There are traces of a brick wall with at least one ladder against it and of workmen carrying baskets of building materials on their heads. Too little of the construction remains to allow for its identification, and the text only refers to canals; but perhaps the structure in question was the Ziggurat and its ancillary buildings, which constituted one of Ur-Nammu's greatest achievements in honour of Nanna.

Nowhere on this stela is there any sense of a flowing narrative within the registers. Indeed the composition is almost emphatically static within each division, which has two perfectly balanced groups. The second register has preserved this, but similar composition may be assumed for the top panel, and was probably used also in the third register, where there are fragments of a second group facing the god and the king, and elsewhere.

The scenes on the reverse, again very fragmentary, are often enigmatic to the modern observer. They may also show rituals performed at the dedication of a building or of statuary within it. There seems little force in a once popular suggestion that they illustrate the celebrations of a military victory. The top repeats the obverse design. In the next register down an animal is slaughtered, perhaps an ox or bull, in front of a statue. In the middle register a bound man is led away from an enthroned figure on the left. At the other end a bearded man stoops or kneels, whilst a priest, with a folded cloth over his arm, cups his hand towards the bearded chin. A naked priest, again with a folded cloth over his right arm and a fly-whisk held high in his left hand, performs some service or ritual for an enthroned

A mud-brick column of the Third Dynasty

figure on a podium. In the next register two groups are preserved, each showing two men beating a large drum. In the lowest panel a fragment from the left-hand end illustrates libation and adoration before a standing god or statue.

As I have said, the stela is the most important piece of sculpture found by us at Ur and its historic interest is the greater because we have very few monuments of the Third Dynasty. But artistically it cannot rank as high as I was inclined to put it in the first excitement of discovery; its technique is excellent but it is wholly uninspired. A generation or so earlier Gudea, the governor of Lagash, had made for himself a stela which like this one recorded the achievements and virtues of the ruler, and the formula used was identical; the scenes and the treatment of them are the same. Ur-Nammu's sculptor was a skilful worker in stone, but he worked in a stereotyped tradition and could make no original contribution to art. Ur as the capital of the empire could command the best, and we may well imagine that no former age in Sumer had produced buildings so vast, combining such solid strength with an architectural finesse, probably, with a wealth of ornament that no previous Sumerian ruler could have afforded; but if we compare Ur-Nammu's stela, correct and conventional, with the fresh invention of the shell plaques from the Royal Cemetery, just as if we set the finely cut but dull cylinder seals of Ur-Nammu's time against the Sargonid seals with their vivid and dramatic pictures, we shall realize that under the Third Dynasty Sumerian art was uninspired and static.

Further Reading

The excavations of the Third Dynasty buildings other than the Ziggurat area were published in *Ur Excavations* VI: *The Ur III Period* (1974); the Ziggurat and related buildings in *Ur Excavations* V: *The Ziggurat and its Surroundings* (1939).

*Alabaster head of a woman, probably dating
towards the end of the Ur III period*

The Isin-Larsa and
Old Babylonian Periods
c. 2000–1600 B.C.

That Nanna shows no respect for his people as
numerous as ewes,
That of Ur, its shrine of the great offerings, the
offerings be changed,
That its people no longer inhabit its dwellings, that it
be made inimical soil
That the Su-people (and) the Elamites, the enemies,
inhabit their dwellings,
That its shepherd (living) in terror in the palace be
seized by the foe
That Ibbi-Sin be brought back to the land of Elam in a trap

S.N. Kramer's translation in J.B. Pritchard (ed.),
Ancient Near Eastern Texts (3rd edition, 1969), p.612.

So did a contemporary poet give voice to the bitterness of his spirit and
there was no poetic exaggeration in his lament; there is not a single
building of the Third Dynasty but bears the marks of violent overthrow.
Ur must have been very thoroughly destroyed, but such was its importance
that when the city of Isin took over the kingship of Sumer and Akkad and
when later the city of Larsa wrested the hegemony from Isin, practically
every ruler of either line was at pains to restore one or other of Ur's ruined
monuments; and when the native dynasty of Larsa was ousted in its turn
and a tribal ruler with Elamite connections, Kudur-Mabuk, installed his
son Warad-Sin as king (1834–1823 B.C.), he proved himself the most active
of them all in the piety with which he rebuilt and enlarged the temples of
the ancient capital.

Royal inscriptions on bricks, clay cones, and hinge-stones from temple
doors found by us amply proved the zeal of successive kings. Shu-Ilishu

(1984–1975 B.C.) boasts that he brought back from Anshan (modern Tepe Malyan in Iran) the statues of Nanna, carried off by the Elamites, and that he rebuilt *Dublamakh*, the place of judgement, and set up its doors. Iddin-Dagan (1974–1954 B.C.) makes a dedication to Nanna. Ishme-Dagan (1953–1935 B.C.) speaks of himself as 'he who exalts the head of Ur' and we have an alabaster vase dedicated to Nanna by him. His daughter Enana-tuma, was, as we have seen, High-Priestess of the Moon-god at Ur, and *Giparu* which she built, will be described later. Her brother, Lipit-Ishtar (1934–1924 B.C.), calls himself 'the just irrigator of Ur'. Sumu-El (1894–1866 B.C.) built a store-house and a temple: Nur-Adad (1865–1850 B.C.) restored and built temples. Siniddinam (1849–1843 B.C.) was particularly active both in the restoration of existing shrines and the building of new ones; seven buildings are recorded as having been the objects of his care and the wide dispersal of bricks stamped with his name bears further witness to his energetic building programme cut short by his relatively brief reign. Warad-Sin (1834–1823 B.C.) was the most energetic of the kings; his great gate-tower for the Ziggurat terrace has been described in the previous chapter, and a dozen other works by him are known; Rim-Sin I's (1822–1763 B.C.) inscriptions claim nine temples to his credit. Clearly, during the two centuries or so of the Isin-Larsa period Ur more than recovered from the disaster that ended the Third Dynasty. It may well be that the temples of that time, when Ur was the capital city and its kings enriched by successful war, were more splendid than those put up by alien rulers, but two centuries of comparative peace enabled the townspeople to attain by trade and manufacture a prosperity less sensational perhaps but scarcely less real.

Our excavations produced no material evidence for such a city wall as some of the inscriptions seem to imply. Ur-Nammu's great wall had been carefully destroyed, not a brick remaining in place, but his rampart, being really the revetted slope of the town mound, was indestructible. The easiest and most economical form of defence was what the people of Ur actually put into effect; along the top of the rampart they built their houses in a more or less unbroken line, and the outer walls, blank at least to the level of the second floor, made a satisfactory substitute for a purely military fortification. Such was indeed a normal thing in the Near East; we may call to mind Jericho, where the house of Rahab the harlot was 'on the wall' and had a window of the upper storey looking out over the country.

On the north-east side of the city we dug houses which gave us a continuous wall line for the space of nearly 200 yards; then there was a salient made by a later (Kassite) fortress, but behind it the house walls ran on and were followed by us for another 200 yards, beyond which we only tapped it at intervals, but with the same result. Sometimes, where the rampart broadened, it might be surmounted by a public building, but even so that would be incorporated in the system of defence. Thus towards the south limits of the town there stood on the wall line a temple dedicated to Enki, the Water-god of Eridu—Eridu, by tradition the oldest of Sumerian cities, lies 12 miles away to the south, its ruins visible from the mounds of Ur, so that the site of the temple seems to have been chosen as one from which Enki could see his own Ziggurat rising in the distance. This was a Third Dynasty foundation restored in the Larsa period; fallen against the wall we found clay foundation-cones which presumably had been embedded in the brickwork higher up, and in one corner of the building an intact box of burnt bricks set in the mud-brickwork of the wall's core in which was the copper figure and inscribed stone tablet of Rim-Sin I, king of Larsa. At the very south end of the town there was another temple, also originally of Third Dynasty date and restored in Larsa times (it was again restored in the Kassite period and finally rebuilt by Nebuchadnezzar) unfortunately not identified by any inscriptions, which too stood on the rampart and was incorporated in the wall.

The Ziggurat terrace: the bastion of Warad-Sin

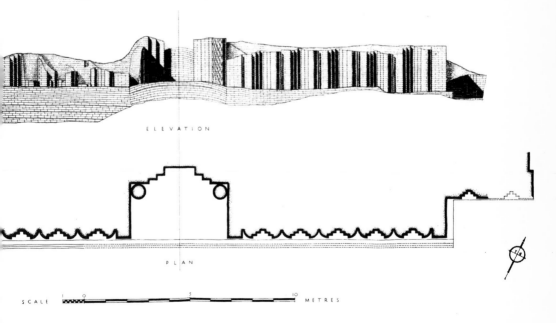

ELEVATION

PLAN

SCALE   0   5   10   METRES

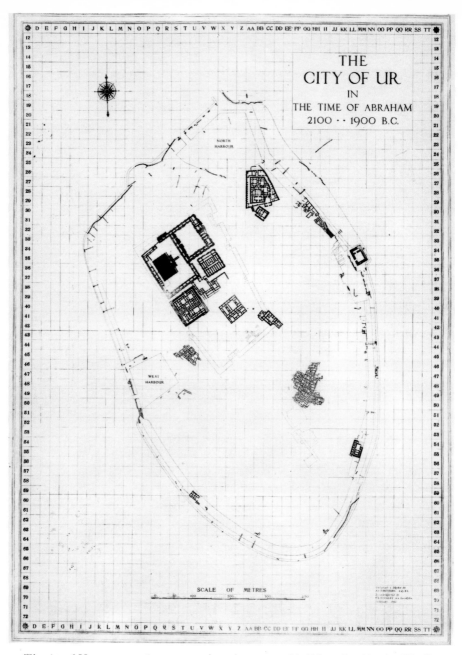

THE CITY OF UR IN THE TIME OF ABRAHAM 2100 ·· 1900 B.C.

SCALE OF METRES

The city of Ur, c. 2000–1800 B.C., to show the excavated buildings (in this plan Woolley inadvertently included much later buildings near the 'North Harbour'). The title is Woolley's own

I think that when we started work at Ur we assumed that all the temples would be found inside the Temenos, or Sacred Area. The Isin-Larsa building inscriptions were enough to show the error of such an assumption, because that area was not large enough to contain so many temples. And now the discovery of temples on the city wall made the truth evident. The Temenos was the peculiar precinct of Nanna and his wife Ningal; the minor gods of their court might be honoured in chapels attached to the shrines of the great deities, but they were inside the Temenos only because they were in the Moon-god's service. Other gods of course were worshipped at Ur and had their temples there, but those temples might be anywhere in the town. And they were not necessarily inside the old city walls. Since very nearly all our work was done inside the walls, we had small opportunity to find them, but the one bit of serious excavation outside proved the point. A small trial dig just a mile away from the Temenos, to the north-east, hit on the scanty remains of a very large and important building with elaborately buttressed walls of burnt brick. We called it the 'Treasury of Siniddinam' on discovery; but this was later found to be inappropriate as bricks with the same inscription as we found here occurred as part of *Enunmakh* on the Temenos, their true home. The niched and revealed façade of this building is appropriate to a religious structure, so we may classify it as such, even though it lies far outside the city proper. We may safely imagine that throughout the whole of the sprawling town there were scattered temples dedicated to one or another of the innumerable gods.

None the less, the first efforts of the Isin kings were directed to the restoration or repair of major buildings lying inside the Temenos. Outstanding among these was the *Giparu*, residence of the High-Priestess of Nanna. It happens that the ruins of the Isin-Larsa period building are so complete that we get from them an unusually detailed picture of a complex structure incorporating shrines, domestic accommodation, and burial vaults.

The *Giparu* was built in its present form by Ur-Nammu, and elaborated by his grandson Amar-Sin, in mud-brick. Now King Ishme-Dagan's daughter, Enanatuma, *entu*–(High) Priestess of Nanna, determined to rebuild it on the old lines but in better material, using burnt brick throughout. Excavating the site, we found her building standing on the stumps of the older walls which had been used by the new bricklayers as a foundation, and so recovered at one time the ground-plan of both buildings.

It was a rectangle of 80 by 76 metres, and was surrounded by an enormously heavy wall through the heart of which a narrow paved corridor ran round three sides of it, leading from a gate-tower over the main entrance to two fortified towers at the far corners; a similar corridor cut straight across the building, dividing it into two unequal parts and affording quick access from one tower to another. From the outside at least the *Giparu* must have looked more like a military than a religious structure.

The north-western unit (A), with its outer and inner court, its two little antechambers (1–2) and its long rooms at opposite sides, bears some resemblance to the comparable parts of *Ekhursag*, described in the previous chapter. At the same time it presented certain curious features. Between the outer and the inner court were two long chambers (A4–5), of which the first (5) had a wide doorway opening on to the outer court, and against the back wall, facing the door, a brick niche for a statue. To reach the inner court one passed through the second narrow chamber (4), round which ran a raised brick bench waterproofed with bitumen and having along its edge a runnel for water; the floor was also covered with bitumen and sloped gently to the door leading to a tiny room in the centre of which was a terracotta drain going deep down into the earth. Obviously this was a lustral chamber, and here the suppliant would purify himself before passing either to the inner or to the outer court. The outer court (A6) contained no objects or structures of any kind. This section of the building is built on the model of a private house and may well have been the living-quarters of the High-Priestess serving the Ningal temple in block C. The inner court (A11) and the sanctuary beyond had been terribly ruined, but enough remained of them to show the place of the great altar in the court and, inside the sanctuary (A18), the bases for statues, the stepped altar, and the 'vestry' or treasury adjoining. A19, in which one might have expected a podium for the god's statue, was badly ruined. What cult was celebrated here remains a mystery. It may be that these were palatial reception rooms, where the high social status of the *entu*-Priestess involved her in more public rituals than would have been appropriate in the temple of block C: the home of the goddess proper.

In all this part, and in the next section of the building, excavation was made difficult by the presence of later walls whose foundations went down nearly as deep as the old work, while in some places the old floor-level had actually been re-used and the new walls simply set on the existing brick pavement. It was no easy matter to unravel this tangle of ruinous brick-work and to assign each fragment to its proper period, but when this was done, the early plan was found to be remarkably regular and what had seemed mere confusion took on a very definite character.

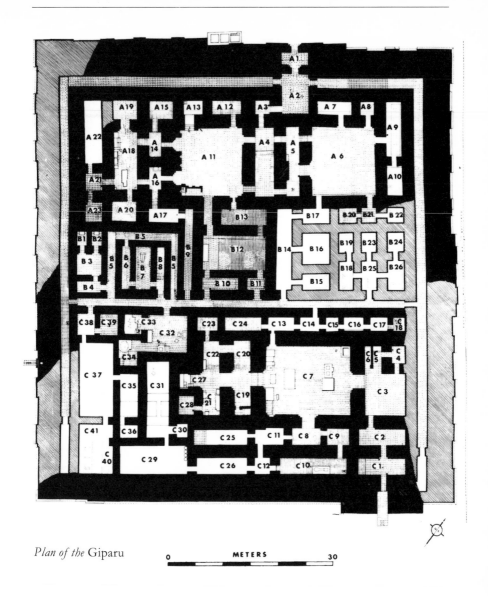

Plan of the Giparu

0   **METERS**   30

    To the south-east of the outer court (B15–16, 18–19, 23–26) the residential quarters of the priestesses were the most ruined of all, for there had been here a motive for more thoroughgoing destruction. In accordance with the fashion of the time the priestesses had been buried beneath the floors of their houses, and the brick vaults must have contained riches which tempted the avarice of the enemy who plundered the building. In every case the pavements had been dug up and the tombs broken into and rifled so completely that there was virtually nothing of this period left.

Next to this domestic quarter we found, very much better preserved, a unit (B5–8) of quite a novel sort, entered from the corridor running across the building. Three narrow interconnecting rooms were isolated by an encircling corridor. It was a regular little maze of which the long central room contained the secret. Standing between its two doorways, one looked down the length of the chamber, now of course roofless, and with undecorated brick walls standing some $1\frac{1}{2}$ metres high. The pavement was of brick, but the farther half of it was covered with bitumen on whose surface could be distinguished the impress of reed mats which had once been spread there. Standing upright above the pavement, in which it was firmly bedded, was a large round-topped slab of white limestone and side by side at its foot there lay fixed into the bitumen of the floor two other round-topped slabs of grey marble, and on each of the three stones, in characters intentionally defaced but still legible, was an inscription giving the name and titles of Amar-Sin and his dedication of the building to Ningal. It seems very unlikely that in the Isin-Larsa period these stelae occupied a shrine for the deified king Amar-Sin, whatever may have been the case earlier in the Ur III period. Even then one might have expected them to be in a temple courtyard. The plan of this unit is quite exceptional for a shrine and none of the doorways is niched as was customary in religious buildings. It seems likely that these stelae had once been set up in the temple courtyard and moved here subsequently. These were probably store-rooms linked across the main passage with the storage units of block C. It is, however, likely that the small adjacent block of four rooms (B1–4), consisting of an antechamber, a small court, and a pair of smaller rooms with niched entrances, was indeed for deity statues housed in the two little rooms at the back. Documents make clear that a number of deities apart from Ningal were revered in this building.

The rest of the great four-square building beyond the central corridor consisted of the major sanctuary and rooms behind it. The main temple was entered through a doorway between the monumental gate-towers which stood near the east corner of the south-east façade. From the main court (C7) three arched doorways led to the sanctuary. One set of rooms formed the kitchen (32–34): in an open court there was a well, and by it a bitumen-proofed tank for water, and a big copper ring let into the pavement may have been for the rope, so that the bucket might not be lost down the well, but perhaps more probably was for the rope fastened round the neck of the bullock intended for sacrifice. Against one wall were two fireplaces for boiling water, and against another the brick 'cutting-up table', the criss-cross marks of the butcher's knife clearly visible on its top; in a side-room was the beehive-shaped oven for baking bread, and in another room the cooking-range with two furnaces and circular flues, and in the flat top of it rings of small holes where the cauldrons were to be set.

But it was the sanctuary and the courtyard that gave us the best results. We had been a long time getting down to them, for close under the surface there were remains of the late Babylonian period which had to be planned and noted before they could be removed, and they were so fragmentary that we were hard put to it to make sense of them.

Below this, more shoddy buildings had to be removed, and then we came on a series of fairly massive mud-brick walls which proved to be those of a great house built probably for the temple priests in about 1400 B.C., with separate dwellings all giving on a central court. We were still high up in the mound, some 6 feet or more above the level of the pavements of Enanatuma's temple, and this was a good sign. In this part of the building the walls, except for the open space of the courtyard, were

Room B7 of the Giparu *with the stelae of Amar-Sin, dedicated to the goddess Ningal*

close together, enclosing small chambers, and the walls were very thick; consequently when the upper parts of them were overthrown, the debris filled the rooms to a considerable height and the builders of the succeeding age could not be bothered to remove it; it was simpler to build on the top of the mounds and where the old court left a low-lying hollow, to put in a flight of brick steps down to it. Thus we found the walls of the chambers round the sanctuary standing 6 feet high and the fallen rubble between them undisturbed, and as we went down through this, we were delighted to come across a layer of ashes and burnt wood spread over the entire area.

Restoration of the courtyard C 7 in the Giparu *looking into the inner shrine, C 27 (see p.185)*

Nothing helps an excavator like violent destruction. If a building has fallen slowly into decay, one can be sure that the impoverished inhabitants have removed everything of value. The best thing that can happen is a volcanic eruption which buries a place so deeply that nobody goes back to salve his belongings; but the ideal conditions of a Pompeii are seldom met with, and one must be thankful for smaller mercies. If an enemy sacks a temple or a town, he is sure to overlook some objects at least which were of small intrinsic value for him, but may be very precious for the archaeologist; and if he was so considerate as to set fire to the place and overthrow its walls, there is the further probability that his search was hurried and that no one else troubled to look for what he left behind.

So it was here. The ashes represented the ceilings and the panelling of the walls, and below them, lying on the brick pavement, there were hundreds of fragments of alabaster and soapstone vases and splinters of broken statues. One small statue we found entire, a heavy and clumsy figure carved in black stone representing a goddess, perhaps Gula or Bau, seated on a throne supported by geese; only her nose (which was made separately) was missing, and round the head were the small drilled holes to secure the gold crown which the robbers had torn off before discarding the statue. This figure in her flounced and pleated dress reaching to the ankles was squat and thick-set. It is far from being a first-class work of art, but as it is one of the very few Neo-Sumerian female statues in the round which time has preserved to us, it must rank high amongst our discoveries.

More fragmentary, for most of the head had vanished, but of far finer work, was a little seated figure of a woman, perhaps the donor herself, which bore a long inscription stating that it had been dedicated to Ningal by no less a person than the lady Enanatuma, the second founder of the temple. This was pieced together from many fragments widely scattered. As the splinters of stone were collected and cleaned, there began a regular jigsaw game, and it was most exciting to watch them gradually growing up into complete vessels, sometimes inscribed with the names of ancient kings. A Sumerian temple, like a modern cathedral, was a veritable museum of antiquities; for centuries pious kings and others had been offering their treasures for the service of the gods, and the temple strong-rooms would contain objects of all ages. It was here that we found the alabaster lunar disc of Sargon's daughter, and here too the limestone relief showing sacrifice being done by a princess of much older date—the latter was nearly seven hundred years old and the former five hundred when the robbers broke into the treasury where both were preserved.

One object was of particular interest. We found part of a granite bowl inscribed with a dedication by the daughter of King Shulgi, herself perhaps a High-Priestess of the Moon-god; another cup fragment bore the name of Naram-Sin, the great king who reigned over a century before Shulgi; and then it was found that the two fragments joined together and that both inscriptions belonged to one and the same cup. How it came about that the princess owned what had been so long before the property of King Naram-Sin we cannot tell, but that she did so is another proof of the way in which in the ancient as in the modern world objects might long survive their generation: we shall see later how another royal priestess of Ur indulged in a passion for 'antiques'.

The stone fragments lay thickest in the neighbourhood of the sanctuary, but in the courtyard also they were fairly abundant: at one end of this we found bits, unfortunately not very numerous, of a large alabaster slab inscribed with a list of the royal benefactions which had enriched the temple, and in the middle of the court scanty remains of a much more interesting document. There stood here a big base of solid brick, and on it and round it we picked up pieces of fine-grained black stone covered with inscription; clearly the stone had originally been erected on the base, and enough remained of the text to show that it enumerated the conquests of the famous king and law-giver Hammurabi of Babylon. Hammurabi reduced Ur to subjection, and this was his war memorial set up in one of the chief temples of the city.

Scattered at random in the chambers of the temple we found a number of inscribed tablets, part of the ordinary business records of the building. Such tablets, from here and elsewhere on the site, are very often dated by the years of the reigning king, and on these we had represented most of the kings of Larsa, several years of Hammurabi; and the reign of his son, Samsuiluna, almost continuously down to year 10 and the beginning of year 11.

In the thirty-first year of his reign Hammurabi of Babylon (1792–1750 B.C.) recorded the defeat of his old rival Rim-Sin I of Larsa (1822–1763 B.C.), who had for so long controlled Ur. After capturing the city from Rim-Sin, Hammurabi set up the victory stela, which we found in fragments in the *Giparu*. The name of the thirty-third year of his reign records the construction of a great canal to provide water for such cities as Eridu, Uruk, Nippur, and Ur, with the implication that this area had suffered from agricultural decline, and perhaps depopulation, in the previous few generations. It is not clear from our excavations in the private houses to what extent Hammurabi's capture of the city had involved their destruction. Of about seventy-three houses which we excavated, only twenty-nine had archives of tablets, some large, some small, and among these only four extended beyond the reign of Rim-Sin I. From this we may conclude either that the majority of houses had suffered at the time of the Babylonian assault and Hammurabi's victory, and had not all been subsequently occupied, or that they had been reoccupied, but for some reason there had been no archives at this time. In about the ninth year of his reign, Hammurabi's son, Samsuiluna (1749–1712 B.C.), was threatened by a rebellion of the southern cities led by Rim-Sin II of Larsa. The Babylonian king's eventual victory was overwhelming. His eleventh year is named 'the year in which [King Samsuiluna], at the command of Anu and Enlil,

The foundation-deposit of King Rim-Sin I (c. 1822–1763 B.C.) in the Enki Temple; the copper figurine, with an inscription on the body, carries a basket of earth on his head

destroyed the walls of Ur and Uruk'. Not only was the great defensive wall at Ur thrown down; the whole city was given over to fire and destruction. Its public monuments were ravaged and the houses of its private citizens extensively damaged. Though badly crippled, as the Babylonian king had intended, by this assault, Ur struggled on. The archaeological traces of reoccupation are elusive and the textual evidence is meagre. Houses were patched up in time and again to an extent which makes the close dating of repairs impossible, whilst the traditional religious shrines exhibit evidence of partial restoration in often crude and makeshift brickwork. But for something like three hundred years after the sack by Samsuiluna, Ur faded into oblivion.

It is thanks to the city's violent destruction that our excavation of the private houses proved so illuminating. We can picture the life of the ordinary citizens of Ur in the earlier eighteenth century B.C. with an accuracy and a vividness such as is surpassed only by Pompeii or Herculaneum; even the well-preserved houses of Tell al-Amarna in Egypt tell us less, because they do not yield the tablets which at Ur give the personal touch that really brings the past to life.

In the season 1926–27 we dug a group of houses that lay just outside the Temenos, against its south-west wall, occupying most (probably all) of the relatively narrow space between the Temenos and the West Harbour (the 'EM' area). The houses were in all respects normal, and there was nothing in the lay-out that would suggest an official quarter, but the position, on the outskirts of the Sacred Area, might justify one in supposing that there was here something in the nature of a cathedral close. Certainly the inhabitants seem to have belonged to the priesthood and may have been those most closely concerned with the temples inside the Temenos; several of them possessed small libraries of ecclesiastical literature and from them we recovered a whole series of hymns in honour of different gods such as were used in temple services.

In the season 1930–31 we excavated an area about half-way between the south-east end of the Temenos and the city wall; the space cleared measured something like ten thousand square yards and gave us a very fair idea of the character of the residential part of the city (the 'AH' area).[6]

Anyone looking at the plans can see at once that there was no such thing as town-planning at Ur. There may have been, there probably was, a Processional way leading to the Temenos, but the town in general pre-

The kitchen in the Giparu, *showing cistern and well, cutting-up table, cooking-range, quern and grindstone. Woolley's Arab workmen act as kitchen staff in this photograph*

served the form, or lack of form, of the primitive village, and there are no straight streets or broad thoroughfares, only winding lanes whose course has been dictated by the accidents of landownership. Sometimes the building-blocks which they enclose are so large that there had to be blind alleys giving access to houses in the middle of the block. The streets were unpaved, with surfaces of trodden mud which in wet weather would make deep slush, and they were so narrow that no wheeled traffic along them was possible. Wheeled vehicles had of course long been familiar (incidentally, a model chariot was found in the quarter), but they must have been debarred from the city, where everything must have been carried by human porterage or on donkey-back, for which reason the masonry at street corners is nearly always carefully rounded so that passers-by should not graze themselves on sharp brickwork; for those who did not care to go on foot, donkeys or asses took the place of carriages, and accordingly we find against a house wall a low flight of brick steps which is clearly a mounting-block for the convenience of riders. Ur was, in fact, a typical Middle East town; its narrow winding lanes are the prototypes of those of old Baghdad, and in Aleppo no more than a century ago the sight of a wheeled cart or carriage in the streets was so rare as to draw a crowd. One difference was

The inner court of the Giparu, *looking towards the sanctuary; the brick base is that of Hammurabi's stela*

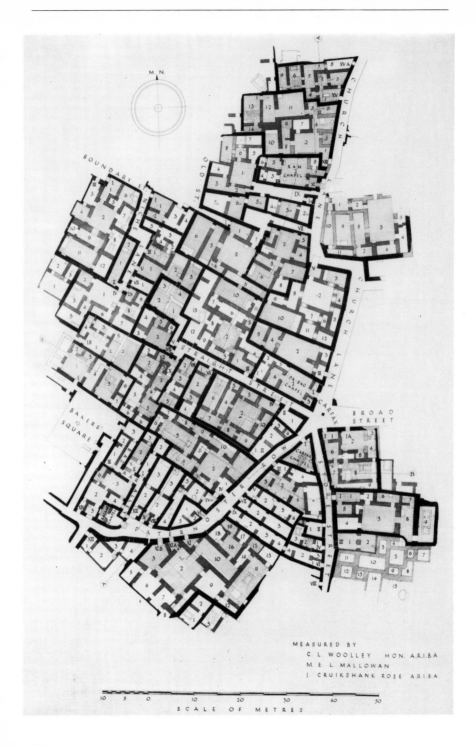

MEASURED BY
C. L. WOOLLEY   HON. A.R.I.B.A
M. E. L. MALLOWAN
J. CRUIKSHANK ROSE A.R.I.B.A

SCALE OF METRES

that there were no domestic drains emptying into the roadway and there running down an open channel, as in so many oriental towns today, but then as now the sweepings of the house floors and the contents of the rubbish-bins were simply flung into the streets and, since there was no system of municipal scavenging, remained there to be trodden under foot. The result was the gradual raising of the street level, a phenomenon common to all old towns, London being no exception, but at Ur the process was more than usually rapid. A new house would naturally be built rather above the level of the street, but the rise of the latter meant that in wet weather a stream of filth would invade the house, so that the only thing to do was to raise the threshold by adding a fresh course of bricks. This

LEFT *Plan of the A.H. House site in the Larsa period, early second millennium B.C. (cf. p.182) Woolley's Pasag chapel is now called Hendursag chapel*

RIGHT *Diorite statuette of a goddess with a goose, perhaps Gula or Bau, from the* Giparu

worked for the moment, but in time another course was needed, and then another; there was indeed no end to it. During the time that the houses fronting on Paternoster Row were inhabited, the street level rose more than 4 feet, and the threshold of No. 15, for example, had been gradually raised to match, so that entry was effected by a flight of six steps leading down to the original house floor. We found that the relation between house floor and street was a most useful factor for dating the building. It also explained the rebuilding of houses. The time came when with the raising of the threshold and the lintel remaining as it originally was there was not enough headroom to allow of entry at all; reconstruction became imperative. The method employed was to pull down the old walls to the level of the ceilings of the ground-floor rooms and rebuild on them, laying

the new ceiling-beams at the proper height above a new floor made flush with or above the existing street; constantly we found that if we pulled up the brick pavements of a house, the walls were seen to go down with no apparent change to a buried pavement 3 feet below, and perhaps to a third pavement lower still.

For the building of the houses both burnt brick and crude mud-brick were used. The front, facing on the street, was of burnt brick throughout —at any rate, to the height to which the walls were preserved, which is virtually that of the first-floor rooms; it may have been of mud-brick above that level. The interior walls were of burnt brick below and mud-brick above; the former might be no more than a damp-course three bricks high, or it might go up for 4 or 5 feet, this apparently depending on the wealth of the owner more than on any structural consideration; the mud-brick at any rate, and perhaps the entire wall, would be plastered and whitewashed. No house windows opened on the street, at least on the ground floor; if there were any upper windows (but the walls do not stand high enough to give evidence on this point), they would have been blocked with shutters of reed-work set in a wooden frame (we found such in a Kassite window) corresponding to the wooden lattices of the modern Arab house. Consequently the streets were uninteresting, shut in by continuous walls blank except for the doorways of the houses; occasionally there might be an open-fronted shop, but most shops were in the regular bazaars where narrow passages, probably sheltered by awnings, were bordered by little lock-up booths, the whole being provided with doors that were closed at night; the only example that we found is Bazaar Alley,[7] between Paternoster Row and Baker's Square, but this must have been typical.

No two houses are exactly alike; the builder had to accommodate his ground-plan to plots of very different sizes and often of irregular shape, but he always kept before him an ideal type approved by experience and suited to local conditions and approximated to it as closely as he could. The type is that of a house built round a central courtyard on to which all the rooms open. Three conditions seem to have dictated this form, namely the climate of southern Mesopotamia, the desire for domestic privacy which has always characterized the Middle East, and the custom of domestic slavery; we shall easily see to what extent these factors influenced the building.

LEFT ABOVE *A street in early second millennium B.C. Ur, peopled by Woolley's Arab workmen and their wives, carrying pottery vessels of the period*
LEFT BELOW *Steps down from the street into No. 15 Paternoster Row, one of the houses in early second millennium B.C. Ur*

A characteristic house of medium size such as No. 3 Gay Street will serve to illustrate them all so far as its arrangements go, though for detail I shall draw freely upon other houses. The front door was small and unpretentious and opened inwards, and you passed into a little brick-paved lobby having in one corner a drain over which would be set a jar of water so that you might wash your feet before going farther; the second door, leading to the house proper, was in a side-wall so that there might be no clear view in from the street; either you or the porter on duty would give warning so that the womenfolk might decently retire. Against the jambs of the second door there would be hung terracotta masks of the god Humbaba, a charm against the south-west wind which brings fever, and there was a step down in the doorway taking you into the central court. This was brick-paved, the pavement sloping slightly to the middle where was the intake of a drain that carried water away into the subsoil and all round it were the doors of the ground-floor rooms. The uses of all these rooms can be determined.

On the side of the court facing towards the front of the house a single doorway, wider than the rest, is that of the reception-room to which visitors were admitted. It is always a wide and shallow room with the door in one of the long sides, precisely like the modern Arab *liwan* or guest-room; in the daytime a 'runner' rug would be laid against the back wall for guests to sit on, and its width is such that at night mattresses could be laid across it for the guests to sleep in a row. In some of the richer houses such

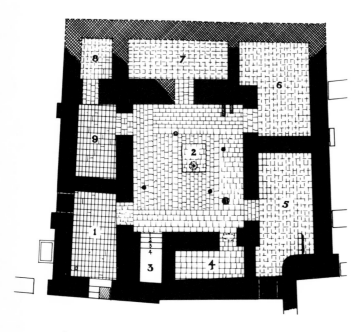

LEFT *Ground-plan of No. 3 Gay Street (cf. p.201)*

RIGHT *Cross-section of No. 3 Gay Street as restored by Woolley; the upper storey is conjectural*

198

as No. 3 Straight Street there is at one end of the guest-room a door into a brick-paved closet provided with a drain, the visitors' lavatory and wash-house, and at the other end a recess probably for the storage of bedding. Facing the guest-room there are two doors in the courtyard wall, one that of the household lavatory, a narrow chamber with a paved floor in which is just such a latrine opening as can be seen in any modern Arab house. The second door is that of the staircase. The stairs run over the lavatory; they start in the doorway, brick-built, and, because in order to secure head-room for the lavatory it was essential to have the maximum possible rise before the turn of the stairs, the bottom step is made too high to be practical and a movable step had to be placed in front of it—which again is precisely what one sees in the modern house, where the same arrangement holds good.

Of the remaining ground-floor rooms one (marked No. 5 in No. 3 Gay Street) was the kitchen, identified as such by its two fireplaces and by the querns found on its mud floor. One, having low brick benches for beds against the wall, was the slaves' sleeping-quarters; another was a general working-room in which might be found querns and store-jars.

It is clear that the ground-floor of the house was given over to the domestic staff and to visitors; the family proper lived upstairs.

This is an unexpected conclusion. Later Babylonian houses were of one storey only, so far as we know; the same is true of houses of the Sargonid

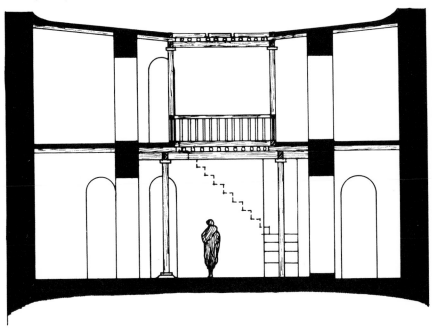

age excavated at Tell Asmar by the Oriental Institute of Chicago; it might therefore seem rash to assert that at Ur in the Larsa period the majority of the houses were on two floors. The existence of a staircase is not in itself a conclusive argument, for it might have led to a flat roof which could be used in fine weather for sitting-out and for sleeping; the Neo-Babylonian roofs were flat and doubtless were so used. But they had no staircases, and access to the roof must have been by wooden ladders (as is often the case today). At Ur there is a solidly built flight of stairs and it takes up the space of a room which could ill be spared when the ground-floor accommodation was so limited; the only justification for such a staircase is that it led to a part of the building not less important than the rooms on the ground-floor. The thickness of the walls is amply sufficient for them to rise to second-storey height, but as the ceilings were hardly calculated to support the weight of walls, the plan of an upper storey must have reproduced that of the ground-floor. There was no space for an internal passage and although all the rooms could be communicating, that is inconvenient, but somehow one must be able to get at the rooms.

The analogy between the ancient houses of Ur and the houses of the modern town Arabs has hitherto proved so close that one can fairly apply it further. In the modern house the stairs lead up to a wooden balcony that runs all round the court, and the doors of the upper rooms open on to that; we asked ourselves whether this could be true of the Larsa house. In No. 3 Gay Street we found, towards the south corner of the courtyard, a single brick bedded to the pavement with stiff clay, and round it were fragments of charred wood; in all likelihood the brick had served to jack up a post which had been cut too short for its purpose. Restoring posts in corresponding positions in the other corners we found that they were so arranged as not to obstruct any of the ground-floor doorways and would support a gallery 3 feet wide, which is just the width one would expect; incidentally, for the short post jacked up on a brick modern analogies would be innumerable.

I have perhaps gone into overmuch detail on one point to show on what sort of arguments we had to base our reconstruction; actually every point had to be argued out in the same way. In the end we could practically prove that the roof was not flat but sloped gently inwards, projecting beyond the walls so as to shelter the balcony, and having along its inner edge a raised coping through which at intervals gutters projected which would direct the rainwater into the drain in the middle of the courtyard; the central opening in the roof, not unduly large, provided all the light and air required. One fortunate discovery was that of a burnt-brick arch fallen

View of the remains of a house in early second millennium B.C. Ur, called No. 3 Gay Street by Woolley

almost complete in a doorway, proving a fresh architectural point. A rough brick compartment in one corner of the courtyard, a feature common to many houses, puzzled us until in one we found the fragments of huge clay pots; clearly, the day's water-supply brought from the public wells was stored here in the porous vessels that would keep it cool; and a very modern touch was given by the presence in one courtyard of flower-pots bedded with clay to the pavement round the central drain.

The picture that we have of a private house of the period is indeed remarkably complete so far as the actual structure goes; of furniture we naturally found nothing, but it would have been for the most part of a very simple nature. Folding chairs and tables are represented on seals and we know of chests of wood or wickerwork for storing clothes; many-coloured rugs would be laid on the floors and plenty of cushions; for light at night there were oil lamps, little saucers with a wick floating on the oil. Granted that the streets were narrow and dirty and that the house-fronts presented little of interest, yet when once one had crossed the threshold, things were very different. Such a house as I have described, with its paved court and neatly whitewashed walls, its own system of drainage, its ample accommodation of a dozen rooms or more, implies a standard of life of a really high· order. And these are the houses not of particularly wealthy people but, as the tablets found in them prove, of the middle class, shopkeepers, petty merchants, scribes, and so on whose fortunes and idiosyncracies we can sometimes trace quite vividly.

Among the buildings we excavated were a number which could, with tolerable certainty, be identified as shops. These always had a narrow frontage on the street but ran back to a considerable depth; in front was a very small room, behind it a long store-room which might be simple or might be divided up into compartments by cross-walls. In No. 14 Paternoster Row, when the private house which had occupied the site was turned into a cook-shop, a proper window was cut through the front wall with its sill about a metre above street level. The actual cooking was done in the front room, as in the modern Near Eastern cook-shop, where the kitchen is always open to view. The standard shop is a small booth whose whole front is taken up by a 'window' opening and a door, and behind it a magazine in which goods could be stored. The front of the booth would be closed by a wooden shutter—of which of course no trace would survive, and most of its interior would be taken up by a raised wooden bench serving at once as a counter and as a seat for the shopkeeper; a few shelves or pegs against the wall would complete the furniture. The owner of No. 9 Church Street had a whole range of magazines attached to his house, and it is difficult to explain these otherwise than as store-rooms for merchandise, though there is nothing here in the way of a shop.

In No. 1B Baker's Square the entire house had been remodelled and turned into a workshop and one old room served as a stoke-hole, and in another room and in the courtyard were kilns. Although a miniature set of

LEFT *and* RIGHT *Baked clay plaques of the early second millennium B.C. showing human figures and gods; note the elephant on the left-hand plaque and the monkey to the right*

metal tools were found in a grave under this building, the craft of the owner is not certainly established. It might have been metalworking, as was originally suggested, but the tools suggest other possibilities like leatherworking or even the shaping and decoration of pots. Perhaps the most interesting case of the remodelling of a private house to adapt it for another purpose is No. 1 Broad Street.

This was a house, larger than most, belonging to a certain Igmil-Sin, a scribe or priest. We were puzzled at first by various alterations that had been made in the building; the doorways of the ground-floor rooms opening on the court had been bricked up, thus isolating from the main living-quarters the court itself, the lavatory, and the guest-room, which was now entered by a door in its south end, the only means of communication between the two parts of the house; and in the north wall of the court a new doorway had been made giving directly on the street. The explanation was given by the tablets found in the building, nearly two thousand in all. Igmil-Sin was headmaster of a boys' school and had adapted his house accordingly; classes were held in the courtyard and guest-room while the remaining quarters were reserved for domestic use. Some hundreds of the tablets were of the regular 'school exercise' type, the flat sun-shaped tablets used for fair copies, etc.; there were very many religious texts probably used for dictation or for learning by heart, some historical texts, mathematical tablets, multiplication tables, all these belonging to the school, while a number of business tablets apparently referring to temple affairs showed the schoolmaster's standing.

In No. 1 Old Street structural alterations were due to quite another cause. This house, approached by a long narrow passage from Old Street proper, was an old building (its foundations went down very deep) originally of considerable size; but towards the end of the Larsa period the

doorways on the south-east side of the central court were bricked up and the rooms there were incorporated in the next-door house, No. 7 Church Lane. Here again the tablets came to our help. In the reign of Rim-Sin I of Larsa the house belonged to one Eanasir who was a merchant primarily engaged in the copper trade. Eanasir travelled regularly to Bahrein (*Dilmun*) in order to buy copper both on his own behalf, perhaps mainly as an agent of the palace, and for other dealers in Ur, who corresponded with him and at times rebuked him. He spent periods of time on the island and arranged for the shipment of the metal, which came from somewhere further up the Gulf, perhaps Oman, to Ur.

In a few cases the houses did not conform to the usual pattern. No. 11 Paternoster Row, owing to its size and complication, we called 'The Khan' (Inn), being unprepared for a private house with nineteen or more ground-floor rooms; but it must be admitted that the presence at the back of the building of a large shrine with many burials under it is against such an identification and this may have been merely the home of a citizen wealthier than others living in the quarter and may be no less typical of its class than are the more modest houses of theirs. The walls of this building were exceptionally thick and suggested that it rose to the height of a third storey. For contrast we had No. 1 Niche Lane, the meanest and shoddiest building in the area. While digging the site we got the impression that in Rim-Sin I's time (1822–1763 B.C.) this quarter of Ur was socially on the downgrade, with the result that what had been the best houses tended to be divided or to be turned to non-residential uses. We do not know how far a like tendency could be observed in other parts of the city, but it is probable that the fast-growing power of Babylon under Hammurabi's rule was curtailing the trade and undermining the prosperity of Ur.

Thus far I have described the domestic part of the Larsa period house, but there is another part of it which is even more interesting. In this period some people were buried inside the houses. In the sixty-nine houses which we cleared in the two areas 'EM' (17) and 'AH' (52) there were 209 burials, though they were by no means regularly distributed within the houses. Only twenty houses had brick-built burial vaults beneath them, sometimes one, sometimes two, and very occasionally as many as four. Some large town houses had no vaults, and some small houses had concentrations of them; nor is their placing consistent, for they appear under various parts of

RIGHT *Lyre from the 'Great Death-pit', with gold bull's head projecting from sounding-box (see p.76)*

the house. The standard vault may be briefly described. If you pull up the floor-bricks above such a tomb and dig down, you find yourself in front of the door of a brick-built vaulted tomb the roof of which is only 2 feet or so below the pavement. The door is blocked with rough brickwork and against it are two or three clay pots for food and drink; inside there may be as many as ten or a dozen bodies. It is a family vault, brought into use whenever an adult of the household dies; then the tomb was reopened, the bones of the last occupant somewhat unceremoniously shoved into a corner, and the newcomer laid in seemly fashion in the middle, only to be put aside in his turn when next a burial took place. Very often against the side of the vaulted chamber there are one or two more clay coffins containing single bodies; this, I imagine, was because two deaths had occurred in a short space of time and the opening of the chamber seemed inadvisable; for small children (and the rate of infant mortality was high) the chamber was never opened, but the body was put in a clay pot and buried below the floor.

Certain critical questions about these burial vaults remain open. Were they built as an integral part of the house or subsequently, as seems sometimes at least to have been the case? Were they perhaps in houses already deserted and no longer used for living in? Why are there remarkable variations (some houses with burials, some without, both large and small), if it was the custom now to bury below the house rather than in cemeteries away from inhabited areas? Does this conceal ethnic groups, religious beliefs, or social rank?

In many of the larger, more pretentious houses there was a room whose fittings suggest it may have been set aside as a household shrine. Against the back wall of such rooms there was a low bench of brickwork on which we sometimes found cups and small dishes *in situ*. Immediately above this there was in the back wall a square recess like the modern fireplace of a western house from which an open channel ran up the wall but ended before it reached the roof. In one corner was an 'altar' built of brick (usually mud-brick) and mud-plastered, the plaster elaborately moulded so as to give the effect of panelling. In one instance we found fixed to the pavement bitumen-holed sockets for fixing horizontal rods just above the floor. In some cases there was in the other corner a door leading to a tiny room in which we commonly found a large number of tablets; a depository

LEFT *Limestone statuette of a woman from a soldier's grave of the Early Dynastic III period (see p.94)*

Burial vault of the kind found in houses of the early second millennium B.C.

for the family archives. Although crudely modelled or moulded small baked clay plaques and figurines representing deities and apotropaic demons were found in some houses, they are by no means invariably within these shrines, whose identity is only vouched for by the panelled 'altars', known also from scenes of worship on seals and from some of the better-preserved Mesopotamian temples. As there is no regular association between these private shrines and the burial vaults in houses, there is no compelling evidence here for any cult of deceased kin, although we know of the existence of such cults in Babylonia from scattered documentary references. Most of this comes from the incantations used by exorcists in rituals for averting the harmful effects of ghosts on their living relatives and others. These private shrines might equally well have been for minor deities under whose special protection the household placed itself.

Another discovery important for our understanding of the religion of the Babylonians was that of the popular wayside shrines. Every now and then there would be opening off the street a doorway distinguished (sometimes if not always) by large terracotta reliefs attached to the door-jambs, replacing the modest Humbaba heads found in private houses. A few brick steps in the doorway led up into an open paved court which might be a court and nothing more, as in the cases of the Bazaar Chapel at the corner of Paternoster Row and the Carfax Chapel, or might be a more

The altar, offering-table, and incense-hearth(?) of a domestic shrine

elaborate affair with a walled-off sanctuary and subsidiary chambers as in the Ḥendursag Chapel and the Ram Chapel in Church Lane. A description of the Ḥendursag Chapel will serve for all.

Like the other chapels it was of a date late in the Larsa period. One came into the court not directly but through an entrance lobby; in the corner to the left what had been a mere recess had been turned into a closed cupboard in which we found numerous votive objects, a clay model of a chariot, model beds, a clay rattle, whetstones and rubbingstones, and more than thirty stone mace-heads, two of them inscribed with a dedication to Ḥendursag. Facing you as you came in was the sanctuary, its doorway, distinguished by jambs having bold reveals, flanked by two brick pedestals $2\frac{1}{2}$ feet high, one flat-topped, the other having in its top a rectangular bitumen-lined hollow, clearly meant for liquid offerings. Immediately in front of the sanctuary was a brick altar, its top covered with bitumen; by it was a clay cup, and other clay cups and the skull of a water-buffalo lay close by. Near the sanctuary door lay a rectangular limestone shaft $2\frac{1}{2}$ feet high having a cup-like hollow in its top and on each side crudely carved reliefs of birds and human figures—it is a libation-altar such as is shown in one of the scenes on the great stela of Ur-Nammu. Towards the east corner lay a (very ugly) limestone figure of a woman which seems to have been set on a wooden base; in the middle of the wood ash was a small bronze statuette of

The Hendursag chapel seen from the street, with statuettes of worshippers in situ

the goddess Lama. Its arms, probably in some other material, were missing. A few more clay pots, some large querns or mill-stones of black lava, and some stone pounders were found also in the court. The sanctuary had been closed by a door consisting of a wooden frame set with panels of reedwork. In the back wall, facing the door, was a niche of which the lower part was filled by a base of bricks, mud-plastered and whitewashed; on this stood the limestone figure of a woman worshipper. It was a small figure, not very well carved, and it had been broken in half in antiquity and roughly mended with bitumen; its feet were missing also, and it had therefore been embedded in the mud base so as to keep it upright in position; a poor thing artistically and never of much intrinsic value, it had nevertheless been respected, and the best had been done to make good the damage it had undergone. On the floor were found numerous small beads (the necklace of the goddess), various clay pots, including an incense-burner, and 64 inscribed tablets.

Statuette of a worshipper found in the Hendursag chapel

We have long been familiar with the character of the great temples of Sumerian and Babylonian cities. They were dedicated to the major gods, they were built by kings, and they were immensely wealthy, the city god himself being one of the chief landowners of the state. At the other end of the scale we now have the domestic altars. The wayside shrine is different from either of these. It may have started from private initiative, but serves a public end; it is dedicated not to any of the great gods nor to the patron god of a family but to one of those minor deities whom the Babylonians could count by the hundred. Hendursag for instance had as his function the protection of the silent street at night and of travellers in general; only if one were proposing an excursion would one have any need to invoke his aid, but in that particular juncture he would of course be invaluable and a prayer put up and an offering made in his shrine would be but a prudent measure of insurance. These minor gods were departmentalized powers, the need for whom was casual but real enough when it did arise; because they were minor they could be approached by the private suppliant, but they held no position such that the state was obliged to make provision for them; that their temples were founded and maintained by the piety of lesser citizens is proof of their importance in popular religious belief. There was nothing in life that did not come within the special province of one god or another—that is why there are so many gods—and the wise man or woman would invoke the appropriate deity for help whatever he or she proposed to do. The little bronze statue of the goddess Lama, who interceded for mortals with greater gods, was a very appropriate companion for the stone statue of a female suppliant found with it.

Our understanding of these little shrines may be extended by reference to Babylonian texts, where the word *ibratu* signifies a shrine outside the temple, in streets or private houses. An essential part of its furniture was a raised mud-brick structure upon which was set the *nēmedu*-altar. Such shrines appear to have been a particular resort of women, for one Sumerian proverb runs 'since my sister stays at the corner shrine and my mother is chatting at the river, I must die of hunger'. The special attraction of these shrines for women may have been their regular dedication to goddesses, for in Babylon the great goddess Ishtar possessed one hundred and eighty of them.

Our excavations in the residential quarters have given us a very detailed picture of the conditions of life at Ur in the Larsa period, but the excavated area was comparatively small and to get an idea of the town as a whole we must call for other evidence.

The ruin-mounds of Ur are very extensive, but even they do not represent the entire town, for quarters which were inhabited for a relatively short period did not form mounds at all, or mounds so low that they have been obliterated by the general rise in the level of the plain. Thus, we dug in the flat ground half a mile south-west of the Ziggurat and found Larsa houses there. A mile away to the north-east of the Temenos we found the so-called 'Treasure-house' of Siniddinam of Larsa, and to the east of this again there was a wide extent of low-lying land in which the houses of the same period are as densely built as those in the Paternoster Row area. The walled city of Ur—the 'Old Town'—formed not more than one-sixth of

'Greater Ur' as the latter is defined by our trial digs; but beyond the closely built-up area stretched more open suburbs—thus, we could distinguish traces of more or less scattered buildings right up as far as the temple of al-'Ubaid, which is 4 miles away, and there were small satellite towns within 5 or 6 miles of Ur (we tested several of these) which themselves can have been little more than suburbs of the capital city. If we assume that our excavated area is fairly representative of the 'Old Town' as a whole so far as density of population is concerned, then the 'Old Town', excluding the Temenos, would easily have contained 4250 houses; allowing eight persons to a house, which is a moderate figure for a country where large families were held desirable, concubinage was freely practised, and slavery was the rule, we arrive at a total for the walled city of 34,000 souls. At that rate the population of Ur must have exceeded a quarter of a million and may have been twice that; it was indeed a great city.

It is obvious that all those people could not have made a living by agriculture. Ur was a trading and manufacturing centre and its business extended far afield, as is shown by the tablets found in the houses of its merchants. Raw materials were imported, sometimes from overseas, to be worked up in the Ur factories; the bill of lading of a merchant ship which came up the canal from the Gulf to discharge its cargo on the wharves of Ur details gold, copper ore, hard woods, ivory, pearls, and precious stones. It is true that the sceptre had passed away from Ur, but neither Isin nor Larsa could be commercial rivals for this city with its old traditions of trade and its key position with navigable waterways keeping it in touch with the sea; the Ur of Rim-Sin I's time was actually larger and probably more prosperous than it had been in the days of Ur-Nammu.

Further Reading

The archaeological remains of this period were published in *Ur Excavations VII: The Old Babylonian Period* (1976); the texts relating to trading activity at this time were discussed in A. Leo Oppenheim, 'The Seafaring Merchants of Ur', *Journal of the American Oriental Society* 74 (1954), pp.6–17; and W.F. Leemans, *Foreign Trade in the Old Babylonian Period as revealed by texts from southern Mesopotamia* (Brill, Leiden, 1960). The history and function of the *Giparu* building have been treated by Penelope N. Weadock, 'The *Giparu* at Ur', *Iraq* 37 (1975), pp.101–28.

The Kassite
and Assyrian Periods
c. 1600–600 B.C.

The eleventh year of the reign of Samsuiluna of Babylon, son of the great Hammurabi, the year 1740/1739 B.C. according to our reckoning, was officially named 'the year in which [King Samsuiluna], at the command of Anu and Enlil, destroyed the walls of Ur and Uruk'. The ruins bear eloquent testimony to the thoroughness of that destruction. The fortifications were dismantled—this indeed one might expect; every temple that we found had been plundered, cast down, and burned; every house had been consumed with fire; the whole of the great city ceased to exist. In the houses it often happened that where walls were not left standing very high, we could note lying over the tops of them horizontal strata of dust and sand and ashes, sure proof that for some length of time the ruins had been undisturbed, long enough for the gradual processes of wind and rain to fill in the hollows and thereafter start the ordered burial of the dead town. Of course people did come back to what had been their home, but they had neither the morale nor the means to rebuild it. Where the house walls were still standing fairly high, they would squat in the ruins, patching the broken walls with old bricks, stamping a new mud floor over the wreckage that filled the old rooms, but would content themselves with the one storey which meant less work and less material; we never find in Kassite houses those staircases which had characterized the houses of the Larsa age. Even the later Kassite houses which were not mere adaptations of old ruins but independent foundations set up when Ur was comparatively prosperous were on one floor only; the ground-plan might be traditional, with the central court and rooms opening off it, but so far as we could tell (admittedly, the number of such houses dug by us was limited, and to generalize from them is perhaps dangerous) the two-storey building had passed out of fashion.

Of course too there had to be temples; whatever happened, the gods must have somewhere to live. One might have supposed that the problem would be solved easily enough, for the land at least was still there and the gods were the great landowners, so that in the hardest times there ought to be revenues sufficient for a good building programme. But this seems not to have been the case at all. Whether or not it was that Babylon laid hands on all incomings, Marduk as conqueror appropriating the wealth of Nanna, at any rate Nanna's priests could not meet the charge. The *Giparu*, the residence of the High-Priestess of Nanna, was the only one that gave us concrete evidence of attempts to make good the damage done by the Babylonian troops, and there it is only too clear that the means of the restorers were straitened to the last degree; their building is the poorest patchwork, there are no dedication-stamps on the bricks and old material is freely employed. In the temples we found no traces of such work, Kurigalzu I's brickwork being laid directly on that of Larsa; where the old ground-plan was so faithfully followed, one imagines that there must have been a building standing above-ground to serve as a guide, something more than mere tradition as to the temple's form: I think that there was something, but something of such poor quality that when proper reconstruction was in view, the first step was to sweep away the shoddy walls which had been all that impoverished piety had been able to set up.

Samsuiluna utterly laid waste the city of Ur, but the effects of his victory went far beyond this. I have constantly, and especially in the last chapter, had to refer to the tablets found by us in the course of the excavations; there were thousands and thousands of them. Down to the time of Samsuiluna these documents, letters, contracts, accounts, and what-not are written in the Sumerian language, the language of the people of Ur. After that date the tablets are in the Akkadian language. Even under the kings of Larsa the old native speech, it is clear, was being hard pressed by that of the Semitic North and the businessman of Ur might profit by being bilingual; but after the downfall of Ur the supremacy of the North was complete. The linguistic transfer was a complex process occurring in stages over many years. Not surprisingly it was texts from palace chancelleries, law codes, and royal inscriptions, which first appeared in Akkadian, whilst some texts were provided with interlinear Akkadian translations. The Sumerian language was only retained for religious purposes, much as Latin was long preserved for the services of the Roman Catholic Church, but it was a dead language. Outside the temples nobody used it at all, and even the priests had to learn what had been the natural tongue of their kinsmen a few generations before, and they did not learn it very well; even when they were copying an old text, they might be guilty of the veriest schoolboy 'howlers'. The old expression for universal dominion, 'King of Sumer and Akkad', was now an anachronism, for Sumer had ceased to exist. We cannot be surprised that the stragglers who returned to the ruins of Ur and even the later generations who built themselves houses more or less on the old model on the mounds that hid the forgotten tombs of the Third Dynasty kings had not the heart, even if they had the means, to repair its ancient monuments. Certainly the gods had to be housed—mere prudence insisted on that insurance policy; but there could be no idea of reviving the glories of a past with which every link had been broken.

The First Dynasty of Babylon petered out ingloriously. Samsuiluna himself had been hard put to it to control raids and settlements on the central Euphrates by a people called the Kassites. His successors found their dominions filched from them, by the 'kings of the Sealands' in the south, by the Kassites in the north and north-west, but in time the latter established themselves as sole rulers and heirs of the Babylonian empire. The early Kassite period is a blank page in the history of Mesopotamia; politically the kings were insignificant, the arts stagnated, no great buildings gave lustre to the names of the rulers, and no records were kept of their uneventful rule. Thus it is that at Ur for the space of nearly 250 years the rather squalid houses of its private citizens are the only evidence that excavation could produce to show that the city was in existence at all.

And then, about 1400 B.C., we have a complete change. There arose a Kassite king, Kurigalzu I, who was an impassioned builder. Ur is full of his monuments, and he was no less active in the other southern cities which had so long been neglected by the central government. It is always interesting to speculate why a ruler should suddenly strike out a new line for himself, and Kurigalzu must have had his reasons. Perhaps it was that Assyria, a vassal state of Babylon, was beginning to show signs of independence, that to the north-west the Mitanni had grown to be a formidable power, and that, in the heart of Asia Minor, the Hittites had built up a state which had already interfered in Syria and was evidently prepared to back its political intrigues by physical force without regard to distance. With storm-clouds gathering in the west and north the Kassite king may have felt that to consolidate the south in his interest was the course of wisdom; the easiest and the traditional method of ingratiating himself with the subject cities was to espouse the cause of their gods, and the rebuilding of temples would appeal both to the people and to the gods themselves. I imagine that Kurigalzu's motive was more political than strictly religious, but in any case he did embark on a very ambitious building programme. In its execution quality had to be sacrificed to quantity. It is true that Kurigalzu worked for the most part in burnt brick, which is more than his successors did, for mud-brick is the standard material of the Late Babylonian builders; but he could very seldom afford bitumen mortar, plain mud taking its place; and whereas in the Third Dynasty temples the brick courses are carefully laid right through the wall's thickness, the Kassite walls, which have so solid a look, generally consist of two skins of properly laid bricks enclosing a core of brick rubble and mud; the broken bricks for the filling are taken from the old buildings which were being repaired, and any unbroken old bricks were used in the face of the wall, so that one can see there bricks of different ages and different sizes indiscriminately mixed. In spite of this, however, much of Kurigalzu's work survives in better condition than that of any former age.

Naturally the king's first care must have been the restoration of the central shrine of the Moon-god. Of the Ziggurat itself we can say no more than that, for the remodelling of the building in the Late Babylonian time involved the sweeping-away of everything subsequent to Ur-Nammu and his son Shulgi; but in the surrounding buildings the hand of Kurigalzu is much in evidence.

The revetment which the Larsa kings had added to Ur-Nammu's buttressed wall upholding the Ziggurat terrace had fallen away in ruins; this was now refaced with specially moulded bricks reproducing the half-columns and niches of Warad-Sin's gateway tower. When we excavated the terrace edge, we found Kurigalzu's wall and at first supposed that our job was done; then in places where the wall-face had fallen away exposing the packing of brick rubble behind it, we found that the latter hid an older but similar burnt-brick wall which was of Larsa date; and finally, where this too had perished, we could see behind it Ur-Nammu's mud-brick terrace wall studded with his clay cones of dedication; it was a curious case of vertical stratification.

Not only the retaining-wall of the terrace but also the whole circuit of the chambered wall above was rebuilt, and so too was the whole of the great courtyard of Nanna lying below the terrace, with its surrounding magazines and its monumental gateway; this was done following the old lines, but no attempt was made to reproduce on the external walls the elaborate decoration of attached half-columns which had distinguished the Larsa work. None the less, the solid double buttresses which relieved the plain stretch of the walls must have been quite as imposing as the rather fussy effect of the columns; certainly this was the impression we got when, clearing the façade of the great court, we found Kurigalzu's square-buttresses wall actually resting on the older columned wall which served it as a foundation; the contrast was all in favour of the later work.

Kurigalzu was primarily a restorer, as he is always at pains to state, and his brick-inscriptions record that 'he has renewed for Nanna *Egishnugal*, his beloved house' (which is the whole Ziggurat enclosure) or, as a gate-socket says more explicitly, '*Egishnugal*, the temple that from days of old had been in ruin he built and restored to its place', but the reconstruction was on such a scale that he could fairly claim—as he does on another door-socket which we found here—that he 'had built *Egishnugal*'. At least three inscribed bricks from its vicinity mention that he rebuilt the dilapidated temple of Ningal on its old foundation. Except for one wall of the outer court we recovered the whole plan of this temple, a small and compact building unlike any other at Ur; judging by the thickness of its walls and the arrangement of its rooms it had a central dome surrounded by barrel vaults, an architectural design curiously like what we find in early Arab times; the suggested reconstruction on page 221 is not at all what we should have expected to find in Mesopotamia of the fourteenth century B.C. The axis of the shrine was at right-angles to that of the building as a whole, the sanctuary being on the north-west side of the central chamber; in a niche in the back wall was a brick altar or statue-base embedded between the bricks of which we found fragments of gold foil, a little silver vase, vases of glazed frit and of variegated glass, objects put here according to some ritual of dedication. For the service of the Ningal temple a new gateway was made through the double enclosing wall of *Egishnugal*, an imposing entrance surmounted by a gate-tower; a smaller and simpler gate, approached by a flight of steps, about 40 yards away to the east, led straight on to the open terrace, taking the place of that which once had passed through *Dublamakh*, 'the Great Gate'.

Kurigalzu's reconstruction of *Dublamakh*, the ancient building which had been built long ago, was most striking.

When we first came to Ur, one of the most prominent features of the site was a little mound not far from the east corner of the Ziggurat which we could identify as one which had been excavated by Taylor, the British consul at Basra, when he dug here for the British Museum seventy years before. He reported having found in it a small two-roomed building of burnt brick with arched doorways, which he had taken to be a house of late date; the walls stood so high that his workmen had roofed the place with mats and used it as a shelter. We cleared away the drift sand which had filled the two rooms and then proceeded to lay bare the outer face. Of the brick arches over the two side-doors noted by Taylor one had since fallen, but the other was intact, and the bricks of the door-jambs and of the walls, good burnt bricks set (exceptionally) in bitumen mortar, had stamped on them the dedication-inscription of Kurigalzu, which Taylor of course could not read; it was not a late building but one of the fourteenth century before Christ. For us at the time the outstanding feature was the arch, by nearly a thousand years the oldest arch standing complete above-ground; since then we have found, in the Royal Cemetery, other arches a thousand years and more older than this, but in the winter of 1924 we could hail our discovery as one which revolutionized the history of architecture.

The little building, whose walls were relieved by the T-shaped vertical grooving which in time we learnt to recognize as the peculiarity of a temple, was surrounded by a brick pavement. Following this outwards we came to its edge, formed by a fresh wall, also having the T-shaped grooves, which went down for some 5 feet and ended at another brick pavement; it was the containing-wall of a platform or pedestal which jutted out from the high level of the Ziggurat terrace and it was on this platform that Kurigalzu's building stood, high above what proved to be a great paved court in front of it. As the floor of one of the two rooms had been destroyed by Taylor's workmen, we dug down through it and immediately below what had been floor level found that the character of the wall-bricks changed and they bore the stamps not of the Kassite king but of the Isin king Ishme-Dagan; deeper down still were one or two courses of bricks stamped with the name of Amar-Sin, of whom we found also one of the inscribed door-sockets. What had happened is accurately described by Kurigalzu on his bricks: '*Dublamakh*, the ancient building which had been built long ago and had grown old, I built on the four sides, I restored to its place, I made good its foundations'. The old temple was in such parlous state that even the lower courses of its walls would not have stood up to the weight of a new building erected on them—but, piety demanded that the new building should be founded on the old. Kurigalzu therefore built a new wall round the temple and filled the space between them with solid mud and rubble packing, laying over this a pavement flush with the floor of the Ziggurat terrace; he filled up the inside of the temple likewise, to the same level, and trimmed down the old walls to a course or two below the pavement; thus solidly encased they would serve perfectly well as foundation for his new work, and since the 'Great Gate' had long ceased to be a gateway at all, the fact that it was now raised up on a pedestal did not matter.

Scattered about in the rubbish at the foot of *Dublamakh* we found a number of Kassite bricks with patterns moulded in relief; most of them had parallel zig-zag lines, others high embossed motifs of which we could not make any sense at all. The explanation came from another site. At Uruk, the ancient Erech, the German excavators found a Kassite building the façade of which was decorated with life-size figures of deities, standing out in high relief from the wall face, built of specially moulded bricks; they stood in a row, holding vases from which came streams of water represented by just such zig-zag bands as we found at Ur. We unearthed only a few fragments whereas the Uruk reliefs could be rebuilt in their entirety, but the identity of the two discoveries could not be questioned; somewhere in the immediate neighbourhood of *Dublamakh* Kurigalzu set up a building adorned in this striking and apparently original manner. The moulded bricks did not belong to *Dublamakh* itself; of this we could be sure, for Kurigalzu's walls were still standing 8 feet high and showed no signs of ornamental reliefs; possibly they came from the façade of a small temple adjoining it on the east which was a new foundation dating from the Kassite time and so badly ruined that nothing could be said about its appearance—at least, there was nothing to disprove any theory regarding its decoration that one might care to put forward. What had happened was this. Up to the end of the Larsa period there had been an open space between the ancient temple *Enunmakh* and the wall of the Ziggurat terrace; Kurigalzu repaired *Enunmakh* and for the most part followed faithfully the original plan, but he pulled down the south-west wall and extended the building right up to the terrace wall, the new wing forming an attached but possibly separate shrine. The addition did alter the look of the façade, which now continued beyond the old south corner so as to include the gateway of the new shrine and beyond that, to abut on the side-wall of *Dublamakh*; along the façade ran a broad road—a 'Sacred Way'—spanned by two double gateways, which led through a third gateway into the great courtyard in front of *Dublamakh*. The greater part of the lay-out had been decided by the Larsa kings and was followed by Kurigalzu, but whereas the Larsa work had been systematically destroyed, the Kassite remained in fairly good condition; it was possible to recover not only the ground-plan but, to a considerable extent, the elevation of the buildings in this area, as shown on page 222. The brick-paved courtyard, with magazines round three of its sides and in its south corner what may have been an office building, was not merely a temple court but served as a continuation of the Sacred Way that ran past *Enunmakh*. In its west corner a gateway through the Ziggurat terrace wall gave access by means of a flight of brick steps to *Etemennigur*, the terrace itself, and a second gateway in the south-west wall gave on a broad passage running right through to the wall of the Temenos; on either side of the passage were gate-towers, that on the right leading into Kurigalzu's temple of Ningal on the Ziggurat terrace, that on the left to his version of the *Giparu* of Ningal. The *Giparu* built by the Larsa priestess Enanatuma had been so ruthlessly laid waste by the Babylonians that its repair was out of the question; tradition preserved the memory of what had stood there, but the shapeless heap of ruins must have daunted even so conscientious a restorer as Kurigalzu, and the building which he erected on the site had very little in common with the old. Even the outlines were not the same: the Kassite building is rather longer and much

Ground-plan and restored elevations of the Temple of Ningal built by Kurigalzu

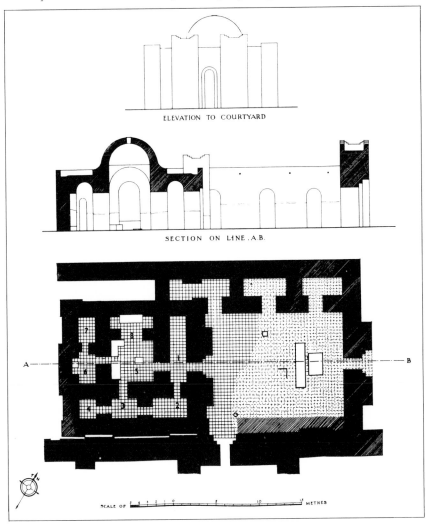

ELEVATION TO COURTYARD

SECTION ON LINE.A.B.

A —————————————————— B

SCALE OF ⊢⊢⊢⊢⊢ 0 ——— 5 ——— 10 ——— METRES

Restoration of the courtyard of Kassite Dublamakh

narrower than that of Larsa; it has none of the massive fortress-like appearance that Enanatuma gave it, and it contains one temple only instead of two. The whole of the south-east end of the block is given over to somewhat flimsy buildings in mud-brick which perhaps served as living-quarters for the priests; there had been such in the Larsa temple, as we know from the tombs beneath the pavements of the living-rooms, but now they cover a much larger area and are quite differently planned. It was perhaps because he suppressed the second shrine in the *Giparu* that Kurigalzu built on the Ziggurat terrace the temple of Ningal which I have described above (p.218); the fact that the doorways of the two buildings face each other across the Sacred Way would seem to associate the two shrines almost as closely as when they were under the same roof.

Indefatigable builder as Kurigalzu was—and there are few monuments at Ur that do not show signs of his handiwork—either he cared little for the arts other than architecture or else there were no other arts for him to patronize. Judging by what remains, the Kassite period was one in which artistic production had sunk to the lowest level and nothing that we have found gives evidence of any imagination or originality. The one example of stone carving is a 'boundary stone', typical of Kassite times, an oval-topped stela bearing a long inscription which is really the title-deed of a landed estate giving the owner's name, the definition of the boundaries and the stereotyped curses on whosoever should remove his neighbour's landmark; at the top are carved in relief the symbols of those gods who in the text are called upon to protect the landowner's rights.

We excavated many Kassite tombs, built like those of the Larsa age underneath the houses wherein the family lived, but not one of them yielded any object of note; undecorated clay pots, generally of coarse and clumsy make, and the few purely personal things that decency would leave upon the body—a string of beads, a copper finger-ring, or a pin fastening the shroud, these and nothing else constituted the grave furnishings. So far as the evidence goes, it was not the wealth of the people of Ur that was responsible for the rebuilding of the old temples; on the contrary, the rebuilding seems to have been the only thing that averted the complete decay of the city. Whether or not it fulfilled the king's political purpose it did enable the chief monuments of Ur to survive yet another long period of neglect.

The Kassite rulers who succeeded Kurigalzu I were not interested in the buildings of what must now have counted as a second-rate provincial city, and there is a long gap in our records. It is true that Nabonidus states that in the course of his work on *Dublamakh* he discovered the foundation-inscriptions of Nebuchadnezzar I (1125–1104 B.C), and presumably the statement is correct, but our excavations produced nothing to corroborate it. Marduknadinahhe (1099–1082 B.C.) certainly did repair *Enunmakh*, for we found his inscribed door-sockets in position in the ruins and a copper cylinder discovered by us, also *in situ*, in the foundations of Nanna's temple kitchen on the north-west side of the Ziggurat terrace bears his name. Adadaplaiddina (1068–1047 B.C.) calls himself 'the Nourisher of Ur' and claims to have 'renewed *Egishnugal*', but a patch of brick pavement against the north-east face of the Ziggurat and a second patch in the great courtyard below are all that today bear witness to the truth of his boast. There was then in the twelfth and eleventh centuries B.C. a certain revival of royal interest in the wellbeing of Ur, although so far as material remains go, the part played by the late Kassite rulers and their immediate successors was not a very important one. Ur was now primarily a cult city, with royal interest concentrated on its age-old shrines.

Documentary sources offer no better guide to the fortunes of Ur over a period of something like 350 years from the later eleventh century B.C. Archaeological remains of the same period are as elusive. In this time in southern Babylonia peoples known to history as the Chaldaeans and Aramaeans emerged as major political forces. The city of Ur retained some vestiges of independence within the territory of the Chaldaean tribe of Bit-Jakin. This was the period when it might most appropriately have been known as 'Ur of the Chaldees'. Like so many cities of this region in the late eighth and earlier seventh centuries B.C. its inhabitants were divided in their loyalties as Assyria strove to control it.

By the earlier seventh century the governorship of Ur seems to have been a hereditary position; it had been held by one Ningaliddin in the reign of the Assyrian king Esarhaddon (680–669 B.C), and his son Sinbalassuiqbi succeeded him in office, perhaps before the end of the same reign, though most of his tenure fell under Ashurbanipal, king of Assyria (668–627 B.C.). Sinbalassuiqbi evidently found the monuments of his city in a parlous state and, being an unusually active person, he embarked on a comprehensive scheme of restoration. It is interesting to note that of the many foundation-inscriptions of his that we found only two say that the work was done 'for the breath of life of Ashurbanipal, King of kings, his King'; in all other cases the governor gives his own name and title and the name of his father, implying that the building was carried out by him on his own initiative and, presumably, at his own expense without the aid of any subvention from the central government; he seems to have enjoyed a large measure of independence. And how necessary the work was is clear enough.

> The great walls of *Etemennigur* [the Ziggurat terrace] and its platform were in ruin since long ago, its foundation was buried. I sought for the place of its destroyed gates, I built the retaining wall of its platform, I raised its superstructure. A door of boxwood, best wood from distant mountains, which was planted on a bronze shoe—its battens were strong, its prop was of gold, its bolt of clear silver—I set with silver, that the gate of the oracle chamber built in the house of divination might stand for ever.

So he boasts in the inscription of a door-socket which we found in position in *Dublamakh*, the actual socket that had served his door of boxwood and precious metal. The stone itself was really fine, a bright green stone like felspar capable of taking a high polish; but it had cost the governor little, for it was only the upper half of an old 'boundary-stone' which had been cut down and re-used. The door, of course, had disappeared, and it may have been as splendid as Sinbalassuiqbi describes it; but every building of his that we could identify was shoddily constructed in mud-brick; undoubtedly he was doing his best, but his work was in sad contrast to that of the earlier kings.

Dublamakh was restored, but also enlarged, new chambers being added on either side of the old two-roomed shrine. The fact illustrates the condition of the long-neglected monuments, for these new rooms extend beyond the high pedestal on which Kurigalzu's *Dublamakh* stood. In the

Kurigalzu's shrine of Dublamakh *as excavated*

course of the centuries that had elapsed the open courtyard in front of the Great Gate had been so filled with gradually accumulated rubbish that the 5-foot pedestal was buried and the new ground-level was flush with the shrine's pavement, and it was on this flat ground that Sinbalassuiqbi built his new wings. He built, as I have said, in mud-brick, but he copied faithfully the grooved walls of Kurigalzu's shrine (which was still standing, apparently to its full height), gave a coat of mud plaster to new and old work alike, and whitewashed it all over; the effect must have been excellent, even if obtained cheaply.

'I built the retaining-wall of the platform [of *Etemennigur*]', declares the governor, and here too our discoveries attest the truth of his claim. On the south-west side of the Great Court of Nanna, where it backs on the Ziggurat terrace, the Assyrian work is quite well preserved. He raised the level of the courtyard, which was deeply buried in rubbish, and laid down a mud floor; the wall was rebuilt in mud-brick, but again the elaborate half-column decoration first introduced by the Larsa king a thousand years before was reproduced. We found it standing 4 or 5 feet high with the whitewash still fairly fresh upon it, and a clay foundation-cone discovered under the floor of the northern gateway confirmed the authorship.

The terrace wall must have been rebuilt, as Sinbalassuiqbi says it was, all round the *Etemennigur* platform, but nothing of it remained. On the north-west side of the Ziggurat, in the tangle of walls of every period which made the site so complicated, we did find patches of a brick pavement which he had laid down over the top of the ruined walls of the Larsa and Kassite kings, but the wall itself had been swept away by the builders of the Temenos wall of Nebuchadnezzar and even its position was uncertain. The same was true of the south-west side of the Ziggurat; we found no trace of Assyrian work there. But on the terrace, in the area lying south-east of the Ziggurat, Sinbalassuiqbi was much in evidence. Here Kurigalzu had built a special temple for Ningal, the Moon-goddess, but it was in ruins and apparently so deeply buried in rubbish that the governor, departing from his usual practice of clinging to precedent, merely cleared the outer face of the containing-wall of Kurigalzu, levelled the rubbish inside it so as to make a solid platform 4 or 5 feet high, and on the top of that proceeded to build an entirely new temple on up-to-date lines.

An entrance at the north-west end, now destroyed, led into a paved outer court with small shrines or service-chambers on either side and in the north corner a brick-lined well with a well-house above it. Facing the entrance was a lofty pylon gateway flanked by two smaller doors which gave access to side-chambers; the pylon doorway opened on the fore-hall or Holy Place and corresponding to it in the back wall was the door of the sanctuary; the latter was at a higher level, approached by a flight of steps filling the door passage, and on this raised platform a rectangular screen of burnt brickwork formed the tabernacle in which stood the statue of the goddess.

The temple as we found it had been restored by Nabonidus, but without any serious change of plan; only an inch or two below his floors we found the Assyrian pavement of bricks stamped with the name of Sinbalassuiqbi. These gave little more than his name, but a fuller text occurred on the clay foundation-cones; we found thirteen of these still in position, set upright, bedded in a little bitumen, in holes beneath the walls and floor of the sanctuary.

> For Ningal the Queen of *Egishnugal*, divine Lady of the crown, beloved of Ur, his Lady, Sinbalassuiqbi, governor of Ur, has built anew the temple of the beloved bride of Sin [i.e., Nanna]. A statue after the likeness of Ningal he made and into the temple of the 'Wise God' he brought it. In *Enun*, a dwelling built for her lordliness, she made her abode.

Again, however, one must admit that the actual work did not come up to the governor's description. Not only were the walls of mud-brick only, but the quality was so bad that the individual bricks could not be distinguished; they were so soft and crumbling that a stroke of the finger would produce a deep rut in the wall's surface, and in most cases the walls could be planned only by the edges of the (fortunately well-preserved) pavements laid against them; Sinbalassuiqbi's brickwork was, without exception, the worst that we encountered at Ur. Even the hinge-socket stones of the doors were all old ones re-used, bearing the names of kings of the Third Dynasty of Ur, and though this may have been due to piety, it was certainly economical. Perhaps the most interesting part of the building was the well. Only the upper part of it was the work of the Assyrian governor—it had originally been made by Ur-Nammu and repaired by later kings—but there the bricks bearing his name, instead of being all alike, showed no less than eight different texts, dedications of chapels or statue-bases to eight different minor gods; the side-chambers of Ningal's temple may have housed these subordinate deities who formed her court, but since the well served them all, the governor was at pains to insert in its lining written witness to the presence of each. The little collection of texts gave us a very distinct picture of the catholicity of worship in a single temple.

The foundation-cones of Sinbalassuiqbi are the latest in date that we found at Ur and represent the final development of an ancient custom. From very early times such cones had been employed, and always with a certain change of fashion. Let into the sloping face of the mud-brick wall which held up the terrace of Ur-Nammu's Ziggurat we had found quantities of nail-like cones, the inscribed shaft buried in the brickwork and only the rounded heads at regular intervals making a sort of pattern on the wall-face—and even they may have been hidden by a coat of mud plaster. Where one of the Larsa kings had built out from the same terrace a fort and postern-gate, we found his cones not in the wall-face but buried in its core, arranged in neat rows behind the burnt-brick skin of the gate-tower; and these cones were much larger than Ur-Nammu's, and instead of the small nail-like head had a broad flat disc of clay on which the inscription of the stem was repeated. The Assyrian cones had no base at all and were placed under the floor instead of in the walls; in the following age barrel-shaped cylinders take the place of cones, and these are immured in the angles of the building.

In every case the inscription is hidden from sight, and it would seem that the intention of the king is not to parade his achievements before his fellow-men, but to keep the record of his piety fresh in the mind of the god, who presumably can see through a brick wall; and probably there was, if not originally, at least as time went on, a second purpose. Everyone knew that the temple which the king built 'for his life' could not last for ever, but that its crumbling walls would one day have to be restored by another; if that later ruler discovered in the ruins the record of the first founder, he would in all likelihood respect it and even perpetuate it in his own inscriptions, and so his new building would acquire merit for the old king. This is what actually happened in a land where the continuity of tradition was so prized. In the very latest times, when Nabonidus repaired the Ziggurat he was careful to give full credit for its founding to Ur-Nammu and his son, and he has left on record the delight that he felt when deep in the foundations of an ancient temple which he was repairing he unearthed the foundation-tablet of Naram-Sin, son of Sargon of Akkad, and looked upon that 'which for three thousand years no human eye had seen'.

We cannot accept Nabonidus's date for his revered predecessor, for he is about a thousand years out in his reckoning, Sargon having reigned about 2330 B.C., but we can sympathize with his archaeological enthusiasm. We had found plenty of Ur-Nammu cones scattered loose in the soil, but when for the first time we pulled one out from the mud-brick wall and saw on its stem the writing which had been deliberately hidden there more than four thousand years before, we experienced quite a different sensation, and though the cones of the Assyrian governor were set merely in the soil below the pavement, not bedded in brickwork, it was with a certain hesitation that we lifted them from the spot where the builders had placed them.

As we dug away the remains of Sinbalassuiqbi's temple, we found evidence again of the piety which respects an ancient record. Lying together close to the foundations were four tablets, two of copper and two of stone, inscribed with the dedication of a building by Kurigalzu. They must have been found in the course of some work of demolition, perhaps of a temple which was not to be rebuilt on the old model or on the old site.

Magical clay figurines from below the floors of seventh-century B.C. buildings

Useless now and of no intrinsic value, they had been given careful reburial in the temple precincts with the idea, so it seems to me, that they might still bear witness before the gods to the merits of the dead king of Babylon, enduring after his works had perished.

Possibly the same spirit of piety may account for our finding below the temple floors a stone foundation-tablet bearing an inscription of Gudea, who was governor of Lagash in the twenty-second century B.C., part of a stela with a dedication to Ningal by Ur-Nammu when he was still a vassal ruler and had not started his successful revolt against his overlord, and the head of a small statue of a priest finely carved in diorite which dates from about the same time. Such things had been consecrated as temple furnishings, and when they in the course of time were broken or simply outmoded and had to be discarded from the temple treasury, there was still a natural reluctance to treat them merely as rubbish; it is not uncommon to find buried somewhere in the temple precincts a hoard of objects that had once adorned or been used in the building. A discovery like that is a stroke of luck for the archaeologist, but it is apt to be misleading; one is tempted to assume that if the temple is accurately dated, the objects, in that they belonged to it, should be of the same date. But this does not follow at all, rather, it is the reverse of the truth. Just as in a modern cathedral you may be shown treasures representing every period in the lifetime of the building, so the Babylonian temple was a store-house of treasures handed down from a remote past and the offerings made by the faithful would not be lightly cast aside. The excavator who finds a temple hoard must make allowances for such piety and assume that the objects may be very much older than the temple.

Under one of the floors we found a small copper figure of a dog. This is something quite different; it is a contemporary object set here as a charm to protect the building. Another discovery that we made illustrated the custom. Sinbalassuiqbi, amongst his other works, rebuilt the ancient *Giparu*, or at least set up a building of his own on the site of the completely ruined *Giparu* of Kurigalzu; as usual, he employed mud-bricks of lamentable quality and the walls had for the most part vanished altogether, so that only by the edges of the burnt-brick pavements, where those survived, could we work out even bits of the ground-plan; it was difficult to decide where any one room began and ended. But when we had done our best and started to pull up the floors, we found further evidence which confirmed our rather theoretical sketch. Along every wall there was a row of brick boxes placed immediately below the pavement so that a pavement brick formed the lid of each box; the box was made of three bricks set on end, the fourth side, that facing inwards on the room, being left open, a sort of sentry-box; in each was a figure of unbaked clay which had been cast in a mould and then dipped in a bath of thick white lime on which such details as the features and the folds of garments were later painted in black with occasional touches of red. The work was extremely rough and the figures, impregnated with salts from the soil, were flaked and split in every direction, some of them in such bad condition that it was impossible to preserve them; but they were interesting none the less. There were snakes and dogs and griffins, human figures and figures of men with the heads of lions or of bulls, with bulls' legs or fishes' bodies, every kind of well-disposed demon that might guard your house or keep off sickness and ill-luck; and with each there were a few calcined grains of barley and fragments of bones of small animals or birds. Cuneiform texts tell us about these figures and the ceremonies of their instalment with prayers and magic formulae; now for the first time we had found them in position with concrete evidence of the little sacrifice that was solemnized when the guardians took their place in the sentry-boxes below the floor. And there was another point. The boxes were made of plano-convex bricks, the old bun-shaped bricks which had gone out of use more than a millennium and a half before. They must have been dug up from the older ruin-strata of the city and because of their antiquity were credited with some peculiar magic power that would increase the efficacy of the protecting demons. We shall see further examples of the archaeological spirit that prevailed in the latter days of Babylon, but undoubtedly it was reinforced by a pathetic super-stition that looked back across the uncounted ages to the fabulous begin-nings of things when men and gods were scarcely to be distinguished and 'there were giants in the land in those days'.

A baked clay drum-shaped object with copies of the inscriptions on bricks of Amar-Sin found when Sinbalassuiqbi was searching for the ancient ground-plan of Egishnugal. *This was found in a Neo-Babylonian building by Woolley, who called it a 'Museum label'*

Further Reading

The excavations of this period were published in *Ur Excavations* VIII: *The Kassite Period and the Period of the Assyrian Kings* (1965). J.A. Brinkman wrote an important review article of this volume from the historical point of view in *Orientalia* 38 (1969), pp.310–48; see also his earlier 'Ur: 721–605 B.C.' in *Orientalia* 34 (1965), pp.241–8. Two fundamental general studies, also by J.A. Brinkman, include the evidence from Ur: *Materials and Studies for Kassite History* I (Chicago, 1976); *A Political History of Post-Kassite Babylonia 1158–722 B.C.* (Rome, 1968).

Woolley and his wife cleaning and recording graves, surrounded by their Arab workmen

Nebuchadnezzar II
and the Last Days of Ur
c. 600–300 B.C.

In the earlier sixth century B.C. Babylon was by far the greatest walled city that the world has ever known, and Nebuchadnezzar had built it. He swept away all the works of his predecessors and set up in their place his enormous buildings; the modern excavators were hard put to it to find, under the deeply sunk foundations of the uppermost level, anything that was older than Nebuchadnezzar. And his activities were not confined to the capital; at Ur also he embarked on an ambitious programme which seems to have aimed at the reconstruction of the entire city.

I think it probable that his work at Ur was begun only towards the end of his life. Naturally Babylon had to be considered first, and he would hardly have started operations in the provincial cities until good progress at least had been made in the capital—and for the rebuilding of Babylon many years of labour were required; most people would consider that his reign of forty-three years (604–562 B.C.) was none too long for the task. What is certain is this; that while of his three short-lived successors there is at Ur no record, when Nabonidus came to the throne just over six years after Nebuchadnezzar's death, there was still a vast amount of building to be done there, which would not have been the case had Nebuchadnezzar completed his programme; indeed, we know that Nabonidus (555–539 B.C.) was sometimes finishing what Nebuchadnezzar had begun. It was not always easy, or possible, to assign a particular piece of building to the one king or the other, and really it matters little; what is of interest is to know what Ur was like in the sixth century after the two monarchs had done their work. The question is even more complicated because Nebuchadnezzar, as his complete rebuilding of Babylon shows, was an individualist and an innovator and even in matters of religion was quite ready to strike out a line of his own, as will be made clear hereafter. Nabonidus, on the other hand, was an antiquary and a traditionalist who prided himself upon restoring an ancient building exactly according to its original plan, 'not a finger's breadth beyond or behind', as he says himself; and he might well disapprove of and correct unorthodox changes made by his predecessor. Thus, in the case of the Ziggurat, Nebuchadnezzar claims to have built '*Egishnugal*, the temple of Sin [=Nanna] in Ur', and that would necessarily include the principal monument of the Sacred Area; we know that he rebuilt the great courtyard, and built (perhaps for the first time) two shrines occupying the angles between the three great staircases that led to the top of the Ziggurat; it is incredible that he should have done no work on the Ziggurat itself, but actually not a brick of his has been found on it. It is possible, though scarcely likely, that he left the restoration of the Ziggurat to the last and had not the time to carry it out; it is more probable that he did, or started to do, something that Nabonidus thought all wrong and so removed bodily; the study of the remains make it clear to my mind that he did not simply attempt to reproduce the original Ziggurat of Ur-Nammu (and that would have been out of keeping with his character), but it yields no evidence at all of what he did do. But of the Neo-Babylonian Ziggurat so much is left that we can picture it in very fair detail.

The Ziggurat of Nabonidus restored

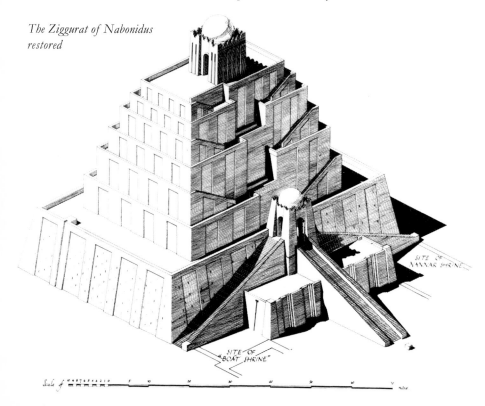

SITE OF NANNAR SHRINE

SITE OF "BOAT SHRINE"

Scale of

Nabonidus found that the lowest stage of the ancient tower was remarkably well preserved. Today, when another two and a half millennia have passed, Ur-Nammu's walls of burnt brick and bitumen still defy the effects of time; then, all that the Babylonian king had to do was to relay the treads of the triple staircase, repair the coping wall, and rebuild the domed archway at the head of the stairs. But above this everything was in hopeless ruin; whether or not he had to clear away a superstructure devised by Nebuchadnezzar as well as any remains of work done by other late builders such as Sinbalassuiqbi, he could not follow his favourite practice of restoration 'to a finger's breadth' because there was nothing to guide him. It is true that we by careful digging were able to recover the plan and character of the Third Dynasty Ziggurat, but the methods of modern science were not those of an ancient king in a hurry; he dug down in a corner of the first platform and discovered in the brickwork there (we found the hole he made, neatly filled in with his own bricks), as he tells us with great satisfaction, the foundation-tablet recording the original building of the tower, begun by Ur-Nammu and finished by his son Shulgi, but there was nothing to show him what the tower had been like. All that Nabonidus could do was to preserve and use the lowest stage, treating it as a base for a Ziggurat of his own construction. In the course of centuries fashions, even for ziggurats, had changed; Nabonidus followed the fashion and the Ziggurat which he set up was entirely different from that which he proposed to restore.

Instead of three stages the Neo-Babylonian Ziggurat had seven. Viewed from the front the effect was dramatic in the extreme. From ground-level the three ancient stairways led up to the domed gate-tower at the top of the lowest stage; above that towered up six more stages, diminishing in size as they went up, with what looked like a spiral staircase encircling the building and leading from one stage to another and so to the topmost platform whereon stood the little shrine of Nanna, a small square building of bright blue-glazed bricks surmounted by a golden dome. So seen, the building corresponds very closely with the description given by the Greek historian Herodotus of the Ziggurat at Babylon, and it may be that, like that, our Ziggurat was painted throughout, each stage a different colour, answering to the colours of the planets; certainly the lowest stage was painted black, for some of the bitumenous coating is preserved, and the blue-glazed bricks of Nanna's shrine littered the site.

The visual appearance did not altogether correspond to constructional fact. Had the staircase really gone round the building in an uninterrupted spiral, bricks and mortar would never have supported the weight of so stupendous a pile;[8] actually the steps were confined to the front of the building. Fortunately, terribly ruined as the Ziggurat was, there yet remained enough of Nabonidus's work to show us its nature. When you had mounted one of the three main staircases and had passed through the arched gate on to the first terrace, there was on your right a little brick-built flight of steps leaned up against the wall of the second stage; the steps ran only as far as the corner of the tower and from that point a level gallery took you right round the tower to the centre of its façade where there was just such a shallow recess as Herodotus mentions in his description of the Babylonian Ziggurat. Then you made a left-about turn to mount a second little flight of steps, this time leading up to the left, and so round the building on the flat to where, on the façade, a third flight running to the right took you up to the gallery forming the fourth stage; then round the building again to another 'sitting-out' recess, and so on. The total height of the 'Mountain of God' on which stood Nanna's Holy of Holies was just over 160 feet. What we found was the brick pavement of the lowest stage, showing that Nabonidus made this uniform throughout, obliterating the stepped form of Ur-Nammu's first stage, so that at either end the Neo-Babylonian floor was nearly 10 feet above the old, and on the whole conformed his second stage to that of the original; but here, on the façade, we found the first little flight of steps virtually intact and, on the left-hand side, what at first seemed an anomalous feature, the front wall of the second stage (which, like the containing-wall of the little staircase, was relieved by the same sort of shallow buttresses as Ur-Nammu had used in the lower stage) stepped forward actually beyond the line of the staircase wall. Above this, everything had vanished. The problem of reconstruction bothered us for quite a while, but at length we realized that if we planned the third stage exactly on the lines of the second, but in reverse, and the fourth in the same way with its steps on the right-hand side, as in the second stage, and so on for seven stages, we not only could explain all the features of ground-plan that survived, but we had an absolutely symmetrical building, of a reasonable height, and one to which Herodotus's description of the contemporary Ziggurat at Babylon would very aptly apply. This cannot be coincidence, and I think that we can fairly claim to have recovered the likeness of Nabonidus's 'Ziggurat of *Egishnugal*, which I have made anew and restored to its place'.

Nebuchadnezzar's main work at Ur was the building of the Temenos wall. There had been a Temenos wall in the time of the Third Dynasty, but this had long since fallen into decay and nowhere did we find any evidence of its having been restored by later kings. Nebuchadnezzar, so far as we can

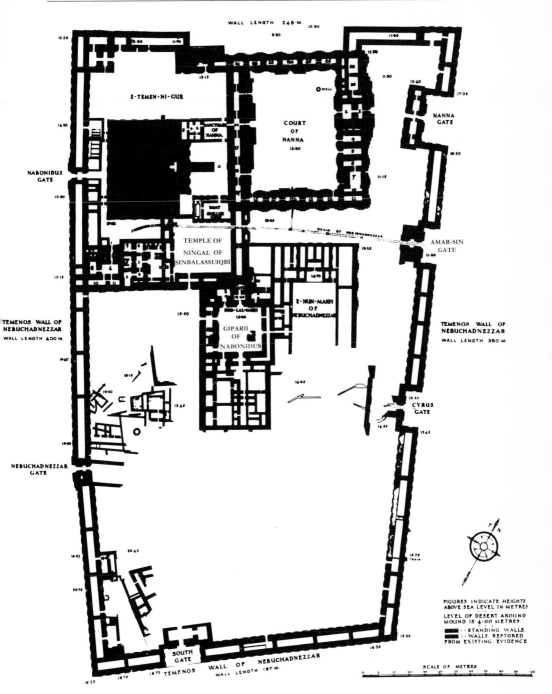

The Temenos of Ur in the Neo-Babylonian period, earlier sixth century B.C.

tell, found a Sacred Area, dedicated to the Moon-god, which consisted of religious foundations of all sorts grouped together and in theory forming a unity, but the unity was ill-defined; sometimes the outer walls of adjacent temples were continuous, sometimes the buildings were more loosely disposed, and it would seem that in fact the Sacred Area in many places merged imperceptibly into the lay quarters of the town. Nebuchadnezzar reformed all this. A space 400 yards long and 200 yards wide was marked out, a rough rectangle which enclosed all the important buildings of Nanna's enclave, and round this was built a wall of mud-brick. It was a double wall with chambers in the middle of it, the flat roofs of which would make a broad passage along the wall-top available for the manoeuvring of troops in its defence; it was 33 feet wide and probably about 30 feet high, the face of it was decorated with the double vertical grooves which were traditional for the external walls of temples, and it was pierced by six fortified gateways; the main gate, having a high tower set back in a deep recess, led directly to the entrance of the Great Courtyard in front of the Ziggurat.

Parts of this great Temenos wall are well preserved and stand 6 feet high and more, and in other parts where it ran over high ground and was therefore more exposed, it was difficult to trace it. We have not dug it right out all the way round—that would teach us no more than we know and would only mean the total destruction of the mud-brick by rain and wind—but having excavated carefully certain sections, we traced the rest by means of shallow trenches which revealed only the upper courses, and so were able to complete the entire circuit of the Temenos in eight days. Sometimes in the course of tracing we were temporarily baffled by unexpected changes in direction, and it is indeed difficult to explain the minor irregularities in the line taken by the wall. In places, where the back of an old temple projected outside the area pegged out, it has been ruthlessly cut away, and the wall of enclosure makes the new back wall of the building; elsewhere the line is deflected as if to enclose some monument which had to be respected, but as only too often the denudation of the surface has resulted in the complete disappearance of the monument, we cannot accept the explanation as certain.

Possibly there was a simpler reason. Examination of the wall proves that it was built by various gangs of workmen each having his own section, and

RIGHT *Ostrich shell cut to form a cup, decorated with mosaic inlays, reconstructed from fragments found in the 'Royal Cemetery'*

the collaboration between them was not very good in that the foundations of adjoining sections are laid at different levels and the projecting footings are not continuous; the irregularities of line may be due to faulty methods.

But the Temenos wall was an imposing structure, and with its completion the Sacred Area took on a new character; it was much more a place set apart than it had been in the past. But the proper privacy of the Moon-god could have been secured by something much less extravagant than this enormous line of brickwork, and the wall must have been planned also as a work of military defence. Indeed, in the east corner of the Temenos there was an immensely solid square structure which cannot be regarded as anything other than a fortress-tower; it could hardly have served any religious purpose. In girdling Nanna's Sacred Area with a work of defence such as might be built round the palace of an earthly king the Babylonian monarch was certainly reviving a very ancient conception of the god as Ruler of the city and its leader in war whose house would be the final rallying-point for resistance against an enemy; his innovations were sometimes tied up with a curious respect for tradition.

I have said that he rebuilt the Great Courtyard of Nanna. He followed pretty faithfully the lines of Sinbalassuiqbi, the last worker on the site, but made one important change. The court had always been at a low level, so that in its south-west doorway a flight of steps led up to the Ziggurat terrace; Nebuchadnezzar raised the level so that the pavement of his court was flush with the terrace and the whole building became an extension of that terrace, *Etemennigur*, to which it had formerly been subordinate. When we dug down here, we were astonished and at first very much puzzled to find, a little way below Nebuchadnezzar's paving tiles and above those of Sinbalassuiqbi, a thick layer of soil containing masses of broken sherds of the painted pottery of the al-'Ubaid period.

Usually when a builder raised the floor-level of a building it was because the old floor had been buried by rubbish accumulated in the course of years; he might throw down the upper part of the ruined walls and lay his floor-tiles over the top of the levelled rubble. But the al-'Ubaid sherds could not have drifted in, nor could they have fallen from above; it was evident that Nebuchadnezzar was raising his floor-level not as making the best of existing conditions but on a deliberately thought-out plan, and he had imported soil expressly for the purpose.

LEFT ABOVE *Part of the mosaic frieze from the Temple at Tell al-'Ubaid (see p.108)*
LEFT BELOW *Gold cup from the grave of Queen Puabi (see pp.64ff)*

In one case then, Nebuchadnezzar could be piously conservative, but in others he was very much of an innovator. A striking instance of this was given by his treatment of the ancient temple *Enunmakh*.

This happened to be the first building excavated by us at Ur. A low hillock rising close to the Ziggurat mound seemed to promise good results, and a trench driven into its flank at once produced walls of burnt brick enclosing paved chambers. It was a small square five-roomed building; the door led into an antechamber, against the back wall of which, facing the entrance, was a brick base for a statue, and four doors, two in the back wall and one at either end, gave access to the other rooms which ran back the depth of the building. The two inner rooms were an exact pair; each had a bench near the door and was divided into two parts by a screen; in the farther part there was a brick altar against the wall and in front of it a brick table; obviously each was a shrine for religious services. The outer rooms were also a pair, but here there were no particular features to show their use. The duplicating of the arrangements in the temple was explained by the inscriptions on the bricks: it was the common shrine of Nanna and his consort Ningal, and in it each deity had his or her special sanctuary.

In front of the building stretched a brick pavement half enclosed by two projecting wings which had been added in mud-brick to the original square of the shrine; immediately in front of the door stood an oblong brick altar for offerings, and to one side remains of a second and larger altar from which a covered drain led right across in front of the temple door. This could only mean that the altar was that for blood offerings—the victim would be sacrificed on the altar and its blood, passing in front of the shrine, would come directly before the god, just as would the other offerings placed on the central altar. On the line of the frontage of the mud-brick wings of the building there was a step down and the pavement, at a lower level, broadened out and ran on as that of a large open court.

The bricks of the pavement bore no stamp of authorship, but their size and character proved them to be Persian, belonging to the very latest date in the history of Ur, and as the gate in the Temenos wall close by had been restored by Cyrus the Great, we can probably attribute to him the last reconstruction of the temple also. It was interesting to observe that the position of the building and the details of its arrangement agreed almost exactly with the description which Herodotus gives of the great temple at Babylon in Persian times, but subsequent discoveries were to prove more interesting still.

It was clear that though the floors were Persian, the walls of the shrine were very much older; in the outer court there was an earlier pavement visible where the new had been broken through, and the same might be true of the chambers also. The order was given to test this by pulling up twelve bricks in one of the sanctuaries and digging down beneath them. Our Arabs, who were new to the work, and had always been told that on no account must they disturb any brick that was in place, could not understand this sudden sacrilege, and when they found the order was serious, jumped to the conclusion that we were looking for buried gold, nor would they believe me when I said that what we wanted was a second brick pavement. I went off, leaving the men at work, but within a few minutes one of them came running to fetch me. 'We have found the gold!' he said, and sure enough just below the paving-slabs there was a whole treasure of gold beads and ear-rings and pendants and one gold pin topped with a little figure of a woman wearing a long dress. The interesting thing about it (which in our inexperience we could not recognize at the time, but came to see it later) was that the little cache, perhaps a votive deposit rather than a hoard hidden for safety, contained objects of many dates; some of them were of Neo-Babylonian or Persian manufacture, but some of the beads were of types characteristic of times as remote as the reign of Sargon of Akkad; it illustrated well the fact that in temple treasuries things of value might be preserved not only for hundreds but for thousands of years. The discovery was as unexpected as it was interesting and, coming in the early days of our work at Ur, established our reputation. Nothing of the kind was found anywhere else in the room or in the other rooms of the temple, and nothing would convince the Arabs that we had chosen to lift those twelve bricks without knowing what lay beneath them.

Fortunately, the second pavement was there as well as the gold, and about one in every four of its bricks bore the long stamp of Nebuchad-nezzar, and this lower floor reproduced in every particular that of the Persian period: there were the same benches, altars, and tables, and in the court outside the same altar in front of the door; only the second altar and the drain were missing, but the level between the wings of the building dropped as before to the wide outer court which reached to the temple walls.

The outer court was in bad condition, much of the pavement gone, and what remained curiously irregular, all in ridges and hollows. The reason for this was obvious from the outset and was proved as the work was carried down deeper: it had been laid over a series of chambers, and where the floor rested on the wall-tops it kept its level and where it had beneath it only the rubbish with which the old rooms were filled it had sunk or broken up altogether. These buried rooms were the store-chambers of the

Enunmakh of Kurigalzu's time, built by the Kassite king exactly on the lines laid down by his Larsa and Third Dynasty predecessors; all those early rulers (whose work has already been described in my former chapters) had preserved the original ground-plan unchanged. According to that plan the small five-chambered sanctuary was a thing apart; it lay at the back of the building and was reached only by a passage which ran round three of its

Part of a hoard of gold jewellery found under the Persian, but above the Nebuchadnezzar, pavement in room 5 of Enunmakh

sides; on the other side of the passage there were store-rooms and priests' chambers occupying the whole of the rest of the temple area and completely masking the sanctuary—it was hidden away and made as difficult of access as might be. Only the priests would enter here and in privacy wait upon the twin deities.

This ancient tradition was completely set at naught by Nebuchadnezzar, when he restored the temple; a comparison of the plans on pp.141 and 237 will make this evident.

The sanctuary itself, the small separate block with its five chambers, was preserved, but all the magazines in front of it were swept away. On either side of the sanctuary new wings were built, projecting so as to form three sides of a square, but the whole front of the original shrine was opened up; where the passage had been there was a raised pavement in the centre of which an altar rose, a statue-base was erected in the antechamber of the sanctuary facing its door, and where had been a maze of chambers the wide lower court afforded accommodation for a crowd of spectators. In the old temple everything had been secret; now a numerous public could watch the priest making his offerings on the open-air altar and behind him could see through the dim sanctuary's open door the image of the god.

It seems fairly certain that some of the innovations made by Nebuchad-nezzar were disapproved of by his more orthodox successor Nabonidus—possibly the unpopularity of the later king was in part due to his reversing a religious policy which had found favour with the priests, but did not accord with the ancient traditions which Nabonidus so sincerely reverenced. This would account for the rebuilding by Nabonidus of temples which had been 'restored' so recently that they could not have required any further work unless indeed it was to correct what had been in his opinion wrongly done; it also accounts for the difficulty which we sometimes experienced in attributing a building to one rather than to the other king when the names of both appeared on its bricks. The 'Harbour Temple' was a case in point.

To the east of the harbour basin at the north end of the city there was a low mound, much disturbed by modern seekers after treasure, on which were lying bricks stamped with the name of Nabonidus; many were loose, but some were still in position, patches of pavement belonging to a building of which no walls were visible. Obviously if the pavement lay at modern ground-level, there could not be much of the building left, but reckoning that the foundations of the walls must remain below-ground and would give us the plan of the structure, we started to trench the area and the brickwork duly appeared. To our great surprise, however, it was the brickwork not of a few foundation-courses but of walls which went ever deeper down until at last we found their footings 21 feet below the modern surface. The excavation was the simplest job possible, for all that was required was to clear out the mass of perfectly pure sand that filled the building; when it was done, we had what at first sight seemed to be a normal Babylonian temple so well preserved that we spread a matting roof over it, from wall to wall (not merely for effect, but to protect it from drifting sand), and one could walk about in it forgetting the centuries. It was a mud-brick building, but the external walls were faced with a 3-foot skin of burnt brick. The entrance was from doors at either end of a passage on the south-west side and so into a forecourt at the south-east end in which stood a brick altar or 'table of offerings' and two more 'tables of offerings' flanked the great doorway leading to the inner court. Here again was a central altar of brick and a table of offerings; beyond was the sanctuary with two more tables and, against a niche in the back wall, the massive brick base on which the statue of the god would be set. The burnt bricks of the outer walls and of tables and altars bore the stamp of Nebuchadnezzar, so that the authorship seemed to be undoubted; the plan was quite conventional, the walls, smoothly mud-plastered and white-washed (the whitewash was wonderfully well preserved), presented no difficulty at first except that one might perhaps have expected a somewhat more ambitious decoration for the temple sanctuary. But there was a great deal that did call for explanation. Those whitewashed walls had no founda-tions at all; they rested on the sand, and the whitewash went down to cover the bottom course. There was no pavement or floor, only the sand which we left on the level of the walls' base. The filling had shown no stratifi-cation, it was all uniform clean sand, right up to the pavement laid by Nabonidus 20 feet above our 'floor'. But the strangest thing concerned the furnishings; the altar, the tables, and the statue-base were built up to the height usual for such (the tables 18 inches, the altar 3 feet) with bricks carefully and truly laid; but above this there was more brickwork very irregularly laid rising to the full height of the surrounding walls; thus the table in the outer court, which was of the normal long and narrow shape, took on the effect of a brick screen and the altar in the inner court became a brick column; no one could have placed offerings or done sacrifice on them. Clearly an explanation was called for.

Towards the end of the third millennium B.C. Ur-Bau, governor of Lagash, describes his building of a temple:

He dug a foundation pit [?] to a depth of x cubits; he heaped up the earth from it like stone and purified it with fire [?] like precious metal. As with a measuring vessel he brought it to the broad place. He put the earth back and filled in the foundations with it. On it he built a substructure ten cubits high, and on this he built 'The House of Fifty Gleaming Anzu Birds', thirty cubits high.

The builder of our Harbour Temple began by digging a deep rectangular pit, in the bottom of which he laid out the ground-plan of the temple, and accordingly he built walls to the height of just over 20 feet; these were neatly plastered and whitewashed. In the temple he built in burnt brick the proper tables of offering, altar, and statue-base, fixed doors in the door-ways, and put on a temporary roof perhaps, like ours, of poles and matting—we found high up in the walls holes for brackets that would have supported the roof framework. Undoubtedly there was a service of con-secration in the building, with the god's statue set on its base. After that,

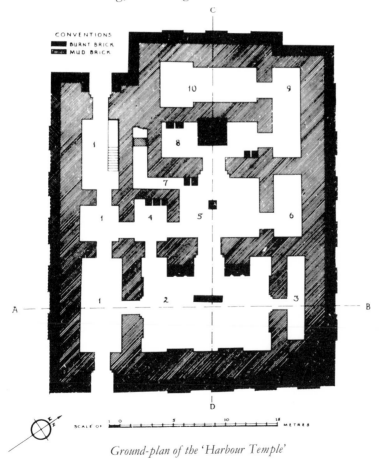

Ground-plan of the 'Harbour Temple'

247

the roof was taken off and the whole building was filled with sand; the old earth that had been dug out could not be purified, considering the mixed nature of the soil here inside the city walls, but clean sand would be a perfectly good substitute. As the sand was poured in from above, workmen laid bricks on the altar and tables, keeping pace with the rise of the sand (the fact that they were working from above would account for the irregular bricklaying) until, when the whole was filled, there could be seen only as it were a ground-plan formed by the tops of the walls and of the temple furnishings, flush with the smooth sand surface. Then there began a new phase. The sand was topped with a pavement of burnt bricks, on the top of the walls, now become a foundation, new walls were built (to the height of 60 feet, if the ancient precedent was faithfully observed) and new tables and altar, built above-ground, rested on the bricks piled above the old. This was the temple in which man worshipped his god and did sacrifice; it derived its peculiar sanctity from the fact that it not only was a replica of but was based directly on the real house of god, inaccessible to man; the altar on which the priest made his sacrifice was holy because it was one with the altar of that hidden and inviolate shrine.

It was tempting to assume that Nabonidus, with his antiquarian tastes, was responsible for the whole building and had merely, for economy's sake, used old bricks of Nebuchadnezzar for the underground part, but even if Nebuchadnezzar was the original builder, Nabonidus had chosen to set his personal seal on the work when he took it over, as he did, for purposes of his own; he may simply have laid a new pavement of bricks bearing his name in a temple already standing, but the temple was now to serve a new function.

From the entrance-door at the north-west end of the temple passage a brick causeway ran northwards to the wall of a huge building (its maximum measures were about 325 feet by 300) in which paving bricks were found bearing the statement that Nabonidus built the *Giparu*. The construction throughout was in mud-brick. The irregular outline seems to have been due to the existence of other buildings to the east which followed the orientation of the old city wall, whereas the main axis of the new building was to be directly north by south; the sides therefore are not parallel. The enclosing wall is, on three sides, relieved by the shallow rectangular buttresses traditional in Sumerian architecture; but the east side (and a short section of the south side also) present a feature which, so far as we know, is purely Late Babylonian; the bricks are laid not parallel to the general direction of the wall but at a slight angle with it and whenever the brick face projects sufficiently beyond the wall-line (the projection is usually about a foot), the brickwork is stepped back to that line and thence is built out again to a fresh projection; the result is a series of stepped 'buttresses' like the teeth of a saw. This very curious form of decoration—for it must be decorative only, since it serves no practical purpose, whereas the vertical bands of light and shade do most effectively relieve the dullness of an otherwise blank wall—is commonly found in the houses of Nebuchadnezzar's Babylon and also in the Late Babylonian houses of Ur. Inside the enclosing wall but separated from it by a broad passage lies the building proper, this too having two of its walls buttressed in the normal way and two with the saw-tooth type of decoration. There were two entrances to the enclosure. At the north end there was a postern-gate flanked by large magazines; under its pavement we found eight brick 'sentry-boxes' containing the painted mud figures of the protective gods and five mud dog guardians. The main entrance was in the south wall, and this gave directly on the doorway of the inner building which lay back at the far side of a large open court and had against one of its jambs a big bitumen-lined tank for the domestic water-supply. At first sight this inner building with its criss-cross of walls dividing it into sixty-four rooms looked like a meaningless labyrinth; but in reality it is a well-ordered residential complex. The rooms are ranged round light-wells (Nos. 5, 13, 42, and 54 on the plan); the principal residence is to the south, where room 13 is its light-well and opening on to it on the south is a reception-room (14) whose unusually solid walls suggest that it rose to a great height; the other blocks are evidently subordinate to this, but they are similarly arranged though on a smaller scale. Exactly similar arrangements are found in the secular buildings of Babylon (see p.250).

Clearly this is a secular building, but none the less it is intimately associated with the Harbour Temple. Not only are the two close to one another, but south of the building there stretched a great square courtyard enclosed by walls and having a pylon gateway on its south side which included the Harbour Temple also; the latter therefore becomes an appendage of the great residence. But what is the significance of the inscribed bricks referring to *Giparu* (traditional dwelling of the High-Priestess of Ur on the Temenos) found here? Did Nabonidus move this off the Temenos for his daughter into the much larger residential palace we had excavated? Or were the inscribed bricks just left-overs from the reconstruction of the traditional *Giparu*, gratuitously used in this palace which had been designed, not for the High-Priestess, but either for a governor of Ur or for the king himself, for its plan is comparable to that of the Southern Palace at Babylon?

Ground-plan of the Neo-Babylonian palace, near the 'North Harbour', built by King Nabonidus

SCALE OF METRES

Another inscription suggests that the second alternative is the most likely. In describing the dedication of his daughter as High-Priestess of Nanna, Nabonidus remarks that 'At that time [as for the *Giparu*] . . . wild date-seedlings and fruit [-trees] of the orchards grew out of its midst. I cut down the trees and removed the loose earth of its ruins; I discovered the building and ascertained its foundation-terrace; inscriptions of ancient earlier kings I discovered within it'. Of this clearance and reconstruction we found nothing but the eroded ruins of Neo-Babylonian buildings on the traditional site of the *Giparu*. However, Nabonidus further recorded that 'along the side of [*Giparu*] the house of Ennigaldi-Nanna, my daughter, *entu*-Priestess of Sin [Nanna] I built new'. It seems very likely that by this he meant the Neo-Babylonian building complex we excavated to the north-east of the old *Giparu* that had formed the south-east extension of the *Dublamakh* shrine.

This shrine was preserved very much as it had been in Assyrian times, but the courtyard buildings were remodelled and enlarged; one part was clearly residential, other rooms seemed to be offices for the conduct of temple business. Here we found quantities of clay tablets, receipts and vouchers for the issue of goods stored in the temple magazines, inventories, accounts; one large tablet covered with script in vertical columns was a month's record of a factory room in the temple where women were employed in cloth-weaving; the individual names are listed, the amount of raw wool dealt out to each at the beginning of the month, notes of attendance, issues of rations in lieu of wages—bread and cheese and butter, etc.—and the weight and quality of the cloth produced at the month's end; a balance-sheet of a very up-to-date sort. But another discovery threw yet more light on the character of the king's daughter. In a very much ruined room whose mud-brick walls rose scarcely above pavement level, one of the rooms fronting on the court which we had taken to be the business offices of the temple, we found a number of clay tablets of what are called the 'school exercise' type; they are flat discs of clay used for the teaching of writing. On one side the master inscribed his 'fair copy', some easy sentence often taken from a well-known text, and the tablet was then handed to the scholar, who, after studying it, turned it over and on the back tried to reproduce what he had read; sometimes the copy is very faulty and sometimes the boy has made a second attempt on the same tablet. We found a number of these, and with them broken fragments of other 'school' texts, bits of syllabaries giving columns of words all beginning with the same syllable, much like an old-fashioned English spelling-book, and one fragment of a dictionary on which was an endorsement 'the property of the boys' class'. Here was definite proof that the priestesses kept a school on their premises.

And a still more up-to-date touch was given by the contents of the next room. The pavement was very close to the modern surface, which was terribly denuded by weather, and not more than a foot of loose rubbish covered the brickwork; there seemed little hope of finding anything in such a spot. But suddenly the workmen brought to light a large oval-topped black stone whose top was covered with carvings in relief and its sides with inscriptions; it was a boundary-stone described above (p.222) belonging to the Kassite period of about 1400 B.C. Almost touching it was a fragment of a diorite statue, a bit of the arm of a human figure on which was an inscription, and the fragment had been carefully trimmed so as to make it look neat and to preserve the writing; and the name on the statue was that of Shulgi, who was king of Ur 2094–2047 B.C. Then came a clay foundation-cone of a Larsa king of about 1800 B.C., then a few clay tablets of about the same date, and a large votive stone mace-head which was uninscribed but may well have been more ancient by five hundred years.

What were we to think? Here were half a dozen diverse objects found lying on an unbroken brick pavement of the sixth century B.C., yet the newest of them was seven hundred years older than the pavement and the earliest perhaps sixteen hundred: the evidence was altogether against their having got there by accident, and the trimming of the statue-inscription had a curious air of purpose.

Then we found the key. A little way apart lay a small drum-shaped clay object on which were four columns of writing; the first three columns were in the old Sumerian language, and the contents of one at least were familiar to us, for we had found it on bricks of Amar-Sin, king of Ur 2046–2038 B.C., and the other two were fairly similar; the fourth column was in the late Semitic speech. 'These', it said, 'are copies from bricks found in the ruins of Ur, the work of Amar-Sin king of Ur, which while searching for the ground-plan [of the temple] the Governor of Ur found, and I saw and wrote out for the marvel of beholders'. The scribe, alas! was not so learned as he wished to appear, for his copies are so full of blunders as to be almost unintelligible, but he had doubtless done his best, and he certainly had given us the explanation we wanted. The room was a museum of local antiquities maintained by the princess Ennigaldi-Nanna (who in this took after her father, a keen antiquarian), and in the collection was this clay drum, the earliest museum label known, drawn up a hundred years before and kept, presumably together with the original bricks, as a record of the first scientific excavations at Ur (see p.231).

Another antiquity belonged, apparently, not to the Museum but to the temple building. In front of one of the side-doors of the antechamber of *Dublamakh* there lay a round-topped limestone relief on which was represented the god Ea, patron deity of the ancient city of Eridu whose ruins break the line of the horizon some 12 miles to the south-west of Ur. According to the old Sumerian convention the god is shown holding a vase from which two streams of water are pouring to the ground, while fish are swimming up and down in the streams; as lord of the Waters of the Abyss, Ea holds the source from which rise the twin rivers Tigris and Euphrates, givers of life to the land of Mesopotamia. The relief may have decorated the space above the door, but if so, it was re-used, for it has nothing really to do with this Late Babylonian building, but is a product of the great art of the Third Dynasty.

Another object, found this time by the door of the kitchen which Nabonidus added to the sanctuary, was certainly of contemporary date, but it again was a stranger to its surroundings. Crushed together under a fallen brick we found at least a hundred slithers of ivory, many of them minute in size and as thin as tissue-paper, the ivory having rotted and split into its natural laminations: so delicate were they that they had to be hardened with celluloid before they could be picked up from the ground. When put together, the fragments took shape as a circular toilet-box decorated with figures of dancing girls carved on it in relief; Egyptian rather than Oriental in style, the row of maidens hold hands and make a ring around the casket.

Ivory toilet-box, perhaps made in Phoenicia, carved with a row of dancing girls; repaired in antiquity. Found on the Nabonidus pavement in Dublamakh

This box was never made in Mesopotamia; it is the work of one of those Phoenician craftsmen of Sidon or of Tyre whose skill in ivory-carving had made them famous throughout the Mediterranean world; as an imported object it must have been a thing of price indeed, that it was valued is clear, for it had been broken and riveted in antiquity.

In view of the immense amount of labour spent on the construction of

ABOVE *Ivory box-lid incised with a Phoenician inscription including a dedication to the goddess Astarte; found below the Nebuchadnezzar pavement in room 4 of* Enunmakh

RIGHT *Ivory spoon with its handle carved as two nude dancing girls; this, like the box in illustration p.253, may have been made in Syria or Phoenicia rather than in Babylonia. Found in the lower courtyard of* Enunmakh *over room 15 of the Kassite building* the Temenos wall one can assume that all the old buildings inside that Sacred Area were restored by Nebuchadnezzar and Nabonidus. But much of that area—at least half of it—has been so denuded by weather that scarcely a vestige of Late Babylonian work remains. But reconstruction was not confined to the Temenos. Our excavations on the line of the city wall brought to light here and there sections of late walling which were far too fragmentary to give an intelligible ground-plan, but did seem to show that Nebuchadnezzar had made some attempt to put in order the town defences. The ancient rampart, whose sharply sloping face of mud-brick had been patched often enough, was still serviceable, with a certain amount of repair, and it seems now to have been capped with a wall which incorporated the walls of various existing buildings but where there were none such was built *ad hoc*, linking them in a continuous line. One of the buildings utilized in this way was a temple at the south end of the city—the temple which in the time of the Third Dynasty of Ur had columns of mud-brick (see above, p.177); this was restored by Nebuchadnezzar. We found nothing that could tell us to what god the building was dedicated, nor was it of particular interest in itself, but it acquired interest from the method of its discovery, which was one of the lucky accidents of archaeological work. We were clearing the top of the city rampart which at this point seemed surprisingly wide; all upstanding walls had been denuded away and when the men scraped off the few inches of surface sand, there appeared only the smooth level of weather-worn mud-brick. One workman, smarter than the rest, noticed that the bricks were not uniform in colour, some being reddish and some grey, and that the patch of grey bricks which he was working on began to take definite shape, and then that between the grey bricks and the red there was a line of white about as thick as stout paper. Actually this was Nebuchadnezzar's temple. The redder bricks were the foundation of the pavements, all the burnt bricks of which had gone; the grey bricks were those of the walls, and the white line was the whitewash which, applied to the upper part of the now vanished walls, had trickled down between wall and floor. On such evidence we were able to work out the entire plan of the temple, and this we could verify later when we dug away the floors and exposed the wall foundations. In the following year precisely similar evidence enabled the German excavators at Uruk to identify and plan the 'White Temple', one of the oldest buildings on the site; but the credit for first recognizing the importance of a mud-brick colour-scheme must go to our Ur workman.

The Neo-Babylonian period saw the temples and public monuments of Ur restored not indeed to their pristine splendour but at least to a condition better than had been known for many centuries; but the city which was thus adorned by the last kings of Babylon was a very different one from that which flourished in the times of the Third Dynasty of Ur and under the Larsa rulers.

I have described the crowded Larsa period houses (above, pp.191ff) with their evidence of prosperous trade and manufacture. All of them had gone. To what extent they had been preserved throughout the long Kassite period, or what had replaced them, there was virtually nothing to show; in the end the ruins of them, or of their successors, had been razed to the ground and on the higher level so formed a new town had sprung up. None of the houses went back to a time earlier than the Neo-Babylonian— they were all new foundations. It really looked as if Nebuchadnezzar's boast 'Is not this great Babylon which I have built', applied equally to Ur. Of course we have to generalize from rather limited data because in few spots where we dug had buildings of so late a date escaped the effects of time and weather; but two sites did provide good evidence. In the low-lying ground north-west of the Temenos we found poor houses of the period in tolerably good condition—poor houses, because it was a bad site where nobody would live if he could avoid it, in good condition because instead of lying exposed to wind and rain their ruins had been buried by the debris washed down from the Ziggurat terrace. They were small and shoddy huts, one storey high, crowded together without plan or system, the typical slum of any Oriental city. But another dig gave us much more illuminating results. Immediately south of the big group of Larsa houses excavated by us the modern ground-level rose to form a hillock, due, I suppose, to some vagary of wind currents, and excavation here laid bare the remains of houses which can probably be taken as typical of the main part of the late town. It bore a striking resemblance to Babylon. The streets were wide and straight, with branch streets or sometimes rather narrow alleys at right-angles to them separating the building-blocks. The houses were of mud-brick only, lacking altogether the burnt-brick 'damp-courses' of earlier times, and very often their outer walls were built with the close-set 'saw-tooth' re-entrant angles which we found in the case of Ennigaldi-Nanna's palace. They were of one storey only, the flat roof probably being used for 'sitting-out' purposes; the general plan was that of rooms ranged round a central court; on one side of the court, facing the entrance, was the reception-room with a retiring-room behind it and rooms of a more private nature on either side, with kitchen and other domestic chambers in the background. A curious thing was that in several cases the lay-out of the interior, while strictly regular in itself, was entirely askew with the containing-walls. It looks as if the direction of the street, which of course determined the orientation of the house blocks, had been imposed on the builders by some arbitrary authority, whereas everybody knew that a house must be sited in such a way that the reception-room faced the north and had the benefit of the cool breezes in hot weather; I cannot otherwise account for the very awkward clash between town-planning and domestic architecture, and if my explanation is correct, it would support the view that Ur was rebuilt on Nebuchadnezzar's order.

The most surprising thing was the size of the houses. Since all the accommodation had to be on one floor, they would naturally be larger than the two-storey houses of Larsa times; but these are great sprawling structures, one of which may occupy an entire block measuring 150 feet by 130, and take up an area which in the Larsa town would have contained fourteen or fifteen houses. This must mean a tremendous fall in the value of building sites in the city, and that in its turn must imply that the population had been reduced to a fraction of what it had been in the old days. The people who were housed on such a scale were presumably wealthy, but no tablets bear witness to any great commercial prosperity. One family archive, covering several generations, was found in a large clay pot in one of the houses and does suggest at least what happened at Ur. In the reign of Nabopolassar, Nebuchadnezzar's father, the head of the family, Sinuballit by name, lived at Babylon where he was in business—incidentally not too successfully, it would seem, seeing that of thirty-five documents bearing his name no less than seventeen record loans contracted by him. Later the family moved to Ur and occupied one of these great houses. If Nebuchadnezzar was trying to rehabilitate the decaying city, his big programme of temple-building (and perhaps his laying-out of the new town) is likely to have been accompanied by an attempt to recall to Ur families which had drifted away to more prosperous centres; one is tempted to think that a government housing subvention accounted for the spacious quarters in which the returned citizens established themselves.

An influx of people from 'foreign' parts would certainly explain a change in what is generally most conservative, the ritual of burial. We still find in the Neo-Babylonian period, under the floors of the houses, the oval terracotta coffins, sometimes containing, sometimes inverted over the dead, which had been the mode for a thousand years; but side by side with those there are 'double pot burials' in which two big clay jars are laid on their sides, rim to rim, and the body is half in one and half in the other; it is a custom introduced from Babylon, and we do not find it at Ur until the reign of Nebuchadnezzar.

Nebuchadnezzar's motive in restoring Ur was doubtless political—to consolidate the South against any danger from a revived Assyria or from the Medes—also it satisfied his love of building. Nabonidus was actuated by religious zeal; he was not a member of the main line of the Babylonian royal family. He was the son of a nobleman and of the High-Priestess of Sin (Nanna) at Harran in northern Mesopotamia; a lady who may have been a member of the old Assyrian royal family. Ur, as the main seat of worship of the Moon-god Sin (Nanna), could not fail to attract Nabonidus. Neither king considered the economics of the question, but the fact was that Ur had flourished as a trading and manufacturing city and now that trade was leaving it, there was little reason for it to exist; the Neo-Babylonian reconstruction was wholly artificial and could hardly be expected to last. Then came the dramatic end of the dynasty; the governor of the Babylonian provinces east of the Tigris rebelled and marched against the capital; Belshazzar, the king's son and co-regent, fell in battle and Babylon was betrayed into the hands of the enemy and almost without striking a blow Cyrus, King of Persia, added the whole of Babylonia to his dominions. To

Ground-plan of private houses of the Neo-Babylonian period

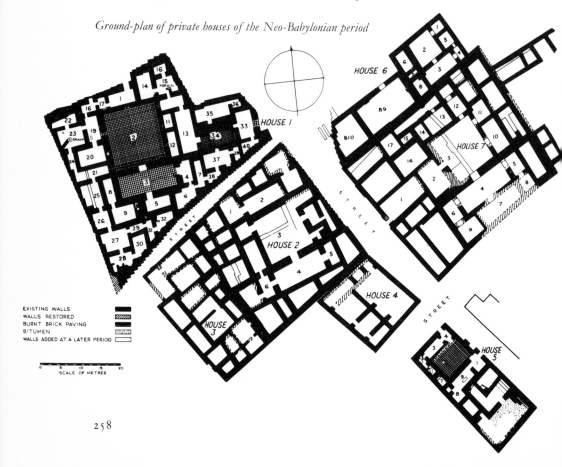

the citizens of Ur it must have seemed that all was over, for the foe against whom its defences had been repaired now held it for his own, and the conqueror worshipped other gods than those honoured in its temples. How then should Ur go on?

But it was the unexpected that happened.

When we were tracing the course of the great Temenos wall built by Nebuchadnezzar, we found in one of the north-east gates the stone door-sockets in position in the brick boxes which kept the earth away from the hinge, and the bricks bore the inscription of Cyrus; the new ruler had repaired the circuit wall of Nanna's temple, and, as we have seen, it was almost certainly he who was responsible for the last restoration of *Enunmakh*, the joint shrine of Nanna and Ningal. The inscription on the bricks has a familiar ring; 'the great gods have delivered all the lands into my hand', it begins, and we think of the proclamation of Cyrus in the Book of Ezra which also had to do with the restoration of a temple: 'The Lord God of Heaven hath given me all the kingdoms of the earth; and he hath charged me to build him an house at Jerusalem, which is in Judah'. That act of clemency, which to the captive Jews appeared miraculous, was an incident in a scheme applied to the whole kingdom: whether the god was Jehovah or Nanna mattered little to Cyrus; his purpose was to placate his people by subsidizing their particular forms of worship, and the temples of Ur gained a fresh lease of life from the catholic generosity of the Persian.

Unfortunately the denudation of the upper levels over the whole site of Ur has left us very little material to illustrate this last phase. The big Neo-Babylonian houses continued in use, handed down from father to son with little or no change. We found in them a fair number of tablets of a business sort, but it is always business on a small scale and of a local sort, the sale of a parcel of garden land, of a house or a slave, the lease of a property or the hire of labour, loans and debts—there are plenty of those—or questions of adoption and inheritance; they are the affairs not of a commercial city but of a country town. Not that people were so poor; in *Enunmakh* we found on the Persian pavement a very beautiful bowl of veined agate and an ivory bowl with a handle in the form of two naked children carved in the round, both of them presumably offerings to the temple made by citizens. It was in a Persian house that we found the finest example of decorative stone carving that our excavations produced, a steatite bowl round which goes a procession of oxen carved in high relief; it is certainly not of Persian date—indeed it goes back to the Jamdat Nasr period, and how it came to be in a Persian's possession we cannot say, but it must have been treasured as an antiquity. Even the domestic pottery suggests a comfortable pattern of life, for it is much better than was in use in older days and in particular we have now vessels of green-glazed earthenware, some of which are highly decorative; that yet finer objects were in use was proved by the discovery in one house of a fluted silver bowl of exquisite workmanship. And another discovery told the same tale. Dug down into the buried ruins of the ancient *Giparu* from a Persian house of which every brick had disappeared we found two coffins each containing the body of a woman wrapped in linen and woollen cloths and adorned with beads of agate and gold and gold ear-rings; with them were glazed earthenware vases and one had also a bronze mirror and a godrooned bronze bowl, and there were too baskets and wooden vessels, these hopelessly decayed. The contents of the graves were moderately but not excessively rich; what was surprising was the coffins themselves, for they were of sheet copper elaborately riveted along the top and bottom and down the sides where there were upright stays; the coffins were of the usual Persian shape, oblong with one square and one rounded end, and at either end they had solid copper handles. Innumerable Persian graves have been excavated but only one other such metal coffin has ever yet been found, and the presence of so rare a luxury must be set against the apparent poverty of buildings when we try to estimate conditions at Ur in Persian times.

Incidentally, our finding of the coffins had a curious sequel. One was in a very bad state, the metal badly decayed, the other relatively well preserved, but we did manage, with some difficulty, to lift them both and bring them back to London. There they remained many years, and at last the worse of the two, being a duplicate, was presented to the Birmingham City Museum. The authorities there were trying to mount for exhibition what seemed to be a sorry specimen when a piece of corroded metal flaked off one of the stays and brought to view an engraved pattern. Systematic cleaning produced on either stay a very lively engraved decoration of animals and flowers; the British Museum coffin was similarly treated and gave similar results. Almost at the same time there was published an object said to have been found at Ziwiyeh in western Iran and now in the Metropolitan Museum, New York, a strip of copper which, as we can now see, is a coffin stay, and it has the same engraved designs so exactly reproducing those from Ur that it may come from the same group of workshops as our coffins. These coffins presented us with a puzzle, since, to judge by their decoration, they may have been a couple of centuries old when used to bury citizens of Ur at the time of the Persian occupation.

Another Persian coffin, found almost flush with the modern surface of the ground, yielded a no less surprising discovery. It had been plundered

'Bath-tub' bronze coffins from below a house of the Persian period; although the burials in them were of this period, the style of decoration engraved on the side-panels of the coffins suggests they were made earlier in the seventh century B.C.

and there were left in it only a few fragments of broken bones and not even a clay pot; but, overlooked in the dust that covered the coffin's floor, there was a collection of nearly two hundred seal-impressions in clay. 'Collection' is the right word, for the lumps of soft clay had been pressed against the gems (the finger-marks were plain on the back and there was no hole through which a string could have passed) and had then been baked to

A collection of ancient impressions on baked clay of seals and finger-ring bezels; some of the motifs are Oriental, some show Greek influence; found in an otherwise empty coffin of the Persian period lying flush with the modern surface

make them permanent; they were illustrations of the gems in a seal-cutter's repertory, probably used to help customers in ordering the designs they wanted cut on seals and ring bezels. The wide variety of designs offered, Mesopotamian, Persian, Phoenician, and Greek, bear witness to the cosmopolitan origin and tastes of Ur's citizens and visitors in the fifth and fourth centuries B.C.

The dated tablets in the Persian houses take our history down to the end of the fourth century B.C.—we have one of the reign of Alexander the Great and one of the seventh year of Philip Arrhidaeus of Macedon, 316 B.C. But though there may have still been rich men and artistic dilettanti at Ur, the city was dying none the less.

Inside the Sacred Area, against the south-west wall of the Ziggurat itself, a potter set up his kilns and plied his trade; we found the 'wasters', the pots damaged in the firing, and the little clay tripods which kept apart the plates piled in the kiln and prevented the glaze from sticking them one to another, mixed in the rubbish with the blue-glazed bricks fallen from the walls of the temple which Nabonidus had built as the Ziggurat's crowning glory. In the west corner of the Temenos where Nanna's shrine had been, we found above the rubbish that buried the Neo-Babylonian court scanty remains of the latest Persian period, walls crooked and irregularly aligned, without regard to the orientation of the Ziggurat hard by, ill-built, sometimes of mud-brick, sometimes of burnt bricks, whole or broken, bearing the names of divers kings, collected from the ruins of old buildings and now roughly relaid in mud mortar; the whole spoke eloquently of poverty and decay. Circular brick-lined pits sunk in the floors of rooms showed that they were used as stores and granaries. Under the floor of one room we found a pot containing unbaked tablets; most of them had reverted to their native mud, but one or two were legible in part at least, and they proved that these miserable chambers belonged to the priests of Nanna and that tithes were still being brought by the faithful to what was probably already a ruined shrine.

It was probably by the close of the fourth century that a combination of events sealed for ever the doom of Ur. In the old days the river Euphrates, or an important branch of the river, washed the walls of Ur on the west, and from it innumerable canals big and small led the water off into the fields which spread far across the plain, and up and down the main canals went the ships bringing trade from the Gulf and from the other towns on the river-banks. For two millennia the Gulf and the Indian Ocean were more important avenues of trade with the East than the overland routes; but with the Persian conquest, and the increasing use of the camel, caravan routes across the Iranian plateau relatively rapidly gained a new pre-eminence. Today the Euphrates runs 10 miles to the east of the ruins and the great plain is a barren desert. The drying-up of the old river-bed, progressively from the Neo-Babylonian period, meant the stoppage of water-borne traffic, the ruin of the whole elaborate system of irrigation, and the end of agriculture; there was not the energy or the capital for the installation of a new system, and the starving city had no longer any reason for existence. Gradually the inhabitants moved away to other homes, the houses crumbled, the wind sweeping across the now parched and desiccated levels brought clouds of sand which they dropped under the lee of the standing walls, and what had been a great city became a wilderness of brick-littered mounds rising from the waste.

Further Reading

For this period the archaeological evidence will be found primarily in *Ur Excavations* IX: *The Neo-Babylonian and Persian Periods* (1962) and *Ur Excavations* V: *The Ziggurat and its Surroundings* (1939).

Footnotes

[1] This may sound improbable, but is really characteristic of the Middle East. Up to 1920 at any rate there was in the centre of Aleppo, facing the Citadel entrance and surrounded by some of the city's finest buildings, a huge empty space which was the regular refuse-dump for the citizens.

[2] Though broadly correct, doubts have been expressed about the details of Woolley's reconstruction (Editor).

[3] This is not certain; it may have been the sounding-box of a musical instrument (Editor).

[4] As was supposed in a reconstruction published in 1927 and subsequently often reproduced (Editor).

[5] So far as they are preserved; it is possible that the upper parts of the walls were of mud-brick, as in the case of private houses.

[6] The following section is typical of Woolley's vivid reconstructions. It has not been radically revised, although scholars would now question some of his reconstructions of two-storey houses and his identification of shops, etc. (Editor).

[7] Such names as these are, of course, Woolley's, not ancient ones (Editor).

[8] The second stage alone would have been 162 feet high, with the other five in proportion!

Select General Bibliography

This short list is confined to books easily available in English; only Sir Leonard Woolley's works are given more fully.

S.N. KRAMER *The Sumerians* (Chicago, 1973).

S. LLOYD *The Archaeology of Mesopotamia* (London, 1978). *Foundations in the Dust* (London, revised edition, 1981).

M.E.L. MALLOWAN and D.J. WISEMAN (Eds.) *Ur in Retrospect: in memory of Sir C. Leonard Woolley* (London, 1960; volume 22 of *IRAQ*).

A. MOORTGAT *The Art of Ancient Mesopotamia* (London, 1969).

D. and J. OATES *The Rise of Civilization* (Elsevier/Phaidon, Oxford, 1976).

J. OATES *Babylon* (London, 1979).

A. LEO OPPENHEIM *Ancient Mesopotamia* (2nd ed., Chicago, 1977). *Letters from Mesopotamia* (Chicago, 1968).

J.N. POSTGATE *The First Empires* (Elsevier/Phaidon, Oxford, 1977).

G. ROUX *Ancient Iraq* (Harmondsworth, 1980).

H.W.F. SAGGS *The Greatness that was Babylon* (London, 1962).

E. STROMMENGER and M. HIRMER *The Art of Mesopotamia* (London, 1964).

C.L. WOOLLEY *Abraham: recent discoveries and Hebrew Origins* (London, 1936). *As I seem to remember* (London, 1962). *Dead Towns and Living Men* (London, revised edition, 1954). *Digging Up the Past* (London, 2nd ed., 1954). *Spadework: adventures in Archaeology* (London, 1953).

The Sumerians (London, 1928).
Ur: the First Phases (London, 1946).
Ur of the Chaldees (London, 2nd ed., 1950).

Ur Excavations

Volume I *Al-'Ubaid* by H.R. Hall and C.L. Woolley (1927).
   II *The Royal Cemetery* by C.L. Woolley and others, 2 vols. (1934).
   III *Archaic Seal Impressions* by L. Legrain and C.L. Woolley (1936).
   IV *The Early Periods* by C.L. Woolley (1955).
   V *The Ziggurat and its Surroundings* by C.L. Woolley (1939).
   VI *The Ur III Period* by C.L. Woolley (1974).
   VII *The Old Babylonian Period* by C.L. Woolley and Max Mallowan (1976).
   VIII *The Kassite Period and the Period of the Assyrian Kings* by C.L. Woolley (1965).
   IX *The Neo-Babylonian and Persian Periods* by C.L. Woolley and Max Mallowan (1962).
   X *Seal Cylinders* by L. Legrain and C. L. Woolley (1951)

Ur Excavations: Texts

Volume I *Royal Inscriptions* by C.J. Gadd and L. Legrain, 2 vols. (1928).
   II *Archaic Texts* by E. Burrows (1935).
   III *Business Documents of the Third Dynasty of Ur* by L. Legrain, 2 vols. (1937, 1947).
   IV *Business Documents of the Neo-Babylonian Period* by H.H. Figulla (1949).
   V *Letters and Documents of the Old Babylonian Period* by H.H. Figulla and W.J. Martin (1953).
   VI *Literary Texts*
      Part I by C.J. Gadd and S.N. Kramer (1963).
      Part II by C.J. Gadd and S.N. Kramer (1966).
      Part III by S.N. Kramer and A. Shaffer (*in preparation*).
   VII *Middle Babylonian Legal Documents and other Texts* by O.R. Gurney (1974).
   VIII *Royal Inscriptions*. Part II by E. Sollberger (1965).
   IX *Economic Texts from the Third Dynasty* by D. Loding (1976).

Concise Topographical Glossary

This list covers only those parts of Ur referred to in this text; for full details the reader should consult the main excavation reports listed in the bibliography.

'*Dim-tab-ba Temple*' on high ground at the south corner of the Third Dynasty Temenos (q.v.). It contained foundation deposits of King Shulgi (*c.* 2094–2047 B.C.) for a temple dedicated to the goddess Shetaba.

Dublamakh meaning more or less 'house of the great collection of tablets': the seat of justice and the home of court records. It was either identical with, or incorporated, the great gate at the south-east corner of the Ziggurat platform found by Woolley in his third season. It led from the lower level of the Temenos up by stairs to the terrace upon which the Ziggurat was built.

Egishnugal (formerly *Egishshirgal*) the main temple of the Moon-god, Nanna, including the Ziggurat at the northern end of the Temenos.

Ekhursag combined shrine for the deified King Shulgi (*c.* 2094–2047 B.C.) and residence for temple personnel, built towards the south-east corner of the Temenos.

Enunmakh combined a double shrine for Nanna, the Moon-god, and his wife, Ningal, with extensive storerooms ('the great and noble abode of treasure') just outside the south-east corner of the Ziggurat enclosure.

Etemennigur: the terrace upon which the Ziggurat stood.

Giparu (formerly *Gigparku*) official dwelling of the *entu*-Priestess, who was a priestess of the highest rank, usually a sister or daughter of the reigning king. She represented Ningal, wife of the Moon-god Nanna, who had a shrine in the building. It was on the Temenos, just south-east of the Ziggurat terrace.

'*Harbour Temple*' adjoined the 'Palace of Bel-shalti-Nannar' (q.v.) on the south; its ancient dedication is unknown.

'*Mausolea of Dungi and Bur-Sin*' the building complex at the north-east end of the 'Royal Cemetery' (q.v.), outside the Temenos at the time, built with bricks stamped for the kings Shulgi (Dungi) and Amar-Sin (Bur-Sin) of the Third Dynasty (*c.* 2112–2004 B.C.). The superstructures are planned like large private houses and have vaults beneath them. Woolley believed these had been the tombs of the kings of this dynasty, plundered and left virtually empty by the Elamite sack of Ur which ended this dynasty.

Ningizzida Temple on the south-west side of the city just inside the main city wall; later a much larger temple, perhaps for the deity Ninezen, occupied the site.

'Palace of Bel-shalti-Nannar' built by King Nabonidus (*c.* 555–539 B.C.), to the north-east of the Temenos near the 'North Harbour'; paving bricks were found there bearing the statement that Nabonidus (re)built the *Giparu* (q.v.). These seem simply to have been left-overs from that building which was to the west of the Temenos. The association of this palace with the king's daughter, High-Priestess of Nanna, now known as Ennigaldi-Nanna, is therefore an open question. It may have been the residence of a governor, or of the king when in Ur for religious ceremonies.

'Royal Cemetery' successive rubbish tips to the south of the later Temenos into which graves were dug from about 2650 B.C. for over six hundred years. It takes its name from sixteen graves, amongst the earliest, with a tomb-chamber of stone or mud-brick, set at the base of a deep shaft, in which the burial was richly equipped and accompanied by the simultaneous burial of male and female servants. Woolley identified them as the tombs of the rulers of Ur just before the First Dynasty in the middle of the third millennium B.C.

'Treasury of Sin-iddinam' the name given to the remains of a religious building roughly one mile to the north-east of the Temenos wall. Inscribed bricks of King Siniddinam (*c.* 1849–1843 B.C.) found there were probably re-used and may originally have been intended for a building near the Ziggurat.

Temenos a Greek word describing a piece of land marked off and consecrated to a god (or gods), and excluded from profane use. Woolley used it to describe the great temple enclosure at Ur. This was at the heart of the city and was surrounded late in its history with a great wall by King Nebuchadnezzar II of Babylon (*c.* 604–562 B.C.).

Ziggurat the Akkadian word, in Anglicized form, for a temple tower rising in rectangular stages of steadily diminishing size; the number of stages varied and some, if not all, ziggurats had a small shrine on the top. None, including that at Ur, survives to full height, so they are reconstructed from views carved on Neo-Assyrian palace sculptures and the description of the ziggurat at Babylon given by the ancient Greek historian Herodotus.

Index

Puabi, queen, 64, 69, 72–4, 76–8, 88–9, 92, 102

Rajeibeh, 24
'Ram-in-a-thicket', 81–2, 95–6
Restoration of objects, 94ff, 108
Rim-Sin I, king, 180–1, 190, 204, 213
Rim-Sin II, king, 190
Rimush, king, 126, 129, 130
'Royal Cemetery', 24–5, 26, 30, 38–40, 47, 51–103, 111–12, 130, 163, 178, 219, 268

Sacred Marriage, 88
Sacred Way, 220, 222
Samsuiluna, king, 160, 190, 214–15
Sargon the Great, king, 15–16, 39, 52, 56, 92, 123, 126, 129, 228, 243
Schools, 203, 251
Seal impressions, 38, 44, 49, 55, 112, 126, 261–2
Seals, 44, 49, 64, 85, 88, 91–2, 94, 126, 128–9, 132, 135
Second Dynasty of Ur, 123, 126, 130–1
Shamash, god, 129
Shells, 41–2
Shetaba, goddess, 267
Shubad, see Puabi
Shu-Ilishu, king, 156, 180
Shulgi, king, 109, 118–19, 130, 142–3, 150, 161, 163, 165–6, 168, 170, 173, 189, 217, 235, 252, 267
Shuruppak, see Fara
Shu-Sin, king, 173
Sidon, 253
Sin, see Nanna
Sinbalassuiqbi, 224–8, 235, 241
Siniddinam, king, 150, 158, 180, 183, 212
Sinuballit, 257
'Standard of Ur', 91, 97–102
Statues, 94, 104–8
Stone: tools, 23–5; vessels, 40–3, 57, 259; passim
Sumer, land of, 19–20, 64, 93, 101–2, 113, 118, 125, 132, 135, 138, 173, 216
Sumerians, 12, 19, 30, 32, 44–5, 59, 67, 88, 93, 98

Sumu-El, king, 180

Tablets, 9, 26, 30, 38, 44, 47–9, 158–9, 192, 203, 215, 251, 257, 259, 262–3
Taylor, J. E., 12, 118, 140–2, 218–19
Tello, see Girsu
Temenos (Sacred Area at Ur), 51, 53, 118, 139–40, 174, 183, 192, 236–41, 255, 256, 259, 268
Third Dynasty of Ur, 14, 36, 113–14, 129, 130, 132, 135, 137–78, 179, 181, 227, 235, 253, 255
Tigris, 19, 32, 135, 252
Tomb-robbing, 56–7, 70–1
'Treasury of Sin-iddinam', 268
Tyre, 253

Umma, 122–3, 126
Ur, site of, 12; identification of, 9, 12, 142; 'of the Chaldees', 9, 224; population of 213, 257; end of, 263
Ur-Bau, king, 130, 246
Ur-Nammu, king, 14–15, 36, 113, 135, 137–9, 142–3, 145, 147–50, 156, 160, 161, 170, 173–4, 183, 209, 213, 217, 227–9, 234–5; stela of, 174–8, 209
Ur-Nanshe, king, 122
Uruk, site, 27, 29, 33, 37, 42, 45, 92–3, 106, 114, 122–3, 126, 135–6, 148, 163, 173, 190–1, 214, 219–20, 255; period, 15–16, 30–1, 36ff; see also under Pottery
Utehegal, king, 135

Warad-Sin, king, 155–6, 179–80, 217
Warka, see Uruk
Wayside Shrines, 208–12
Wood-carving, 56
Woolley, Lady, 17, 25, 67
Woolley, Sir Leonard, 8–11, 264
Writing, 43, 102, 203, 251, 252

Ziggurat, 12, 36–7, 43, 46, 53, 113–18, 121, 122, 137–47, 174, 176, 217–18, 227–8, 234–6, 267–8; terrace, 150–5, 217
Ziusudra, 34